PENGUIN BOOKS

No Brains At All

Keith Dunstan was born in Melbourne in 1925. After completing school, as a boarder at Geelong Grammar, he enlisted in the RAAF and served in Borneo during the Second World War. He joined the Herald and Weekly Times as a cadet reporter after the war. His talent as a writer was quickly recognised by Sir Keith Murdoch, who in 1949 sent him to the USA and England as a journalist. On his return to Australia, Keith Dunstan lived in Brisbane for four years, writing a daily column for the *Courier-Mail*. In 1958 he joined the Melbourne *Sun News-Pictorial* and for many years wrote the popular 'A Place in the Sun' column. Keith Dunstan is the author of several highly successful books on Australian society and mores, including *The Paddock That Grew, Wowsers, Knockers, Ratbags* and *The Amber Nectar*. He now writes regularly for the Melbourne *Age*. He and his wife, Marie, have four children and eleven grandchildren and live on a vineyard on the Mornington Peninsula.

For our grandchildren, Jack, Sam, Charlie, Tom, Hannah, Tim, Isabel, Ned, Henry, Zoe, George, and, with luck, any more who come along.

NO BRAINS AT ALL

AN AUTOBIOGRAPHY

Keith Dunstan

PENGUIN BOOKS

Penguin Books Australia Ltd
487 Maroondah Highway, PO Box 257
Ringwood, Victoria 3134, Australia
Penguin Books Ltd
Harmondsworth, Middlesex, England
Viking Penguin, A Division of Penguin Books USA Inc.
375 Hudson Street, New York, New York 10014, USA
Penguin Books Canada Limited
10 Alcorn Avenue, Toronto, Ontario, Canada M4V 1E4
Penguin Books (N.Z.) Ltd
182–190 Wairau Road, Auckland 10, New Zealand

First published by Penguin Books Australia Ltd 1990
This paperback edition published 1991

10 9 8 7 6 5 4 3 2 1

Produced by Viking O'Neil
56 Claremont Street, South Yarra, Victoria 3141, Australia
A Division of Penguin Books Australia Ltd

Designed by Leonie Stott
Typeset in Highland by Midland Typesetters, Maryborough, Victoria
Printed in Australia by Australian Print Group

National Library of Australia
Cataloguing-in-Publication data

Dunstan, Keith.
   No brains at all: an autobiography.

   Includes index.
   ISBN 0 14 015786 7.

   1. Dunstan, Keith. 2. Journalists –
   Australia – Biography. I. Title.

079.94092

CONTENTS

CHAPTER OPENING ILLUSTRATIONS

Doing this is like sitting naked in the bath while a television crew films you for the 'Today' show. A dreadful experience. So why do it? Vanity? It is an act of vanity, yes. But I must put in a plea of guilty with extenuating circumstances.

Heaven knows how many times I have thought about my great-grandfather John Dunstan, a tin miner who was born in Penryn, Cornwall, in 1833. He arrived in Adelaide with his wife, Nanny Collins, on 20 August 1854 aboard the *William Prowse*, and from there they proceeded overland to Ballarat. Almost certainly John Dunstan would have been at Eureka, but I know nothing of his life, not a thing about that huge adventure of leaving home for ever, sailing out to the new colonies, establishing a life at the diggings. Was he filled with fury over the injustices he found in the young colony? Did he and young Nanny have their triumphs? Did they turn up any gold? Who knows? There are no diaries, no letters. All gone.

Or what about another great-grandfather, Henry Mitchell, a miner also? He came from Brunswick, Germany, in 1855. In 1861 he married Harriet Ann Andrews of Portreath, Cornwall, at Brown's Diggings on 3 March. What a fascinating occasion that must have been. But I know practically nothing about them except that Great-grandfather Mitchell died young. Just ten years after his arrival in Australia he was riding from Scarsdale to Smythesdale near Ballarat when a dog frightened his horse. The Ballarat *Star* of 10 January 1865 described it as a 'yelping cur'. Henry fell, suffered a kick from his horse and died. How did Harriet Ann and their two children survive after that? If only Harriet Ann had written something down.

Every family should have its own historian, biographer, diarist, someone to keep records of lives that may have seemed ordinary in 1850, 1880 or 1900, but are fascinating to us now. There is a modern craze for genealogy, a great desire to know about our ancestors, but most genealogists only uncover bare bones – births, deaths and marriages. We need to put humanity on those bones.

I believe lives are being eclipsed more completely than ever before. When I started in journalism obituaries were all-important. The newspaper's library had its 'dead' file, its morgue. Often there were moments late at night when the journalists appeared to be idle. It was then that the Chief of Staff would cast a searching eye around the reporters' room.

'What are you doing, Dunstan? What are you up to, Bennetts? Have you finished your last story, Tucker?'

'We're not doing anything, Mr Travis.'

'All right, I want obituaries on Mr Chifley, Thomas White and Dr Hurley.'

All three gentlemen were alive and apparently healthy, but it was the custom always to have obituaries of leading figures ready and waiting. That does not happen any more. These days eminent politicians would still get an obituary, but not middle-of-the-road successful citizens. Obituaries have gone out of fashion, and the majority of us live and die without our stories appearing in the newspapers. The best hope of having an obituary published is to have been a Test cricketer or to have played Australian Rules football.

The dearth of information extends further than that. Diaries are not as fashionable as they were in Boswell's day. We do not write letters any more, not the way Lord Chesterfield wrote to his son. We call on the telephone. Or, if we do write letters, we do not keep them in a box as Auntie once did, simply because we do not have the space. Letters are burned, shredded, put in the wastepaper bag for recycling.

So that is one excuse for writing this autobiography. As well, I plead forgiveness for indulgence because this story is designed to evoke an era, a time, a style that has now almost disappeared. We have lived through a period of moral, social and technological change that has been very nearly more rapid than any other in our history. At first it did not occur to me that school life in the

1930s could be interesting to those living in the 1990s, or that a Second World War career in which almost not a shot was fired in anger was worth recalling. For forty-five years I kept dark those events in which I contributed not a whit to the downfall of Hitler or even Emperor Hirohito. They were something to be ashamed of. Then I began to realise the events should be told because to another generation they would seem odd, indeed.

The suggestion for this autobiography came from my son, David, who has a very strong sense of history, and my publishers, but for fifteen years I avoided the idea, gave priority to countless other projects. Not now, next year. Oh yes, there will be more time next year. Only in 1989, while spending six weeks at Montisi in glorious Tuscany, did there seem to be a chance. No longer was there any excuse for escape.

The truth until then was this: an autobiography was too hard, and I had neither the skill nor the courage to write it. A good autobiography requires an honesty, an intensity of emotion, a readiness to reveal things that most of us really do not want to reveal. At least when one becomes older self-revelation is easier. Even self-humiliation causes no pain. But the mind can play many tricks. I found long ago, when writing books such as *Wowsers, Ratbags* and *The Amber Nectar*, that there is always a blend between fact and fantasy. I would take down many a loving memory on the tape recorder, then check the facts in newspapers and other records, only to discover the events never took place. An event can be created, nurtured and cherished with such passion that the creator believes it actually happened. In a mysterious, psychological way I suppose it almost did.

So an autobiographer must watch himself, be a stern examiner and strive for honesty. Two of the Australian autobiographies I most admire are Donald Horne's *The Education of Young Donald* and Xavier Herbert's *Larger Than Life*. Here there is no fear and one senses the truth.

After the writing there was the hunt to find the right title. 'A Fortunate Life' would have been ideal, but unfortunately it had already been taken. 'Tandem' I liked because for more than forty years my life has been in tandem with my wife, Marie Rose. We love tandem bicycling. The cyclist who rides number two on a tandem is known as the stoker. This life would have gone nowhere without Marie Rose as the stoker. Finally we went back to the words of my old science teacher, Charlie Cameron, who had tried valiantly to teach me the mysteries of chemistry and physics. One day in desperation he had said: 'Dunstan, you are stupid. You have no brains at all. But you do have guts'.

There is something in that. Even if it does not require superior brain, just possibly it takes guts to write an autobiography.

CHAPTER ONE

A nice suburb

It is much easier to write a novel or an autobiography if you
have been miserable as a child, persecuted, tortured or banished.
That is why the Russians Dostoevsky, Tolstoy, Turgenev and Gogol
remain the greatest writers. Not only were they able to draw on
their own emotional, anguished lives; they were also able to call
upon the sufferings of their country: upon the poverty, the class
conflicts, the frigid winters, the wars and the subjugation of the
Russian people. Some writers who have found their lives not
sufficiently awful have even gone out of their way to make them
so. Philip Roth the United States novelist has admitted to doing
this.

What a handicap it is to have been happy. My parents were
loving and generous. The climate in Melbourne was only frigid
superficially – perhaps briefly in July or August. The political
suffering under the benign dictatorships of Messrs Bruce, Lyons,
Menzies, Curtin and Chifley hardly compared with that under
the tsars.

What's more I grew up in an utterly affluent suburb.

I was born on the kitchen table on 3 February 1925 at 13 Coppin
Street, East Malvern, a very suburban Melburnian street named
in honour of George Coppin, flamboyant showman, actor,
entrepreneur and politician. East Malvern was considered a very
solid suburb in its own way, but when I was 4 we moved to
Toorak, which was a positive pocket of indulgence and
unquestionably Melbourne's most exclusive suburb. Toorak was
really tiny: it only extended from Williams Road to Glenferrie
Road and from Malvern Road to the Yarra. If you lived in
Melbourne and you wanted to be socially top drawer, it was vital

to live in Toorak. Oh, Camberwell was good, Hawthorn was fine and parts of Brighton were excellent, but if you wanted true prestige and the envy of your fellows you went to Toorak. Its smallness was a great help: it made it harder to get in and it helped push up real estate prices.

The postal address was SE2. South Yarra to the west of Williams Road was SE1, Armadale on the other side of Malvern Road was SE3 and Malvern over Glenferrie Road was SE4. Desperate people who lived on the opposite side of those roads tended to lie just a little and claim they were really SE2 people. Not all of Toorak was perfect. West of Grange Road was plebeian and south-west, around Mathoura Road, was Siberia, beyond the pale. Perfection was the east, beyond St John's Church, up around St George's Road, Lansell Road and Heyington Place, among the Myers, the Baillieus, the G. I. Stevensons, the Grimwades, the Knoxes, the Nathans and the Darlings.

Toorak is an Aboriginal word meaning reedy swamp. The heart of Toorak, of course, is Toorak Village. In the 1920s it really did look like a village. It had a charm of its own. Many of the shops had little gardens out front and the sweet shop just around the corner from Wallace Avenue, where we lived, had its own small picket fence. Flats, units and own-your-owns were unknown. As you left Toorak Village there was a long green fence that went all the way from Grange Road to Orrong Road. In the 1930s as the little Toorak shopping centre grew there was an attempt to retain the charm and to keep the village atmosphere. So it went all Tudor and the developers built several blocks of shops in mock Tudor to give a false impression of upper-crust county England. Toorak, I think, had the only example of Tudor architecture with louvre-glass windows.

Ladies always dressed, complete with hat, gloves and handbag, to go shopping in Reedy Swamp. It was good to own a Packard, a Rolls-Royce or a Daimler, and Toorak matrons did their shopping in the family limousine. There was never a parking problem in the 1930s because only the rich owned cars. The ladies would sweep into the shops and shortly afterwards uniformed chauffeurs would carry out the goods.

We lived at 20 Wallace Avenue, adjacent to Glamorgan, Miss McComas's school for boys. It was just west of Toorak Village or roughly grade three Toorak. We had a vast Victorian house:

bluestone foundations, very, very solid brick walls and a slate roof, with a square, cast-iron look-out perched on top. It was built in 1889-1890, just before the great bank crash. We knew that was the date of its birth because workers found old copies of the *Argus* when repairing the slate roof. The name of the house was Ste Anne's. My mother's Aunt Viola lived at Ste Anne de Bellevue in Montreal, Canada, and the house was named in her honour.

I slept in the attic, which was a roomy space, reached by steep stairs, that included two bedrooms and a play room. Further stairs led up to the roof-top look-out. I slept in the corner room and when my brother was away it was lonely, indeed. The roof creaked and moaned with the changing summer heat. I swore the sound was footsteps and spent sleepless nights with the bedclothes pulled over my head, hoping the awful invader would not find me. I was convinced the house was haunted.

Many years later, when the old house was sold to Glamorgan school, it became the residence of the headmaster and I was invited for a cup of tea.

'Tell me', the headmaster asked, 'did you know this house has a ghost?'.

I pretended innocence.

'You know that room up the front?', he continued. 'I think you called it the Smoke Room?'

'Yes.'

'Often a boy has come to me and said, "Sir, there is someone waiting for you in your study". I walk up to the front room, only to find nobody is there. There is no other exit or entrance, so where could the person have gone? Then sometimes my wife and I wake in the middle of the night and find a woman standing beside the bed. In Victorian dress, she is. Then she disappears – she just seems to go through the cupboard.'

The ghost was harmless as most of them are.

Ste Anne's was a house of lofty, 5-metre ceilings, big verandahs and climbing roses tended by Claude, the gardener, who came once or twice a week. Almost every room had a fireplace, a tribute to the never-ending labour of Victorian and Edwardian serving maids. The maids wore uniforms with white aprons and big cross-over straps. Day uniform was butcher blue, night was black, with frilly apron plus cap.

One of our maids, called Mary, was a country girl very carefully watched over by her father. Thursday and Sunday afternoons were days off for the maids, but Mary sometimes went dancing at the Green Mill on Friday nights. The Green Mill, literally a great shed, was where the Victorian Arts Centre is now. Mary had two evening dresses, one gold and one black, and she wore formidable corsets.

Violet came later. She was devoted to my mother and the victim of every emotion. Weeks never went by without a dinner party and one was so important that my mother hired Mrs Cameron from Toorak Village to assist. During dinner there was a dreadful lull; the second course did not appear. My mother sent my sister, Helen, to investigate. Violet was out in the woodshed, crying. Why had they called in Mrs Cameron? She could do the job herself, perfectly well. Helen had to coax and cajole for some time before she would return to the house and get things going.

Maids were paid only about 10 shillings a week, plus keep, but being a servant in the city was considered good training for motherhood. There were certain daily rituals. Fires had to be constantly tended. An Aga stove in the kitchen burned anthracite. There were fires in my parents' bedroom, the living-room, the breakfast-room and, if there were guests, another fire in the sitting-room. Dad favoured the marvellous, slow-burning mallee roots. Every morning the fireplaces were painted with ochre to present a new, fresh, virginal appearance. The kitchen and the servery had splendid working spaces and benches of unsealed timber. These had to be scrubbed every day to preserve a noble, pristine whiteness. Formica had yet to be invented.

The house had a grand hall, with rooms down either side, including a private section for my mother and father, which consisted of a bedroom, bathroom and dressing-room. There was an east wing with yet another hall, plus bedrooms and bathroom. We called the hall 'the back passage', a term Mum did not like.

'It is not the back passage, dear, it is the back hall.'

The maid lived in the far bedroom at the rear end, so to speak, of the back passage, next to the room with the briquette hot-water service.

My mother, Marjorie Lillian Stuart Dunstan, was a Carnell and, like her husband, William, was born in Ballarat. William, whose father was also William, rated only one Christian name and his forebears were Cornish tin miners. The Dunstans came to Ballarat in the 1850s, looking for gold.

The Carnells were not quite so working class as the Dunstans. There was Henry Charles Carnell, a civil engineer from Perranarworthal, Cornwall, who arrived in Melbourne aboard the *Shropshire* on 30 August 1869. Another great-grandfather was Walter Ratcliffe, a saw maker from Sheffield, Yorkshire. He arrived almost at the same time. He was married to Helen McGregor McIntosh from Fifeshire in Scotland, and legend had it that she came from aristocratic Highland stock who actually had a castle in Scotland. The Dunstans, blue-collar working class, were amused by this, so Dad was irritated when in the 1950s he visited Scotland and discovered the McIntoshes really did have a castle.

Grandfather Henry Carnell was manager of Farmer's Hams and Bacon. There was never the slightest doubt in our minds that Farmer's produced the finest cured ham on God's earth. In our youth there was always a ham on the sideboard, a general purpose, eat-any-time ham. It was considered no crime to steal a slice quietly, every time you walked past.

Henry Carnell always wore a blue serge, three-piece suit with gold watch-chain across his comfortable stomach. There was a little medal attached to the chain, a trophy from the 1880s for being swift in foot running. Grandfather Carnell had competed in the Stawell Gift. A blue serge suit was a sign of respectability, and there were few concessions to vagaries of the weather. Even when the temperature got over 38 degrees Celsius a gentleman did not discard his tie or stiff collar. That was unthinkable. But it was permissible to wear a lighter jacket of black alpaca.

In an era of servants in the house Grandfather Carnell was never known to lift a broom, pull a weed or sully his hands with a tea-towel. On his living-room wall at Ballarat there was a vast picture in a heavy oak frame, showing him with a chain of medals around his illustrious neck. Around the portrait was a constellation of small pictures, like minor planets about the sun. These were of lesser gentlemen in the Independent Order of Rechabites.

Grandfather William Dunstan, a bootmaker, I saw only rarely. He made very occasional visits to Melbourne from Ballarat. He, too, dressed in blue serge and he, too, had the mandatory gold watch-chain. No athletic medals for him. On his watch-chain he had a marvellous gold sovereign case, which he would open for our fascinated inspection. It always held four or five real sovereigns and we gazed on them with wonder. On one occasion Grandfather

Dunstan propped me on his knee and said, 'You know who I am, don't you?'.

'I know your face, but I can't remember your name', I said. It was a remark I was never allowed to forget.

Grandmother Dunstan I never knew. She died in the great influenza epidemic of 1919. She had had six children. Grandmother Carnell, on the other hand, was an amusing, ebullient woman, a born organiser who was on every charity committee. On one occasion, when she was ill with typhoid, every denomination in Ballarat prayed for her recovery. It would be interesting to know which were the most successful with their prayers – the Roman Catholics, the Anglicans, the Presbyterians or the Methodists. Despite the Catholics' prayers for her, they were her pet phobia. Catholics, clearly, were the source of all evil. What went on in Catholic churches, with their bells, incense, strange ceremonies, idolatry and such, she dreaded to think. There was even a suspicion that they sacrificed babies on the altar. Grandma Carnell was paranoid about Catholics. She couldn't even pronounce the name properly, but spat it out as 'KATH-licks'. Never would she go into a fish shop on Fridays for fear people might think she was 'turning'. When my sister ultimately married a Roman Catholic, Grandmother Carnell was never told. The shock would have killed her.

The Carnells were Anglicans and the Dunstans were Methodists. The invasions of the Cornish during the gold-rush ensured Ballarat was always a good Methodist city. In one street there were three Methodist churches in a row. By tradition the Dunstans did not smoke, drink, chew or gamble. Sunday was for church, nothing else: it was a sin to indulge in sport, dig the garden or even sew. Occasionally such godliness had unexpected outcomes. My father recalled a solemn occasion at the Golden Point Methodist church. The minister was in full cry giving his sermon, when one of the Dunstan children quietly entered the church and discreetly made her way to the Dunstan pew. A whispered message passed from one end of the pew to the other. After the service the minister asked anxiously whether some disaster had befallen the Dunstans. No, all was well. Mrs Dunstan had to find out where Annie had put the peas for Sunday dinner. The peas, of course, had been shelled on Saturday. Shell peas on a Sunday and the transgressor was in danger of hell fire.

My father was the first of the Dunstans to break the Methodist tradition and take up the Demon Drink. Yet sometimes curious things could happen. On his return from Gallipoli my father was stunned when his father took him to a hotel in Golden Point and bought him a glass of beer, one only. Fathers pre-war and in the 1920s did this. It was the symbolic recognition that a son had reached adulthood.

Doctors would describe Dad as a perfect case for a heart attack (and that is what eventually brought him down). He was dynamic, restless, one for immediate action. Like all grand Victorian houses we had two living-rooms: one for actually living in and another for not living in – the drawing-room or parlour, which was kept almost like a museum piece for guests. One day, as Dad was sitting in the real living-room, his attention was caught by the light, a single bulb with lampshade, which hung from a pretty ceiling rose of plaster.

'I can't stand that light any longer', he announced.

He left his chair, fetched the kitchen steps and, with one mighty heave, pulled the whole cord out by its roots. Bare wires were left in his hand. Down came lampshade, plus a huge blob of plaster.

'That looks better, doesn't it', he demanded triumphantly. 'We'll have it all patched up tomorrow.'

He did, indeed. Never again was there a ceiling light, and from then on we had floor standard lamps.

There were three children in our family. Bill was the eldest. He was dark, handsome, devoted to shooting and a champion rifle shot. Then came Helen, who had long, blonde hair and was a great beauty. I was the youngest and I frequently complained that the others had collected the good looks. My father, who appeared never to have self-doubts, insisted his children should not have self-doubts either. He saw us all as future captains of industry. He was always feeding us information.

One night Bill was battling with a school essay.

'Not good enough', said Dad. 'Show it to me.'

Thereupon he demonstrated how an essay should be written. Bill took it to school the next morning and it was a triumph. It received such high commendation that his teacher had it published in the Melbourne Grammar magazine, the *Melburnian*. Dad was thrilled with his achievement.

Helen was also impressed. When she received an essay subject at school, entitled 'Will radio replace the newspapers?', she took it to Dad. Immediately the champion essay writer went to work.

'Of course, it won't', he said. 'Radio is just an expedient.'

'Expedient, that's a good word', Helen's teacher remarked after she had read the essay. 'Where did you get it?' The lady smelled a rat, so she wrote at the top of the essay: 'Not up to your usual standard'. Dad was devastated.

My mother was a gentle character, but she knew how to handle my father. She could manipulate him with ease. Her system was never give a man bad news or discuss anything serious the moment he comes home from work. Wait until he has had a drink or, even better, until after dinner when he is feeling good. So delicate was her sense of timing that she would sometimes delay breaking the news of an expensive new hat for several days.

Dad was chairman of a newsprint pool and he often went away on long trips. One time both he and my mother left for six months and our Aunt Nell came in to mind us. Aunt Nell was very warm, very indulgent. She always signed her letters 'Yours lovingly, Nell'. During her stay, Bill was away from school for a week, which required a formal letter of excuse to the school. So Aunt Nell wrote to Mr Plummer, the deputy head at Wadhurst: 'Dear Mr Plummer, I am sorry but I had to keep Bill home from school this week. He has been suffering from a very bad cold'. Then, without thinking, she added, 'Yours lovingly, Nell'. Mr Plummer was so overcome he read the letter to the whole class, while Bill, crimson with embarrassment, listened.

It was not entirely easy for Nell to look after a family of three, so my parents thought they would reduce her workload by boarding Helen at her school, St Catherine's in Toorak. Helen saw this as an injustice while her brothers remained at home. Consequently, every so often she ran away. A good time was on Sunday mornings when the young ladies of St Catherine's were marched off to church at St John's, Toorak. Off they paraded in pairs, the perfect crocodile, while Helen slipped away and ran home. Nell was always terrified when Helen rang the front doorbell. Suspecting the police were already searching for Helen, she would telephone the headmistress. Immediately a car would be dispatched from St Catherine's, driven by a chauffeur in a grey uniform. At the sight of it, Helen would flee up the stairs, into the attic and out onto the balconied look-out, screaming. Bill always had to fetch her down.

Helen had beautiful blonde hair, braided into a thick plait. Every night we used to watch her brushing this glorious, long hair. Brush, brush, brush. Thirty, forty, fifty brushings until it shone. Was she 15 or 16 at the time? In any case, a plait was not modern, not right for 1938, but my father insisted she keep it. One day, while still at boarding-school, she had an excuse to go to the city for a dental appointment. Dad's barber was in Collins Street, close to the Athenaeum. Helen went in and asked the kindly gentleman to cut her plait off.

'I can't, Helen', he said.

'You must.'

'Look, I won't do it. I could never face your father if I did.' Helen looked very menacing, indeed.

'Either you cut it off or I will.'

There was no choice. The barber cut off her magnificent plait, the hair that went almost to her waist. Carefully he put the locks in a parcel and gave it to her. A new era for Helen had begun. She celebrated by crossing the road and purchasing some figs from Mr Jonas, who had the superb fruit shop in Melbourne Mansions. She ate those figs on the way home and forgot about her hair. She left the precious parcel in the tram.

Aunt Nell looked at the short-haired blonde and screamed. Whatever would she tell Helen's parents? Bill was even more shocked. Tears ran down his cheeks.

Although in 1932 I had started school at Wadhurst, the preparatory school for Melbourne Grammar, my best education came from comics. It was the English comic that taught me to read. There was the *Magnet*, the *Gem*, the *Champion*, the *Triumph*, *Chums* and *Boys' Own Paper*. I would get them all. The *Magnet* and the *Gem* were both written by the astonishing Frank Richards.

It was a time of schoolboy closeness and loyalty. The *Magnet* had the story of Greyfriars: of Harry Wharton, the Famous Five, and Billy Bunter, 'the Owl of the Remove', who was fat, lazy, deceitful and always consuming buns. The *Gem* had the story of St Jim's: of Tom Merry and his extraordinary crew. They wore

Eton collars, cutaway jackets and striped trousers and told tales of far-removed upper-class English privilege and the exquisite persecution the English inflicted on their young through their barbarous education system. The *Magnet* and the *Gem* were later castigated by such authorities as George Orwell for being snobbish, racist and the worst kind of literature. At the time they seemed wonderful. The *Champion* and *Triumph* carried shorter episodes, usually from adventure tales about such characters as Fireworks Flynn and Rockfist Rogan. These gentlemen were clearly forerunners of more bizarre people, such as Superman, Phantom and Batman. They could achieve anything and rout all evil. Rockfist Rogan was always depicted throwing a fist straight through a barrel. George Orwell was right, of course. Evil nearly always was something un-British – and frequently French, Chinese or black. Foreigners, if not evil, were strange and absurd. The French were always 'Frogs'.

Regardless of their shortcomings the comics were the most important thing in my life. They arrived at the newsagent on Tuesdays and a small pile, with 'Dunstan' written on the top left-hand corner, was always put aside. Each Tuesday afternoon I walked down Wallace Avenue and round into Toorak Road, with a strange feeling in my stomach, an ache of anticipation. Sometimes, because of a strike or a failure in shipping schedules, the comics were not there. This was a disaster of mega proportions; a day, a night ruined. Close to tears I would trail home again.

Chums and *Boys' Own Paper* were monthlies, more prestigious than the others and better written. Of the two I preferred *Chums* because the writing was superior and it had fewer serials and more complete stories. Every year they were bound as annuals. It was pure joy if a *Chums* or *Boys' Own Paper* annual appeared in my Christmas stocking.

Toys were different from comics. They came in waves of all-consuming crazes. There was the kite craze, the top craze, when every breathing creature had to own a whipping top, and the diabolo craze. The diabolo was like two wooden cones joined together, which the possessor made dance on a taut string, a feat that required great skill.

Hoop bowling was good and all the rage for a time. The ideal hoop was an automobile tyre. Not any tyre, you understand. The best was an old T-model Ford tyre, which was lean and large.

This the enthusiast bowled along by beating it with a stick. My climactic adventure came in Linlithgow Avenue, which takes a sharp turn then drops steeply to Toorak Road. I was hitting my tyre at the top of the hill when it started moving faster and faster until gravity raced it away, far out of my reach. It sped down Linlithgow Avenue towards Toorak Road, gathering awesome speed. As I ran after it I saw to my horror that a tram was approaching along Toorak Road. Could the tyre possibly derail the tram? Actually it struck the tram amidships, bounced inside, tore through and went out the other side. Heaven knows whom or what it struck inside. I fled. In guerilla warfare it is wise to disappear as quickly as possible. I was not brave enough to return to the scene to claim my priceless T-model Ford tyre, and it was the end of my tyre-bowling career.

Then there was the go-kart craze, when we all manufactured go-karts, theoretically out of a soap box. Actually we never saw a soap box. The Elliott soft drink company made the best boxes: very solid, not too deep, and wooden. We attached to the box a stiff board, two cross-arms for the wheels and a rope to control the swivelling front arm. It was the very devil to get the right wheels. Pram wheels were good, but the best were roller bearings, usually acquired at a used-car yard. We considered it an act of honour always to make our own go-kart. Later, when my own children reached this stage, I was shocked to discover that the Myer Emporium sold go-karts, cubby houses and crystal sets all beautifully manufactured, with no need for the children to dirty their fingers.

It is customary for the aged to say that things are not what they used to be, but in the case of sweets this is undeniably true. Take the year 1933. In the glorious summer of that year aniseed balls, rainbow balls and acid drops were twenty a penny. They were always arrayed in 2-kilogram, glass-stoppered jars and it was a matter of immense deliberation how we disposed of a penny.

'Mmmm . . . five rainbow balls . . . ahh . . . five aniseed balls . . . five acid drops, two of them pink – no, make it ten rainbow balls.'

Sweet-shop ladies used to suffer.

My passion was cricket balls and cat's-eye rainbow balls. They cost a whole halfpenny each and, although some manufacturers have tried to make them since, they are not the same. They were made to the precise size of a small child's mouth and the idea was to keep popping them in and out to watch how delicately and beautifully they changed colour. They would last through at least two hours of continuous sucking. If we could get away with sucking them during class, of course, we would. Otherwise we wrapped our cricket balls in our handkerchiefs and waited until recess.

Licorice I adored. The licorice of those days seemed blacker and richer than today's. The *pièce de résistance* was the licorice fishing-line. The thing to do was to put several metres of this fine licorice into our pockets, draw one end up into our mouths, then quietly chew it, no hands. Fizzos, too, were good. They were the size of a ping-pong ball, with a hard, sugary outer crust. We sucked and sucked until suddenly the shell cracked and there was an explosion of sherbet in our mouths.

If I was particularly flush I would buy a revolver. They were almost life sized, made of marshmallow and covered in thin chocolate. We always devoured a revolver by sticking the muzzle in our mouths and chewing up the barrel, into the cartridge cylinder and around through the trigger until finally we enjoyed the solid hunk of the grip.

But the real excitement was the halfpenny box. The halfpenny box was a special cardboard tray of individual treasures created by the MacRobertson sweet company. Every item in it cost a halfpenny. We could buy the entire box for 3 shillings. The thrill was to pick over the treasures. There were such things as mice, whizz-bangs, silver sticks, nulla-nullas, cigars, engagement rings, lipsticks and, perhaps most famous of all, Maurice Tate's boots. Maybe you are too young to remember Maurice Tate? He was the awesome English fast bowler of the day and he wore enormous cricket boots. So, naturally, it gave us a certain sadistic thrill to eat them. They were white with pink soles and made of the same stuff used for clinkers today. Another choice item in the box was the frying-pan and bacon. The frying-pan was made of flat, hard licorice and in the centre was the bacon, superbly real even down to the streaks. The bacon must have been a thin strip of toffee.

Buzz-saws were worth having now and then. They were made of rock-hard candy in the shape of a circular saw. There were two holes in the middle through which we threaded string. Then, by winding up the string and pulling, we could make the buzz-saw buzz.

Oh, I could go on and on, about Fiji bananas, ingots, niblicks, snowites, colt foot's rock – all names that have vanished. MacRobertson's in the 1930s had 2000 different sweet lines. By the Second World War most of them had disappeared. They were too labour intensive. Items such as the frying-pan and bacon were all handmade, and it took three days, building it up layer by layer, to make a really good cat's-eye rainbow.

The crystal set craze started around 1932 with the coming of Don Bradman. It was necessary to have a coil, which we created by winding fine wire round a spent lavatory paper tube, and a cat's whisker, a pair of earphones, a cedar cigar box to hold the set, an earth and an aerial were also essential. The cat's whisker was a fine wire attached to a little handle. The idea was to probe the crystal with the whisker to find the sensitive spot that would create the magic of 'wireless'. Almost every week there was a set of instructions in *The Listener In* on how to build the latest crystal set.

The crystal set was vital when the Australian cricketers were playing in England. Mum would send me to bed at 9 o'clock with strict instructions to sleep: I could read the scores in the *Sun* in the morning. But with Bradman going on to his second hundred how could I go to sleep? A crystal set with earphones was ideal for listening under the bedclothes. My aerial was connected to the steel bed base beneath me, and the earth was a wire that went right down the wall to a pipe outside the bathroom window. So it was possible to listen right through to 3 o'clock stumps, parents unknowing. There was just one problem: the cat's whisker was a fragile creature and any jolt or movement, or just the plain quixotic nature of the beast, could cause me to lose the sensitive spot on the crystal. Naturally this would happen at the most vital moment. How could I fail to wriggle when Bradman reached his century or Walter Hammond lost his wicket? Then there would be a terrible, frantic struggle to get a return of sound.

The cricket broadcasts were important beyond measure in our house. Dad was general manager of the Herald and Weekly Times Limited. He was also a prime force in the early days of 3DB radio, which the Herald and Weekly Times had bought and started operating on 1 June 1929. Dave Worrall was the first manager of 3DB. He had a staff of eight and an income of 20 pounds a week. Commercial radio was very new – so new that during the Great Depression years people who could not afford receivers camped outside radio shops just to listen.

Cricket virtually created 3DB. In 1930 Worrall talked to Oswald Anderson of 2UW in Sydney, and they had the idea that it would be wonderful if they could get some sort of broadcast of the cricket from England. They looked into it and discovered that the cost of urgent cables from the English cricket grounds was 6 shillings a word. This was appallingly expensive and the sponsors fled in terror. However, Worrall and Anderson decided to try it just for a few hours on the first day of the first Test at Nottingham. By midnight there had been no response from listeners so Worrall took the microphone.

'Is there anyone listening out there? Shall we close down now or go on until stumps?', he asked.

The result was unbelievable. Every telephone began ringing at once.

'There are thirty of us here. The beer's running out, but we're still with you', one caller said.

The next day there were several thousand letters, boxes of oranges, cases of whisky and wine. One group sent a keg of beer. So 3DB was made that day.

Worrall was four years ahead of the ABC. Charles Moses did not start his simulated ball-by-ball broadcasts until 1934. Moses would wait until he had cables for a full over then re-create the scene as if he were in the grandstand. He even faked the sound of the ball by tapping the table with his pencil. Worrall never did this. He gave scores the second they came through so that 3DB and 2UW were always an over ahead of the ABC. Anyone who was desperate to know what was happening, of course, went to 3DB.

To keep it all going 3DB had their funniest performers, Charlie Vaude and Ren Millar, cracking jokes and telling tales. Under the bedclothes this was pure excitement. They turned cricket into a dazzling show. There were appropriate songs for every occasion. For example, if the Australians got Herbert Sutcliffe or Hammond, they would play 'Thanks be to God'. For every fall of wicket there was their theme song, 'Rickety Kate', and when there was an Australian disaster they would get together and hurl words of defiance.

We don't worry, we're not cryin',
We're not afraid of the big, bold lion.

Australians still love their cricket, but then it was a passion, an obsession. Dad would go in to 3DB to observe the fun, and he would report the next morning that all over Melbourne there had been Test cricket parties: at 2 a.m. in suburban streets every light would be on. There would be parties, too, at the wireless shops, with people sitting outside round burning braziers to keep themselves warm, all listening in. Passion for cricket was never quite the same again.

This was the Bradman era. My earliest memory was of Friday, 30 December 1932, when I was nearly 8 years old. My father took me to the Melbourne Cricket Ground for my first Test match. Australia was playing England in the second Test, and a record crowd of 63 993 was present, all of whom had come to see this unbelievable young man, Don Bradman.

Bill Woodfull won the toss and opened the batting. He went, after an interminable innings, for ten runs. Leo O'Brien was run out and we were two wickets down for sixty-seven runs.

'Ahhh, now we're in for the experience of a lifetime', my father announced.

We made ourselves comfortable, got ourselves ready to watch Mr Bradman for the entire afternoon. The cheers were deafening. Tall, lumbering Bill Bowes came running in, bowled a sort of long hop. Bradman, not waiting a second to get his eye in, went for the hook, mistimed and dragged it onto his stumps.

There was the most profound silence ever heard at the MCG. The astonishment, the horror, the grief, the shock were boundless. This was not in the script at all, Bradman out first ball for a duck. The day was absolutely ruined. My father, normally not all that interested in watching cricket, was so disappointed we packed up and went home.

Cigarette cards further fanned the sporting obsession. Capstan, BDV, Players, all the best cigarettes carried cards, and we bought special cigarette card albums at the newsagent. There were butterfly cards, animal cards, movie star cards and cards that featured famous castles in England, France and Italy, but unquestionably the most popular cards were those that featured cricketers and footballers. It was vital to achieve a full set, showing off Bradman, Stan McCabe, Alan Kippax, Bill O'Reilly, Clarrie Grimmett . . .

My parents were a failure. My father smoked only a pipe and my mother did not smoke at all. It was an unwritten rule: Dunstan women never smoked. So I plagued uncles and aunts, and like many others of my generation used every penny of pocket-money to buy cigarettes just for the cards. We tried unsuccessfully to smoke the cigarettes, then dumped them in the scrub by the Yarra.

Cards could be gained by swopping, but there was another, more unnerving method: flicking. It was possible to flick a cigarette card in the same way as a frisbee. By careful study of the wind, topography and arc of projection, cards could be flicked over a long distance. So there were card-flicking contests in which the winner took all the cards. I was not good at cricket, a poor performer at football and lamentable as an athlete. However, I was the champion at card flicking and I quickly gathered an immense collection of cigarette cards, which I kept for more than thirty years.

Cubby houses were vital to our games. These, like go-karts, we manufactured out of Mr Elliott's sturdy soft drink boxes, with the addition of old sheets of galvanised iron. Their location was the garage roof. From there we conducted warfare with toy guns and bows and arrows. The only acceptable toys were those that killed other human beings. Every participant had to know how to fall over dead, and we killed or maimed at least 300 victims a day. Somehow it did not seem to harm our psyches.

Yes, I possessed a beautiful collection of weapons. There was the toy Thompson sub-machine gun, so we could be Al Capone and the Chicago gangsters. There were six-shooters that would take caps on a long roll, providing up to sixty useful explosions in a gun fight. My finest weapon, the envy of every child in the district, was nickel plated and a perfect reproduction of a Colt .45 revolver. My father bought it for me on a visit to the United States. When I pulled the trigger, the cylinder that held the bullets revolved exactly as it did in a real revolver. The revolver made a superb explosion, with smoke issuing from the barrel. There was just one problem. It took its own special variety of caps, a disc of six that fitted on the revolving chamber. Fresh supplies of caps could be purchased only in the United States, so my fancy revolver had to be used with discretion; it could be used only for the most serious, the most important killings.

Naturally, this led to a desire for the real thing. When I was 16, I acquired a single-shot Remington .22-calibre rifle. Vastly excited, I took it to Leongatha and at the fifteenth attempt I finally shot a rabbit. Rushing forward to my prey, I found the rabbit half-paralysed, shot through the spine and lying on the turf, squealing in agony. I put another shot through its head to kill it, took home my dazzling new Remington and never fired it again.

It was also important to collect toy soldiers to have on hand a private army. Toy soldiers today seem mainly for adults, for those who like to indulge in war games and re-create the Battle of Stalingrad, Waterloo or Agincourt. Our soldiers were made of lead, now considered too expensive and too toxic for toys. The soldiers, little taller than a box of matches, were exquisite. Mostly they were gentlemen of fine British regiments and brilliant in their micro-detail. It was possible also to get Germans and even Turks, so the lust for genuine battle could be assuaged. Part of our joy was to declare war and fight a battle against our dearest school friends. The shops sold reproductions of First World War artillery pieces. They were spring loaded and fired tiny steel shells. The idea was to line up opposing armies on either side of the room and indulge in artillery battles akin to those on the Somme. The general who was left with more soldiers standing was the winner. I was militarily powerful, the Kitchener or Bismarck of Toorak.

One of my most magical Christmases involved toy soldiers. It could have been 1936. Christmas was always taken very seriously in our house. It began with Mum making her Christmas puddings in November, then, come early December, squadrons of Christmas cakes. The cakes were stashed away in secret kitchen recesses. Sometimes they did not reappear for a whole year, then at the appropriate moment Mum would say: 'I just managed to find a mouldy old cake. It won't be any good'. Of course, always it had matured like a Mouton Rothschild and was magnificent. Every December there was a Christmas tree erected in the, ah, front passage, under the skylight, which was 6 metres from the floor. Decorating the tree was an all-day project, using the Christmas decorations Mum saved from year to year in boxes.

Dad always insisted on being Father Christmas and delivering presents correctly. We put out pillowslips, not stockings, for expected treasure. Dad waited until he was convinced we were all asleep before he did his rounds. Naturally, sleep was impossible. I would wait and wait and wait until I heard his footsteps on the stairs, then feign slumber as he stuffed the presents in the pillowslip. After he left there was the problem of opening the presents in the dark. Children become knowing about the contents of a parcel very early. Some presents were discarded quickly. Aunt Annie always gave handkerchiefs. What on earth could any human being do with handkerchiefs, or even socks?

Christmas 1936 I discovered a large box in my pillowslip. It was filled with toy soldiers: American soldiers, an entire United States Army complete with vehicles, equipment and weaponry, brought back by my father from his latest visit to the States. I dared not turn on the light, but there was a glow from the moon. I paraded my soldiers up and down on the wide sill of my dormer window by moonlight, almost to the dawn. That was my happiest Christmas.

CHAPTER TWO

Education by flagellation

So many people look upon school-days as the happiest time of their life. For me school was little pleasure. I suspect my misery was self-inflicted. Home was such a warm, pleasurable place; school such a hideous, disciplined contrast.

At the age of 7 I was dispatched to Wadhurst, the preparatory school for Melbourne Grammar, which was in the grounds of the senior school. Melbourne Grammar, Anglican, bluestone, was created by Bishop Perry in 1849 and was one of the great public schools. The former prime minister Stanley, Lord Bruce, was a famous old boy, and the school much later could boast another prime minister, Malcolm Fraser.

Melbourne Grammar had a noble record not only on the Yarra with its crew, but also on the football field. Its history was impeccable. Indeed, in 1858 Melbourne Grammar and Scotch College played, very nearly, the first reported match of Australian Rules football. There were forty a side, including six or seven teachers. It took place over a vast area in the Richmond Paddock – so vast neither side could score the necessary number of goals to win, even though the game went for three hours until all were exhausted. They played on 7 August, tried again on 21 August and yet again on 4 September. Even then nobody had scored so they abandoned the game as a draw.

Melbourne Grammar possessed, and perhaps still does, a school song designed specifically to terrify the opposition. It was sung to the rabble-rousing tune of 'Men of Harlech'. The chorus went as follows.

None our ranks will sunder.
Who would shirk or blunder?
For all are true
To our Dark Blue.
Our foeman will go under.

'Under! Under!' was always chanted with terrible force. There were verses for cricket, football and rowing, also designed to inspire stark terror among the Presbyterian Scotch, the Methodists of Wesley College or, worst of all, the students of Xavier College, who were known as the Catholitics. Prejudice did not run as deeply as Grandmother Carnell's, but very nearly.

A Melbourne Grammar boy wore a dark blue cap with badge at the front on which was the school motto, '*Ora et Labora*'. How much praying took place is open to question, but just to be at Melbourne Grammar was essential for social success. Affluent Melburnians did three things for their sons at birth: they put them down for the Melbourne Cricket Club, for the Metropolitan or Royal Melbourne golf clubs and, most essential of all, for a place in form one at Melbourne Grammar.

Travel to Melbourne Grammar was easy. We all went by tram except for the super rich who were delivered by car and chauffeur. The tram fare was threepence for an adult or a penny for a child. My brother, Bill, five years my senior, was told to guard me with his life on my first day. That was an embarrassment for both of us. When the time came to return, he said, 'Nick off'. I knew my way and had to do it on my own. Juniors carried leather bags, which hooked over the shoulders; seniors carried Gladstone bags, which went out of fashion utterly after the Second World War until Barry Humphries revived them by having his Gladstone bag specially made. On the tram, by law and under threat of school expulsion, we had to give our seats to any adult, male or female. Our bags contained our school lunches plus a few books. My lunch was always the envy of all. It contained one of my mother's superb steak and kidney pies, often a piece of home-made coconut ice, and an apple. Sometimes the apple got eaten.

The teacher for form one was Miss Baker, an omnipotent power. Her method of discipline was a ruler that was brought down with a resounding crack on the outstretched hand. She noted at once that I was left-handed. Left-handers notoriously had lamentable handwriting. If I was to have a perfect script and go through life in the correct manner it was essential that I use the right hand like other civilised people. Beware of the left-hander. The Latin *sinister* for left made that clear. The French, too, had the correct idea: *gauche* meant left.

So all attempts by the sinister and gauche to pick up a pen with the left hand met with a crack from Miss Baker's ruler. Actually it was almost impossible to do other than write right-handed, since we sat in rigid desks that had an ink-well in the right-hand corner. Ink-wells were filled with ink every day and we had to use pens with a steel J-nib. Later on we could graduate to a broader, more comfortable relief-nib, but at least until form four the J-nib was compulsory. The ambition of all was to own one of the wonderful new fountain-pens. For example, there was the splendid Swan or the Onoto. Dad brought back from the United States a dazzling new variety. It had a glass centre, so I could see how much ink it contained. Miss Baker confiscated it and it was taken to Mr Caffin, the headmaster. Mr Caffin had a cupboard full of confiscated fountain-pens.

So, right-handed, J-nibbed, I battled, hands always covered in black ink. The desks were heavily etched with initials. We also carved little grooves, into which we poured ink to make fine Ganges rivers flowing in their channels until they made waterfalls to the floor.

Exercise books had to be filled with perfect, flowing italic script; fine upstrokes, thick down. The Dunstan efforts were appalling, ink splashed and illegible. Miss Baker fixed a gold star to pages that were exquisitely neat. Score a gold star on three or more consecutive days and, oh heaven, oh bliss, the boy received a school badge. Miss Baker would take out her rubber stamp with the Melbourne Grammar badge, swat her ink pad with it, then reproduce the insignia over the perfectly executed work.

I never scored a star, never scored a badge. Finally in the second form the teacher, Miss Peters, asked, even pleaded with me to write with my left hand. In 1943 when I was in the Royal Australian Air Force there was a second attempt to force me to write right-handed. It was all part of pilot training. I was told that in all aircraft the Morse key was on the left-hand side so it was necessary to take down messages with the right hand. Unless I wrote with my right hand I could not graduate. As it turned out I flew only single-engined aircraft and never once used a Morse key; all communication was by direct radio telegraphy. But the threat of being dropped from pilot training was so unnerving I did learn to write right-handed, and to this day I can still write with either hand although even Miss Baker, if she were still available, would concede my left hand is the more legible.

Dunstan was a poor student, always lingering at the bottom of the class. As we moved from class four to class five, it was the mathematics that filled me with dread. English, history, even geography were a joy, but algebra, geometry, arithmetic were subjects designed specifically to make life miserable.

The crisis came with geometry. There were the dreadful theorems, particularly the theorem of Pythagoras. We had to learn each theorem, beautifully executed in our school exercise books with the badge on the cover, then write QED, *quod erat demonstrandum*. Every theorem was a mystery to me. I could not work any of them out. The only solution was to go to the textbook and learn each theorem by heart. In geometry class it was the custom for the teacher to call out a boy to go through a theorem, writing it down in chalk on the blackboard as he did so. Dunstan had to do this one Tuesday and he got it right. However, the teacher sensed it was all done by memory, with zero understanding. On Wednesday he called me out again, but this time he changed all the letters on the triangles. I froze. What was I to do now?

'Dunstan, come on, go ahead. We haven't all day, have we?'

My mind was paralysed. I couldn't think. I wanted to be anywhere, any place on earth, except that dreadful school room.

'Come now, Dunstan. The class is waiting for the splendid solution you will give us to this problem.'

Helpless, I drew a few lines, put a few words on the blackboard, but it was obvious that I was a failure, that I knew nothing. First there were a few titters. Soon the entire class was laughing as if they were at the city pantomime.

'You don't know anything, do you Dunstan? I doubt if you have even attempted to study this theorem. I will expect you back here on Saturday morning.'

This was the most dreaded event: a Saturday detention. The sinning student received a printed card, almost as if it were an invitation to Government House. It had to be signed by the parents and brought back. The Saturday prison sentence was not an invitation to more learning, it was more penal – the writing of hundreds of lines. Brother Bill invented the Dunstan Quick Line-writer. He taped together four pencils, perfectly spaced and angled so that I could write four lines at a time. He did try five and even six, but four were the most practical and legible.

Nothing ever again went quite right at Wadhurst. Roald Dahl in his autobiography, *Boy*, tells of schoolboy flagellation and how his Norwegian mother could never believe what the English did to their young. My headmaster, Mr Caffin, taught Latin with a cane on the table. The cane was a metre-long length of bamboo, flexible, thin and capable of inflicting searing pain on the behind. Nothing before or since has filled me with such dread as the thought of that cane. I have often wondered where the school obtained torture instruments of such quality. Were they supplied by stationers along with the J-nibs, exercise books, rubbers and boxes of chalk? Could teachers buy canes individually, like golf clubs, with the correct length and weight for the strength of arm, or did they come neatly bundled by the dozen?

Dunstan sank and sank to the bottom of the class. Arithmetic, algebra, geometry were now my daily terror. Homework was a continuing nightmare. Brother Bill and sister Helen took pity and actually did my homework for me. This, of course, only made the situation worse.

It was in form five that Mr Caffin put me on the daily report card system. The report was like a weekly diary. There was a square for each forty-minute period, Monday to Friday. The teacher for each period had to fill in his square and initial it, then submit this report on my performance. There was a rule: if I scored two 'poors' or one 'bad' I had to report to Mr Caffin and that meant only one thing – a caning.

Then would follow the long walk up the carpetless, bare passage to Mr Caffin's study, the queasy feeling of terror in the stomach, the tremulous knock on the door.

'Wait, boy!'

So I would wait and wait.

'Come in, boy.'

Mr Caffin would look at my card.

'You know what this means, don't you? When are you going to start trying and learn to do better?'

He would go to the cupboard, take out his cane.

'Bend over. More than that.'

Sometimes it was one hit, sometimes two or three.

The first time this happened, I had my bath that night. As usual my mother entered the bathroom to hand me a towel. I screamed and told her to go out. She thought male modesty was taking over and retreated. That was not the story; I did not want her to see the red weals on my behind. I never told my parents what was happening. There was an unwritten law: parents should never be told anything that was not good for them. But I did show my lacerated behind to my brother, Bill. I was getting caned almost every day and he thought something had to be done. Bill, the inventor, this time devised a protector. He found an old car tube, cut out a square of rubber, fitted it with four tapes and tied this across my posterior. We used to wear woollen underpants and shorts of blue serge, so there was no revealing bump.

The W. Dunstan Patent Bottom Protector worked splendidly, but it did not cure the fear of Mr Caffin. I will not say the report card system was an entire failure. In a matter of months I leaped from thirty-second in the class to eighth, but my progress could not be sustained and the following year I slipped back again. The school reports said, 'Has tried this term but could show more application', 'Often inattentive in class' and 'Better than last term but much more improvement required'.

There was only one possible solution: send him to boarding-school. Geelong Grammar would be ideal; 80 kilometres from Melbourne he would be free of all distractions. There he would be able to devote himself entirely to study.

Banishment to Geelong Grammar I saw as a disaster of major proportions.

As a school Geelong Grammar was considered slightly effeminate. The boys wore pretty, pale blue caps, pale blue ties and stiff collars. In the junior school they wore half-belted jackets and, glory be, Eton collars, huge things that came right down over the jacket lapels. I had seen them before. Tom Merry, Bob Cherry and those chaps in the English comics the *Gem* and the *Magnet* wore Eton collars.

And what did Geelong Grammar ever do? It had been known on rare occasions to win the boat race, but in serious matters, such as cricket and football, it was hopeless, never got anywhere. Geelong Grammar had a school song, but not a rollicking rabble-rouser that promised death to the enemy. Instead – could any schoolboy believe it? – it had a school song in Latin. What use was this at a boat race?

> *Salve schola te pia laude efferamus,*
> *Pueri, viri, senes, usque te amamus;*
> *O Corio, praenitens ludo et labore,*
> *Floreas virtutibus floreas honore.*

Ask any Geelong Grammarian what it meant and he had not the slightest idea.

Then there was the problem of leaving my warm and comfortable nest, my close circle of Melbourne Grammar friends, matinées at Hoyts, and skating at the Glaciarium, to say nothing of the bountiful supplies from the Elliott soft drink company.

Dad was a director of many companies – Email, AWA and Prudential among others – but best of all he was a director of the Elliott soft drink company, which meant we had a permanent supply of lemonade, cola beer, raspberry soda and my favourite, creamy soda. These were stored in an ice chest. The ice man called twice a week, a big block of ice in a hessian bag on his shoulder. We had two ice chests, one in the kitchen and one on the back verandah. Some time in the early 1930s Dad became one of the first to get an electric refrigerator. As if the Elliott soft drinks were not enough, there was Sharpe's brewed ginger beer, the most heavenly drink of all. The Sharpe man had a horse-drawn wagon and he called on Thursdays. The ginger beer came in 4.5-litre stone demijohns. With careful management it would last just a week until he called again. There was a steady beat of horse-drawn delivery vehicles up Wallace Avenue. Milk and bread also came by horse power. My mother's favourite was the Chinese fruiterer, a gentle, sweet man, who sold fresh vegetables. Every Christmas he presented her with a green ceramic jar of ginger.

In addition to this, I faced the cultural shock of leaving my mother's cooking if I went to Geelong Grammar. Mum adored to cook and this was a sublime era when it was not considered evil to have a large waistline, when there was no such word as cholesterol in the vocabulary and when people did not try to live longer by not eating. Citizens did not jog, smokers were not pariahs and a cigar after dinner was considered a good smoke. A large breakfast was essential.

For breakfast it was good to have steak and eggs, chops and eggs or sausages and eggs, but Mrs Dunstan's family special was fried eggs with fried bread. We had a cool cupboard in the kitchen, which always contained a large basin of dripping. After the cooking of every roast Mother topped it up, so never did we go short of fat.

A shortage of fat would have been terrible. Fat was necessary perhaps not so much for frying the eggs, as for frying a slice of bread to perfection in the deep, cast-iron pan. This required a lake of fat, very hot. The fried bread came out crispy and crunchy to the tooth. Tears of nostalgia come to the eye at the very thought of that fried bread. Even better were fried scones. Two or three times a week my mother made scones for afternoon tea, always being careful to make too many. This meant a breakfast next day of fried eggs and marvellous fried scones. Cooking them in butter was no good. It had to be the succulent beef dripping.

On Saturday morning, before Dad went to golf for the day, there were brain fritters. Sometimes Mum varied them with beef fritters and home-made tomato sauce, but absolutely the best fritters were the brain variety. Mum mixed up the batter, stirred in the lambs' brains and then, while I watched in wonder, put the fritters into the big frying-pan, with its splendid lake of fat.

Mum always cooked her own Farmer's ham. She did this in a pastry shell that set like iron, providing the ham with an oven of its own. Cooking over, off came the pastry cover, like a plaster cast removed from a broken leg. Mum then decorated the ham with pineapple rings and cherries. On the outside of every ham is a thick, white aureole of fat. These days it is treated as if it is cyanide.

'Absolutely the best part', cried Dad as he carved.

It was, too.

On Sundays there was the ritual of the wing rib of beef, which was massive, thick, red. Dad carved by making one large horizontal slice from which he then took mini-slices of fillet. Nobody usurped his position as carver. He claimed that had he been given the proper education he would have made a brilliant surgeon – except that all the surgeons he knew were abominable carvers. The wing rib was cooked in its own grand cast-iron dish and its own lake of fat, into which went the roast potatoes. That wing rib was always a beauty, a small mountain of meat.

'How did I get it? Well, I sat on the butcher's table and stroked his cheek', Mum would say impishly.

After the Sunday lunch ritual came the Sunday supper. Dad carved further slices from the wing rib and we made them into big sandwiches.

Another special was the Cornish pastie. The recipe had been handed down through many generations of Cornish Dunstans. The ingredients were a whole leg of lamb cut into fine pieces, turnips, onions and potatoes. It was large – two-thirds of a metre long – with a perfect rope of pastry across the top. Much work had to be done, much chopping and infinite slicing, but the Cornish pastie refined and improved by Marjorie Dunstan is still made in Dunstan households.

Mum's cakes were something to behold also: sponge cakes, fruit cakes, coffee cakes, lamingtons. Her lamingtons were not your anaemic, flaccid, kapok, church-fête lamingtons. Hers were made of the best quality cake, thick chocolate and masses of coconut. There was a Madeira cake recipe that had come down through the generations, but Mum made it her masterpiece. Into the mixing-bowl went astonishing quantities of butter. Madeira cake was meant to be long lasting, but if it survived uneaten for three days it was a record for longevity.

'I think it just needs a little straightening. It's crooked', was Mum's favourite line.

So we would straighten the Madeira cake with yet another slice. Fortunately nobody ever achieved the perfect straightness.

My mother was kind. She passed on her recipes and particularly that of the Madeira cake. Yet no one could ever get just the right consistency. It was like trying to repeat a 1961 Château d'Yquem or make your own Johnny Walker Black Label. We never got there and sometimes we wondered whether she had left out a magic ingredient in the recipe.

Then there was Mum's chocolate cake, rich and capped with thick chocolate icing. Always there would be such a cake to greet us when we came home from school. Our house was like a subscription-free club for small boys. They flocked there after school for Marjorie Dunstan's chocolate cake and the endless supply of sweet, fizzy drinks.

Occasionally there would be even more than chocolate cake and soft drink after school if Mum had been entertaining ladies to afternoon tea. Afternoon tea in the 1930s was a serious social matter. Ladies constantly asked each other to afternoon tea, which took place from 3 p.m. to 5 p.m. The ladies dressed in their finest afternoon tea dresses, plus hat and gloves. My mother never approved of any female who set foot abroad not wearing both hat and gloves. The ladies, maybe nine or ten of them, would gather in the best room – the sitting-room or parlour – which was kept for grand occasions. The sitting-room was resplendent with marble fireplace, lustres on the mantelpiece and piano in the corner, complete with pedal Pianola and Pianola rolls that played songs from *The Desert Song, The Vagabond King* and *The Maid of the Mountains*.

There was an hour of polite chat, then, some time after 4 p.m., a signal was given to Mary or Violet and in she came with an autotray. On it was the silver teapot, the silver hot-water jug and the best Minton china. Tea, never coffee, was served. Coffee did not become the vogue until the Second World War, with the arrival of United States troops, and afterwards with the migrant invasion from Greece and Italy. On the autotray there was also the food. There were always delicate sandwiches, cut into diamonds and neatly arranged with parsley on a silver salver. The ladies worked on these first, then negotiated their way through the shortbread, the sponge fingers, the lamingtons, the éclairs, saving just a little room for the splendid climax: the sponge cake filled with thick country cream. Heaven it was to come home from school in time to catch the left-overs.

Of course, as the youngest, I was much indulged in the family. The hard battles had been fought by Bill and Helen. I was particularly the favourite of my Aunt Nell, and legend has it that for my first three years I was raised almost entirely on penny Nestlé's chocolate bars and MacRobertson's chocolate frogs. To say that I got away with murder at home is an understatement; there has to be a stronger term. If school was always something to be escaped, home was something to be treasured. Life began again as soon as I left the gates of Wadhurst.

I had a great team of friends, a regular gang. There was David Campbell, whose father was a wholesale dealer in exotic hardware – all those door knobs, window sashes and such never sold by anyone else. Campbell was an unusual character who liked to do daring and different things. There was also Milton Johnson, whose father was an architect. Milton, who later became a distinguished engineer, could make anything, even boats for sailing on Port Phillip Bay, and his model aeroplanes were always neater, better crafted and more airworthy than mine. And there was Dicky Bland, later to become an accountant. Dick was the brainy one, always top of the class, and his name was in gold on the honour board. It was good to look over his shoulder when we had algebra problems. Campbell lived in Balmerino Avenue near the Yarra, and the river became our special playground, as the Mississippi had been for Tom Sawyer. We spent hours making tunnels through the fennel in the open paddocks around Burnley. However, our greatest thrill – and terror – came from walking kilometres up the great drainage pipe that spilled water into the Yarra. As we walked in the darkness of the pipe we imagined we were under Toorak's stateliest homes.

One of our passions was the new game Monopoly. After school we rushed home to get out the Monopoly board and played until mothers began demanding the return of their children. Monopoly was a very good game for educating the young about greed and money. Yes, 400 pounds for the purchase of Mayfair, 150 pounds for the Waterworks, even 60 pounds for Old Kent Road seemed huge sums then. How fascinating that this power game of money, borrowing and acquiring property was invented at the height of the 1930s Depression. But little schoolboys at an Anglican public school knew nothing of depressions; a great national disaster passed us by. I remember travelling along the Footscray Road by the then-vacant lands that we called Dudley Flats, where the unemployed, the wretched and the near starving lived in humpies made out of galvanised iron little better than the cubbies we built on the garage roof. When I asked why people lived there, the answer was non-committal. Children should not worry about such things.

Weekends at home had a special wonder. Every winter I had a season's ticket to the Glaciarium, the ice-skating rink on the edge of the city, just near the YMCA in South Melbourne. Known as the Glaci, it was the world's seventh ice-skating rink and the oldest in continuous operation. It opened on 8 June 1906. The entrepreneur was Mr H. Newman Reid, late general manager of the Portland and Western District Freezing Company. On that great day in 1906 he spoke of the marvels of the equipment, the mechanical stoking gear for the furnaces, how not a breath of smoke polluted Melbourne's air and how every texture could be given to the ice, from granite hard to cushion soft. At the opening there were 2000 ladies and gentlemen present, including representatives of both Houses of Parliament and the Chief Railways Commissioner, Mr T. Tait, who gave an elegant exhibition of skating.

In the days before drive-ins, bowling alleys, indoor cricket and television, the Glaciarium was the social centre of Melbourne. Many a beautiful Melburnian romance, on skates hired at a shilling a pair, blossomed in the Glaci's Mugs' Alley. It was marvellous to get to the rink very early on Saturday morning and be the first out, when there was a faint fog across the floor and the ice was virgin smooth. We skated to 'The Skaters' Waltz', then put on our tubes for the speed session. At half-time the prime delicacy was hot crumpets soaked in butter and topped with honey. If a skater needed to retire to the lavatory, the correct term was 'Excuse me, I must tighten my skates'.

Skating was rather genteel and polished. Skaters had to be correctly attired, usually in a proper shirt, tie and jacket. In the 1920s, for example, *Table Talk* recommended that lady figure skaters wear properly fitted frocks with fur collars and cloche hats. The opening of the season was always a black-tie affair, and the finish, for the select few, was a sentimental occasion. The ammonia was turned off, the ice melted, water became centimetres deep and we had the excitement of seeing who could skate over the bumps of the pipes.

Then, of course, there were the speed boys. Young Lex Davison indulged his first urge for speed at the Glaci, while the band played 'The Post Horn Gallop'. A really hot skater jumped chairs or barrels; the record for this was sixteen.

In the 1950s the Glaci began to report losses. The 1954 annual report said that the customers were taking to square dancing. In

1957 the Glaci closed down for ever, and a group from Flinders Lane bought it for 135 000 pounds. In April 1963, alas, it burned to the ground.

On Saturday afternoons we went to the Regent Theatre, South Yarra, which had a Saturday arvo matinée designed especially for the young. Hoyts would have give-aways designed to entice the young: balloons, sweets, cardboard gliders, mini-pistols. It was not the main feature that got us there, but the weekly episodes of Tarzan, Zorro, the Lone Ranger, Flash Gordon and Tailspin Tommy.

Tommy Tompkins, the boy mechanic who became an air ace, was our absolute favourite. He had a tiny airline that was always battling against nefarious villains who tried to steal his contracts. I remember in one episode Skeeter, Tommy's faithful mechanic, had his eyes burned by exploding oil. Tommy was pumping fuel into his aircraft to fly Skeeter to hospital when Hoyt, the villain, jumped into the plane and took off, with Tommy still hanging onto the fuel hose. Up they went, higher and higher, Tommy dangling underneath. Suddenly the fuel hose started to break and Tommy started to fall towards earth. 'What has happened to Tommy? Is this the end? Is he dropping to his certain death? Be sure you are back next week for the next episode in this thrilling story.'

We came back next week. Tommy was still hurtling to the ground. But it so happened that Skeeter, back at base, made a sudden and brilliant recovery. He took off in another plane and flew under the plane from which Tommy dangled. Just as the hose broke there Skeeter was, and Tommy dropped safely, right on top of his aircraft. What a relief that was.

Just as a treat Mum occasionally took us all in the tram to the State Theatre in Flinders Street. The State was an amazing example of architecture in the grand Hollywood style. It was the largest theatre ever built in Australia, with over 3300 seats. The exterior had a clock tower, a dome, minarets and filigree bits; you could call it Westminster trying to be a Persian temple. Inside it was more ancient Greece, with statuary plus a few sacred relics, such as Rudolf Valentino's very own sword, later stolen. Up aloft there was an artificial sky with scudding clouds and little stars that twinkled. That was a city adventure, going and returning by tram.

Also important was Luna Park. Regrettably the Dunstan parents drew the line at Luna Park, which they looked upon as junk entertainment. There it was at St Kilda, its entrance a grinning face. Visitors walked in through the mouth, under gigantic teeth, to find the wonders of the Big Dipper, the Scenic Railway, the River Caves and the Giggle Palace, with its long, bumpy slide and funny mirrors. One year a noble parent took the entire class at Wadhurst to Luna Park for a birthday party. Even now I look back on it as an event very close to heaven.

So leaving all this, leaving the comfort and freedom of 20 Wallace Avenue, seemed at the time a living death, like going to Pentridge, Fanny Bay or Boggo Road Gaol. I pleaded with my father to let me stay at Melbourne Grammar. Melbourne Grammar, particularly in fifth form, had been a special kind of hell, but distant Geelong seemed infinitely worse. Protesting made no difference. My father was a kindly man, but his authority was complete. He was never to be crossed.

There was one last glorious summer holiday in 1939 before I went to boarding-school, the last of an era.

Every year, Dad booked the entire family into Erskine House, a large, gracious guest-house at Lorne, which had been there since the 1880s. We stayed there from immediately after Christmas until the first week of February, although Dad sometimes returned to the city and came down at weekends.

Erskine House had its own gate right on the surf beach, its own grass tennis-courts, bowling greens, croquet lawns, ballroom, billiard-room and even its own nine-hole golf-course. There were both ancient areas and modern. There was a new wing, absolutely the latest in art deco, with modern bathrooms and a splendid foyer, but then Erskine House wandered into antique areas, mysterious passages and alcoves, up and down to the picture-theatre-cum-ballroom, on to the games area, and finally out to scattered bungalows among the cypress trees near the tennis-courts. Dad did not like the main building; he preferred the isolation and quiet of the bungalows in the garden.

· The expedition to Lorne was always a grand affair. In the early days we went in an Essex sedan. Several suitcases would be strapped to both running-boards, others lashed on the luggage carrier at the rear. By 1939 our travelling had been refined. Dad sent a Herald and Weekly Times van on ahead. This was loaded not only with luggage, but also with enough whisky, gin, vermouth and beer to last a month. There was also ice. It was tricky trying to find ice for a whisky out in the bungalows so Dad also carted ice to Lorne in large insulated boxes. This way he was able to entertain in style.

The drama and magic of Lorne was the Great Ocean Road, which started at Anglesea and twisted, turned its way along steep cliffs to Apollo Bay and on to Peterborough. It was completed in the depression years around 1936 to become one of the most spectacular coastal roads on earth. In the 1930s it was narrow and required very careful driving. Every year three or four cars went over the edge and dropped to the rocks below. From Anglesea, through Airey's Inlet, the drive was partly coastal, partly in thick bush.

At Erskine House we were always a large community of several hundred. All meals were provided – breakfast, lunch and dinner, plus morning and afternoon tea – in the dining-room. Bells called us to meals. The first bell was the early morning warning bell at 7.30 a.m. The old hands used to say this was not the get-up bell, but the warning bell to advise males to return to their own beds.

Gentlemen dressed for dinner in black tie and ladies wore long gowns. There was a dance in the ballroom every night with a live band, except on Sundays when there were movies. The projector did not run sound so we had silent pictures: the best of Charlie Chaplin, the Keystone Cops and cartoons, such as *Felix the Cat*. Once a week, say Thursdays, there was a fancy dress ball.

Most guests came and departed on Sundays. The service car from Melbourne arrived at noon. Not many people had automobiles in the 1930s so the arrival of the service car, a stretched Hudson or maybe an elongated Pontiac with multiple seats, was a vital social event. Guests sat out on the verandah just to run an eye over newcomers. At 1 p.m. those leaving were farewelled.

No one ever stayed for less than seven days because a whole week's activities were organised. Each Sunday a committee was elected to arrange the entertainments and sports for the following week. Archie Whyte, a born entertainer and compère, was a favourite president. The week's programme included tournaments for bowls, tennis, golf-croquet, golf and table tennis, complete with a treasure hunt and a sand castle competition for the children.

In the summer of 1939 I was brave enough to enter the golf-croquet tournament, a very serious matter, indeed. The croquet lawns, like those for the lawn bowls, were as smooth as velvet, beautifully manicured by George the greenkeeper. Guests never considered walking on them unless in the correct shoes. I fancied myself as an exponent of croquet, having a reasonably straight eye. I can't remember the name of the female champion, but let us call her Hilda Derbyshire. She played pennant croquet in Melbourne. The draw was always placed on the notice-board on Sunday evening. Mrs Derbyshire ran her finger down the list and noticed with some satisfaction that her partner was Mr Dunstan. Unbeknown to her, Dad did not play croquet. That was not his style at all. Mrs Derbyshire was aghast, horrified, even humiliated, when she at length found that the Dunstan in question was a 14-year-old boy. Worse than that, he was little, blond and looked about 10 years old.

Golf-croquet is a mean, ruthless game, ideal for ladies dressed as nuns, in all white. As soon as your opponent gets in a position of advantage the idea is for you to blast this enemy out of existence. Yet the game is full of subtlety, requiring, like billiards, a knowledge of what happens when two spheres collide, of what direction each will take. Then, too, the ball has to be projected through hoop after hoop.

Mrs Derbyshire was so furious she did not speak to me through the first round, which oddly enough we won with ease. The second round she was the martinet, the drill sergeant; every prance of the ballet was directed by her. Of course, Mrs Derbyshire had her own personal weapon, which she always brought to the green in its own protector. Don Bradman could not have looked after his cricket bat half as much as Mrs Derbyshire cared for her croquet mallet.

By the fourth round her fury had subsided. She was calling me not only Keith, but also her little pal. The final took place on Saturday evening and all Erskine House gathered to witness this mighty event. The crisis came at the end. I had to play a 5-metre shot right across the green to blast my female opponent. Mrs Derbyshire said in icy tones, tones that might have been expected from Field Marshal Montgomery at Alamein, 'Keith, you will remove Mrs Watson and I don't expect you to miss'.

There was a long, tense pause, all eyes staring. It wasn't exactly like Greg Norman lining up for a long putt. No, there was a sighting line down the centre of the mallet. I pretended I was at home with my Daisy air-rifle, which I used by the hour firing lead pellets at Havelock tobacco tins. I lined up my opponent's ball.

'Now', hissed Mrs Derbyshire.

My ball went right across the green. A direct hit on Mrs Watson's. Mrs Derbyshire sailed through the final hoop and we won. Never again did I dare enter the croquet competition. I wanted to preserve my record. It was the greatest triumph in my miserable sporting career, and I won a whole pound, a fortune practically beyond my dreams. The prize was presented on Saturday night in the hall at the weekly prize-giving.

Another important event was the Erskine House photograph, which took place at least once every summer. The entire complement of guests gathered on the lawn in front of the verandah at 11 a.m. Carefully the photographer arranged us in appropriate rows. The camera was on a wooden tripod, with a black cloth shade for the photographer's head, and it had an extraordinary lens that operated by clockwork motor. The lens moved in a 45-degree arc so that it could produce a panorama of the guests. My cousin George Farmer and I always made sure that we were positioned in the left-hand corner of the group, then, as soon as the lens started whirring, we sprinted round the back and got into position on the right-hand side of the group. Somewhere in the family archives there is still a picture of the Lorne gathering that curiously depicts twin boys on either side of the group.

The summer of 1939 was drought ridden, hot and dry. Victoria was famous for its dreaded north wind. In the 1850s and 1860s Melburnians had called it the Brickfielder because it blew hot, red dust from the Mallee. Come January 1939 the Brickfielder was ready to break all records.

On Friday, 13 January 1939, the temperature in Melbourne was 42 degrees Celsius and all Victoria was ablaze. Millions of hectares of forest were destroyed, seventy-one people died and 1500 were left homeless. The fire swept through Airey's Inlet and burned right down towards Lorne. The flames raced through the houses we used to call Little Colac and burned the suspension bridge over the Erskine River at the back of the Erskine House golf-course. At one stage it seemed all Lorne would go and we gathered on the beach by the water's edge. From there we looked in awe at the columns of rising black smoke. Everything smelled of burning bush and charcoal and the sky was raining ash.

Dad was in the city, but he was determined to get back to his family. He was a man who would not be stopped by opposition, official or otherwise. He drove his big, eight-cylinder Buick 860 through all the road blocks. He ignored all warnings that getting to Lorne was an impossibility. From Airey's Inlet on he was driving through fire, at speeds of over 145 kilometres per hour. He arrived triumphant, the car singed by the flames.

There were other holidays at Erskine House after 1939, but never again was it the same. There was no formal dressing for dinner, and the balls, the tournaments, the elaborate weekly programme were all gone. After the war the crowd that could afford to holiday at Erskine House went elsewhere. For the Toorakers it became the fashion to have a second house at Sorrento or Portsea, so that people who drank and supped with each other all the working year continued to drink and sup together through the summer break, not having to meet anyone else. The rich took cruises 'home' to England aboard the *Strathnaver* or the *Strathaird*, or sailed on the *Mariposa* or the *Monterey* to California.

For me it was the end of an era, also. Number 20 Wallace Avenue had been like a cosy womb. There I had my own room, my own private territory in the attic. Now that life was over. After the summer of 1939 I had effectively left home.

CHAPTER THREE

Siberia

The Geelong Road in 1939 was the epitome of dreariness. One proceeded out past Flemington race-track, through Footscray, through industrial Deer Park, then on to a treeless, rocky plain. The plain seemed waterless, burnt, grey. The only feature, over there to the right, was those humps, rather mysterious, all alone – the You Yangs. The road passed through Werribee, a small town, but I always had a feeling of passing through a wasteland. The young prisoner was going off to Siberia.

There were various ways of getting to and from the school at Corio, on the Melbourne side of Geelong. Students could go by train and get off at Corio station, only a kilometre or two from the school; they could go by car; or, if they were energetic, they could bicycle. The rich whose parents had houses at Frankston, Mt Martha or Sorrento were known to sail across the bay in their personal yachts. Always I went by car or train, and always it seemed like the trip of the doomed to the Russian wastes. The turn-off to Geelong Grammar came up about 12 kilometres before Geelong. From there visitors could see the, oh yes, quite lovely clock tower.

There were five houses in the senior school: Geelong, Manifold, Perry, Cuthbertson and Francis Brown. Geelong was the house for the day boys, who came in every day from Geelong. The other four were for boarders, and I was allotted to Francis Brown, named in honour of the previous headmaster, Dr Francis Brown.

Boarders had to report a day before school started. I was shepherded in with my parents to meet the housemaster, Mr Jaffray, to become acquainted with the matron, my new mother, and to be allotted a dormitory, a bed and two drawers. On that day in February 1939 it all seemed so stark – long passages, no carpets, no floor coverings, booming feet pounding on timber floors. Mr Jaffray explained that on week days we had to wear grey slacks, open-necked shirt and tweed sports coat. I discovered it was *de rigueur* and utterly Western District to have your sports coat look not new but thoroughly worn and lived in. Best of all was when the elbows wore out and parents were asked to cover the holes with leather patches. Many years later I was delighted to discover that the Queen's son-in-law, Captain Mark Phillips, always wore leather patches on his elbows, and Henry Bucks in Melbourne had Daks sports coats, patches in the correct position, for 800 dollars each.

On all formal days and on Sundays boys had to wear suits with stiff collars and pale blue ties. Suits were combined with religion and had to be worn to chapel. Senior boys were relieved of the misery of the huge Eton collars; these were for junior school only. We had the tough, hard variety worn by Edwardian businessmen. They were separate from the shirt and required a plain stud at the back and a two-piece stud at the front. The stud at the front had a plunger that was pushed in when the collar appeared to be fixed in place and ready to enshrine the neck, before the tie was added.

On the first day, as the deadline of 10 o'clock chapel drew near, my new collar was like an elliptical spring. I would get it over the front stud but, before I could push home the plunger, it would fly out again, springing around my left ear. Finally, when I had the collar harnessed, I could manoeuvre the tie perfectly all the way round under it but nothing would make that tie go into place. What with all the fingering the pristine collar became blacker and blacker. Suddenly it was all too much, the whole disaster only too apparent. I think that was the only time I cried at Geelong Grammar.

Of course, I should have been delighted with the school. The establishment was similar to Greyfriars or St Jim's. The four boarding-houses were little autocracies, with the housemaster as dictator and the two assistant masters as adjutants. Those in a house lived as separate entities, like inmates of a severe guest-house, only meeting boys from other houses in class or chapel or on the playing field.

Among the boarders of each house a strict hierarchy existed. At the top there were the senior prefect and his cabinet of seven

My parents, William Dunstan and Marjorie
Carnell, before they were married in 1918.

Bill, Helen and K. D. (centre).

20 Wallace Avenue.

The Melbourne Glaciarium, opening day, 1906. (La Trobe Collection, State Library of Victoria)

Wadhurst boys George Derham and K. D. (right).

The Number 1 croquet lawn, Erskine House, 1939, on which I scored my greatest sporting triumph. (La Trobe Collection, State Library of Victoria)

Geelong Grammar School.

The music school and chapel at Geelong Grammar.

Geelong Grammar headmaster
and cadet officer James Ralph
Darling.

The Head of the River boat race on the Yarra in the 1940s. (Herald and Weekly Times Limited)

School cadet Adrian Benns.

School cadet Dunstan.

William Dunstan receiving his Victoria Cross from the Governor-
General, 9 June 1916.

Marjorie Dunstan loved this picture of her three children in the services, Bill, Helen and K. D.

or eight prefects. They were awesome figures of terrible authority, who lived in a private corridor next to the housemaster's study. The senior prefect was responsible for order and discipline. He even had authority to use the cane. In the *Magnet* prefects bawled 'Fag!' down the corridor, and the unfortunate, tortured young had to come running. Fag was not in the litany of Geelong Grammar but we were certainly the servant class for the prefects. I had to clean the study for prefect Nigel Pugh, make his toast, run his messages. In the *Magnet* fags were occasionally rewarded with a cream bun or other bounty. I never had rewards from Mr Pugh.

There were sixty-eight boys in Francis Brown. Every boy had a number: the senior prefect was number one, and the most miserable junior was number sixty-eight. And every boy's number was on his tuck locker, his clothes peg, everything. I was among the lowest of the serfs, number sixty-two. After the prefects there came the room heads. There were three large study rooms with a room head and deputy room head in charge of each. First form did all the menial tasks, such as sweeping the study rooms, cleaning the changing and locker rooms and weeding the tennis-court. Room heads and prefects inspected these areas daily.

'Dunstan, there is a smear on that window. Come on, come on! This is not good enough. And pick up that sweet paper in the corner.'

Matron was another authority figure, small, imperious, in her forties. Immediately on rising we had to make our own beds. Until now Mary or Violet had always made my bed. If we were careful and didn't engage in too much rocking and rolling, it was possible to sneak out of bed, pull up the bedclothes here and there and leave it practically made. But Matron had a ruthless, all-seeing eye. She would have made a wonderful senior buyer for Sotheby's, unerringly detecting fake von Guérards, Tom Robertses and Gills. She knew at once a bed that had not been through the full strip. Everything had to be torn off and the bed made again, with corners mitred and not a ripple left on the surface. A dormitory had to look better than the Royal Melbourne Hospital.

Bells rang all day. The first bell was at half past six. My most vivid memory of Corio is of the cold. There were wind-breaks of trees on the extremities of the school property, fraîl things that were supposed to check the gales that roared over the Werribee plains. There was nothing that could withstand the southerly from

Corio Bay, which in full cry brought ready-frozen air direct from Mawson and the Antarctic. We were allowed a hot bath once a week, for which there was a roster. We might be allotted, say, Thursday night at 9 p.m. A cold shower every morning was compulsory. Bell at 6.30 a.m., then out for the shower. It always seemed that Corio water was maintained at a special temperature of 2 degrees Celsius. I developed what was called the stiff-armed technique. I sprinted into the shower, stiff arm outstretched, my hand hit the back wall of the shower and I was immediately propelled out again. Suffering time: one 250th of a second. The true agony came after sport. We could get away with a slight rinse after running or cricket, but football required mud to be removed. On bad days the cold wash could last a minute or more.

There were house assemblies every morn and night. The bell rang and all the boys sprinted in. Everyone had a position according to number. Dunstan in his lowly position of sixty-two was virtually at the end. Finally, when all of non-officer rank were in position, in filed the housemaster, house captain and prefects. Prayers and announcements for the day were then intoned.

For the new boy there were shocks aplenty at boarding-school. For example, prefects conducted body inspections. It was presumed that all small boys had tinea, or 'toe rot', from not drying between their toes. There was also the dhobi itch, a rash that spread around the genitals. At 9 p.m. there would be an announcement that all boys in junior dormitory had to report to senior dorm. We had to run there in our pyjamas, queue outside, then proceed inside, one by one. A prefect sat languidly on the end of a bed, torch in hand. When it was my turn, I had to walk forward and drop my pyjama pants, while he shone the torch on my genitals. My face went as red as a traffic light. The humiliation could not have been greater had I been asked to drop my pants in a Bourke Street window.

The ultimate shock, of course, was leaving my mother's beautiful cooking. At Geelong Grammar there was never quite enough. A glass of milk at meals was an extra. Parents had to pay a surcharge for milk; some boys received it, some did not. Porridge was the regular morning ration, plus toast and jam. There was an appalling dish, much feared, of dried bacon on a piece of fried bread. For dinner there was boiled mutton, called boiled baby, and, just occasionally, a chocolate dessert or blancmange with a smear of artificial cream on top. This we called Yarra mud, and we fought for second helpings. The food was a continuing horror, and not even during the war in North Borneo, when nothing was fresh, did I find the standard of cooking as appalling as it was at boarding-school.

Yet the kitchen staff were remarkably tolerant and helpful when we provided our own food. There were food lockers near the dining-room and we carted in boxes of cornflakes, Wheaties, our favourite jams, Vegemite and even that forerunner of instant coffee, a black poison known as Turban Coffee Essence. Mrs Dunstan could not bear the thought of her youngest going hungry, even faintly. So she prepared hampers that contained her famous chocolate cake, bottles of her best home-made marmalade, a Violet Crumble or two and, oh heaven upon heaven, crumpets. The kitchen staff very kindly toasted the crumpets at dinnertime. The delivery of the hamper was a brilliant operation. A Herald van travelled down the Geelong Road every day to deliver the afternoon paper to Geelong and districts. Dad would ask the driver to divert to Corio to deliver a hamper to young Dunstan. Just as in the chocolate cake days of Wallace Avenue, my popularity with my peers soared. At dinnertime I passed around chocolate cake and that very special bliss, crumpets saturated with melted butter and honey.

In Francis Brown it was the custom to keep track of any young man who was getting, so the term went, above himself. If the members of senior dorm thought the juniors were getting above themselves, they would call them up on Saturday mornings, when it was possible to sleep in. Sometimes they called up the entire dormitory, lectured them, made them do repeated push-ups and applied a little refined torture. Once I was called up and told to remove my trousers and read what were considered *risqué* portions of the Bible. On another occasion – one terrible morning in winter – I and four or five others were hauled out of bed and advised: 'We are going for a little run. Put on your gear'. Out we went, across the frosty grass, beyond the wind-break plantations to a series of icy mud pools. We were told to get face down in the mud and paddle around. Once covered head to foot with icy mud, we ran back to the house to wash. Rocks in the mud left scratches all over my chest. Presumably some lessons are learned, because I didn't get above myself for quite some time.

Three years later, when we were seniors ourselves, it was our turn. A group of young fellows who had been getting above themselves were called to our dormitory. One of the seniors was E. S. Crawcour, who was later to become a brilliant scholar of the Japanese language and culture and a professor at the Australian National University. He had the bed just inside the senior dorm and, as the junior dormitory boys came in, he quietly told them it was a mistake and they were not wanted. The rest of us felt rather ashamed and the dressing down fizzled out. So there was no bullying after that, and I hope the tradition ended for all time on that Saturday morning.

If discipline was overbearing, there were some sides of school life that were inspired, no doubt due to the headmaster, Dr Darling. For example, there were Saturday parties. On Thursday we could give our names to the administration, saying that we wanted to go on a Saturday party and stating our destination. A party had to be composed of three boys. This was a safety valve. Heaven knows what two boys would get up to if they went off together. On Saturday morning a hessian bag would be waiting. This would contain chops, tea, sugar, bread, butter and a tin of jam.

We could bicycle anywhere within 30 kilometres of the school; only Geelong itself was out of bounds. In 1939–1940 there were 12 kilometres of open field between Corio and Geelong. Favourite places for excursions were Fyansford, the You Yangs and Anakie. When not forced into organised sport, I went on these trips almost every Saturday. It was the ultimate escape.

In 1972 Headmaster Tom Garnett brought girls to Geelong Grammar, a courageous and brilliant move. Until then, like all Australian public schools, we had sexual apartheid. Geelong Grammar was as celibate as a priory; boys lived with boys. We were allowed an exeat three times a term. This consisted of escape for a precious six hours, never overnight. The housemaster had to be advised of a boy's intentions and that a parent or appropriate relative would be taking him out. The relatives arrived after chapel on Sunday and the boy had to be back by 6 p.m. in time for dinner and the evening service.

My father and mother always came down in the Buick. In summer there was a huge packed picnic lunch. In winter we went to the Barwon Heads Golf Club where Dad was a member. The club was famed far afield for its sumptuous smorgasbord lunches and boys from Geelong Grammar would fall upon them like starved prisoners.

After four years of this females became strange, mysterious creatures, seen only during school holidays. However, it was an era when every young gentleman had to learn how to dance, so dancing instruction was an optional extra on the school bill. Miss Lascelles came from Melbourne to give lessons on Thursday afternoons. Miss Lascelles was famous. She taught several generations of young Melburnians how to dance. She had a large bosom, poised herself squarely on her two feet and called out, 'Slow, slow, quick, quick, slow'. Her authority was that of a regimental sergeant-major. She taught in the vast, timber Bracebridge Wilson Hall, where earlier in the day we suffered through gymnastics and once or twice a term had suitable adventure motion pictures.

The handicap was no females. Once a year girls were invited from Morongo or the Hermitage girls' schools for a school dance. Both masters and mistresses stood around the dance floor like prison warders, making sure no couples ventured outside. But for dancing lessons we saw no girls; boys had to dance with boys. I was little and blond, so invariably I had the female role.

'ONE-TWO-THREE . . . ONE-TWO-THREE', bawled Miss Lascelles. I would obediently dance backwards. Even now I dance backwards rather better than I do forwards.

There was a fear among all housemasters of that deadly sin, masturbation, and, even worse, the gravest of all disasters, sexual couplings between boys. These were sins too awful even to be mentioned. In 1893 Henry Varley, a Baptist minister, published in Melbourne a pamphlet titled *A Private Address to Boys and Youths – on a Very Important Subject*. He never actually explained what the important subject was. The reader had to guess. Although written half a century earlier, Mr Varley's promises of a terrible fate for all those who indulged exactly capture the spirit of Geelong Grammar's thoughts on the subject. Varley wrote:

> A short time since, a youth wrote me saying that in a large school numbering nearly 1000 scholars, to which he was sent, he was at once taught this hideous sin; another writing of a superior school in a principal city added, 'I do not believe a single boy who entered that school escaped' . . .

Indigestion, bad temper, moroseness, drowsiness and idleness are results distinctly traceable to this deadly practice. Large numbers of young fellows who have committed this sin in boyhood, and who are now more than from 18 to 20 years old, constantly lose their strength during the night by what are known as 'involuntary emissions'. For this condition cure is exceedingly difficult. The memory becomes permanently impaired, mental indolence becomes chronic, often accompanied by a marked want of moral integrity in the character.

It is only true to remark that more youths and young men have become insane through self pollution than from any other cause.

Well, what was the cure? Mr Varley suggested:

Let every father and mother banish intoxicating drinks from their houses, and one of the chief incentives to lust and uncleanness will cease to curse our home life . . .

Cold-water bathing, water as a beverage, simple and wholesome food, regularity of sleep, plenty of exercise, sports such as cricket, tennis, boating, football and bicycling are amongst the best preventatives against these youthful lusts.

Geelong Grammar provided a complete range of Varley cures: cold water, plenty of exercise, cricket, football and bicycling. The dictum of Dr Arnold, headmaster of Rugby, was never let a boy be idle. 'Get out and run boy.' Geelong Grammar boys were always running, and at the Combined Sports the pale blues never won the athletics title but always did well in the long distance events. If normal sports, such as cricket, were not possible in stormy Corio weather, there were always cross-country runs in their place. So we had to pant along in the rain and cold, senior boys making sure there was no flagging, no lagging behind. How curious it was, thirty years later, to take up running for fun.

Sex was a mystery, something never to be discussed in public. In my last year at Wadhurst the school chaplain had called the class together. He had explained carefully about the seed in a mother's stomach and how it grew and that that was why pregnant women looked the way they did. He had not explained how the seed was placed in the mother. After this extraordinary lecture I had discussed the subject with a school friend, Alan Champ.

'Do you know what he was talking about?'

'No idea.'

'I think he was talking about how women get a disease and have a baby.'

'Don't men have something to do with it?'

'Of course they do.'

I was fairly convinced men were involved somehow. Wilson, whose father was a big deal in the city, managed to get hold of a sex education book by Marie Stopes. It was a triumph. Twenty of us fought to get a look behind the scoreboard one morning during recess. The book had some fantastic pictures, particularly of women with no clothes on. But competition for a look was too fierce, so I did not have a chance to read the printed matter to find out how sex really worked.

My true education in sex came at Geelong Grammar in my fifteenth year. I was an amazingly slow developer who was really more concerned with model aeroplanes and photography than the human body. Actually my seduction was entirely due to photography. My first camera was a Voigtlander Brilliant reflex that took 120-millimetre film. Then I inherited from my family a Kodak Retina 35-millimetre, a marvellous camera, so small it could fit in the pocket. It had a German-made lens, focal length 3.5. It is still one of the finest cameras, I think, ever produced by Kodak. Geelong Grammar had its own dark-room, with cubicles for developing film. We did not have such niceties as developing tanks: film was developed by hand in the cubicles. In the large dark-room itself we used several fine enlargers for making our prints.

A fellow camera enthusiast whom I shall call McPherson came from Sydney. His family was very rich. One day in a developing cubicle he showed no interest in 35-millimetre film. He was interested in developing something else. It was the first time I had seen or felt an erection, an experience full of amazement, wonder and, of course, deadly sin. A game of mutual masturbation followed.

This went on for several terms. McPherson and Dunstan became inseparable friends; as I saw it, almost like Harry Wharton and Bob Cherry in the *Magnet*. But a sexual relationship of any kind was a sin beyond measure. There was no question of sodomising. Nobody had given us a book of instruction for things like that. Everything was hand-play. Even so I was laden with guilt and in terror of being discovered *in flagrante delicto*. Our favourite place was a little cubicle under the stairs in Francis Brown. But we always needed a film to develop in the dark, so that there was a perfect excuse not to allow a third party inside.

A mixture of guilt and fear, and the certain knowledge that masturbation caused impotence, blindness, loss of memory and insanity, made me call a stop to our intimate dark-room developing. McPherson was deeply offended, and our friendship came to an instant end. No more Saturday parties together, no outings with parents when they came to visit and a decline of interest in photography. The collapse of the friendship was hard to bear. It took more than a year to find new close friends of a different kind.

Sex and everything associated with it remained the awful, fearful taboo. Soon after the break with McPherson there was an explosion at Geelong Grammar akin to 1963 when Britain's minister of war, John Profumo, was discovered sharing the sexual favours of a gorgeous call-girl, Christine Keeler, with a Soviet spy, Eugene Ivanov. Also involved was the 18-year-old Mandy Rice Davies, who allegedly bedded such people as Lord Astor and Douglas Fairbanks, junior. There was a blond boy in our year who was the boarding-house equivalent of Mandy Rice Davies. He was discovered in the most awful of crimes and turned King's evidence. Mandy named a dozen boys with whom he had enjoyed a liaison. Here was a crisis beyond belief. Not only did it involve sons from some of the most prestigious Western District families but also three house prefects and a room head.

The housemaster called a special assembly. We all walked in, heads bowed: we knew there was to be a fearful announcement in which the housemaster would virtually put on the black cap and announce the death sentence. It was very difficult for him since sex was so sinful it was impossible to use any word associated with it. How could any gentleman, let alone a Christian housemaster, use words such as copulation, coitus, sodomising, homosexual, masturbation or, or – let's not shatter glass – fuck? He did manage to get out the word self-abuse. A number of boys had been involved in self-abuse with a certain boy in the house (the unnamed Mandy) who had turned them in.

There were too many involved for a mass expulsion, and, apart from that, what would happen if the scandal reached the outside world? The three prefects and the room head he demoted to other ranks, and he appointed new prefects with clean, unmasturbatory records in their place. This meant that when those demoted marched into assembly they had to endure the humiliation of being dropped twenty numbers. Furthermore their names would never go up in gold on the honour boards.

For a time Francis Brown House was purified, with no more hint of the unmentionable. But a year later there was another scandal. This time the crime was too awful for the house even to have an assembly. It was not strictly true to say there were no women at Geelong Grammar. There were. There were maids who waited on the table in the dining-room. One healthy young man, again son of a famous and wealthy family, athletic and good at football, was found in bed, not with a boy but, far worse, with one of the maids. The young man was smart. He did not wait for his trial or to be expelled. He caught the first train home and there was no mention of him again. It was as if he had been sunk down a well or buried in concrete. Next year all the maids disappeared and the boys waited on the tables. A wartime measure, of course.

Despite these incidents, sex remained for us a matter of mystery and wonder. Even talking to women was not easy because they were creatures so different, so far apart. Sexual education of any kind was not a subject. My best friend now was Bob Dalziel, a very unusual young man. His father, a retired sea captain, was a pilot in the Port Phillip Pilot Service. Bob's mother had died when he was young and he had been brought up by two maiden aunts at Queenscliff. Dalziel was an independent spirit. His father had made big sacrifices to send him to Geelong Grammar.

'Absurd really', Dalziel would say. 'Had he booked me into the Australia Hotel I would have learned much more that was useful to me, and it would have cost him less. I would have met a lot of women.'

That was true, but there was always the hope of finding something good on sex in the house library. I was the house librarian. Every book was vetted carefully by Mr Jaffray and then by Mr Newman, when Mr Jaffray went off to the war. There were several books that had what we thought were a seduction or a sex act. There was A. J. Cronin's *Hatter's Castle*, thumbed by every boy in the house. It fell open perfectly at page thirty-nine.

It was the spring of 1879. Mary Brodie, a beautiful girl with warm, soft, brown eyes dallied with Denis Foyle, son of an Irish publican. Potato-eating trash Mary's father called him. Yet Mary, disbelieving her father and devoted to this young man, walked home by moonlight with him after the Levenford fair. It was the first time she had kissed a man. Ahh, her lips were soft, warm and dry. The effect of the kiss was sensational, overwhelming. Denis pulled her down beside him. There was no mention of clothes coming off, but it was obvious things were happening very quickly. The contact of their bodies gave them a delicious warmth . . . Her breath was like new milk . . . Her teeth shone in the moonlight like small, white seeds . . . How firm and round her breasts were, each like a smooth and perfect unplucked fruit enclosed within his palm for him to fondle . . . Her spirit rushed to meet his . . . Swifter than a swallow's flight, together, united, leaving their bodies upon the earth, they soared into the rarer air. Together they floated upwards as lightly as two moths and as soundlessly as the river. No dimension contained them, no tie of earth restrained the ecstasy of their flight.

I tell you, all young visitors to the Francis Brown library were deeply moved by this sort of thing.

We also avidly read *Victoria Four Thirty* by Cecil Roberts. Books in the early 1940s were so different. None went into close detail about sexual liaisons; there was hardly a suggestion even that there had been a sexual coupling, but just the knowledge that somewhere it could happen between lovers who were not married caused excitement and set the imagination into high gear.

We had, of course, not seen a female unclad. Apart from the information provided by Mr Cronin and Mr Roberts, we had to rely on the illicit copies of *Men Only* that were smuggled into the school. *Men Only* was a small, dull English magazine. It sprinkled its pages with prim nudes in forced, ugly poses. The subjects always looked odd between the legs where the pubic hair had been brushed out.

There were two chances for a young man to see naked flesh or what seemed to be naked female flesh. There was the painting of the saintly looking nude Chloe, in the public bar at Young and Jackson's Hotel in Swanston Street. Seeing her was tricky. Being under 18, we had to nick in and out of the hotel without being caught. The other opportunity, and again we needed to look 18, was to visit the Tivoli. The Tiv still flourished in the 1940s. It was the last remnant of a long Bourke Street vaudeville tradition. Roy Rene – 'Mo' – was the star, and his earthy humour packed the theatre every matinée. But many did not go there for Mo. Three or four times during the show naked women would be on display.

Victorian law was strict. Nudity was only half legal. The nudes were required to adopt poses and remain as still as Fitzroy Garden statues. Politicians in their wisdom believed anything that wobbled was obscene. Furthermore it was a sin to look straight at the nudes. There had to be a light gauze screen between them and the audience. So they would be there behind the gauze, suddenly, at the grand climax just before the interval. They would be there no longer than twenty or thirty seconds. All we would see was a hazy, Renoir-like impression of nudity. We would gaze fixedly, not wasting a second of the precious twenty seconds, trying to fasten forever that wonderful impression in the mind.

Sport was the antidote to all these unhealthy thoughts. Dr Darling approved of clever, brilliant boys, but unquestionably athleticism was the road to glory. If a boy could run, kick, row or hit a ball with brilliance, then the climb to room head, house prefect, school prefect was swift. If a boy was in a house team he earned the right to wear a house blazer, or, in a school team, the glory of school colours, which meant a pale blue blazer with a badge on the pocket and a fetching white pullover with a single, pale blue band at the neck.

Sport for me was trying, indeed. Just by the process of seniority and the passing of years I should have been in house cricket or football teams. However, for two years I was captain of the house seconds both in football and cricket. The house captain told me tactfully that I was just too valuable where I was, to be moved to the senior team.

The greatest suffering came in athletics. Dr Darling believed athletics should not be elitist, everybody should take part. So the teachers devised a piece of cruelty called qualifications. If a boy qualified in any division of athletics he earned a point for Francis Brown in the inter-house competition. The qualifications were 5 feet for the high jump, eleven seconds for the 100 yards sprint, five minutes for the mile. There were other qualifying tests for the long jump, the shot put and the 440 and 120 yards hurdles.

I trained and trained but could not master any of them. All sixty-eight of us had our names placed on the notice-board, with details revealing how we had fared in each of the qualifications. Against Dunstan's name there was zero. The humiliation was hard to bear.

It was compulsory to be interested, compulsory to watch the school row in the boat race, compulsory to watch school cricket and, above all, compulsory to be there to cheer on Geelong Grammar in school football. Bob Dalziel was a passable rower but as inept as I was at running and football. The most serious fixture for the entire year was the football match against Melbourne Grammar. All boys were ordered to watch and cheer. Dalziel and I had other thoughts.

On the Thursday before the big match Dalziel expounded the theory that there was something Hitlerian in all this. Why should we be forced to watch a game we did not enjoy? If we did not watch we would receive the charge that we were lacking in school spirit. But school spirit was just another form of nationalism, the sort of thing that caused world wars. We should be above this. Why not prove the theory? I thought. Instead of wasting our time we could be doing something constructive, perhaps something allied to the war effort. Could we not apply to look over the Ford factory, which was between Corio and Geelong? I contacted the management and arranged for Dalziel and me to see over the factory at the exact time of the football match.

There was no point in asking for leave, that would have been an impossible request. For a Roman Catholic it is a mortal sin not to go to church on Easter Day. For a Geelong Grammarian it was a mortal sin not to be present at the battle of the Anglicans: Melbourne Grammar versus Geelong Grammar. The Ford factory was a pleasant, easy bicycle ride, and we had a constructive afternoon looking at vehicles being manufactured for the Australian Army.

We had made no secret of our expedition. When you are trying to make an intellectual point it is absurd to do so without some publicity. Melbourne Grammar at this time was all-triumphant as a football school. It had the famous football coach 'Bully' Taylor and winning the football crown was just a matter of course. Predictably Geelong Grammar had been suitably thrashed that afternoon, so the disappointed pale blues were looking for scapegoats. It was people like Dunstan and Dalziel, lacking in school spirit, who were the cause of everything.

As we made our turn from the Geelong Road and pedalled towards the school gates we could see a crowd gathered. It was the lynching mob. Just near Francis Brown House was the rowing pond. This pond had a little island in the centre, a mock-up of a rowing seat, rowlock and oar. Here it was possible to practise rowing. The lynch mob grabbed the two despicable non-football-lovers, marched them to the pond and threw them in, fully clothed. We were then made to swim round and round the concrete perimeter. We had been swimming for maybe five minutes when the fracas was stopped by Brian S. Inglis, house captain of Francis Brown and splendid all-round sportsman. He called a halt to the proceedings and told us to get out of the freezing water and go away and change. The lynching was over. I always thought there was a sweet irony to the tale. Brian Inglis, later Sir Brian, went on to become chief executive of Ford Australia.

The incident left me with many bitter feelings. I contemplated walking out, disappearing for several days. All life at Geelong Grammar seemed hopeless. Dalziel was the saviour. He adopted a position of intellectual superiority and laughed at his assailants. So we continued to wait, biding our time, for the eventual release.

Geelong Grammar was indeed an Anglican school and, like Melbourne Grammar, had been launched by Bishop Perry. So we were meant to be religious. I was, but Bob Dalziel was different. His intellectual courage was enormous. We had to go through the long preparation for confirmation, which included learning the catechism by heart and faultlessly repeating the Creed and the Lord's Prayer. Bishop Riley, Bishop of Bendigo, had been asked to make the formal laying on of hands. The bishop was a large man, with a face full of lines. I thought he had a face like Spencer Tracy. He was one of the few men who came to the school who could give a sermon and have every boy listening from start to finish. When his son arrived in our dormitory we treated him with cool respect and said little. After lights had been turned off he sat up in his bed and cried out: 'What's wrong with all you bastards? Are you worried because my father's a bishop?'. He had no trouble after that.

Confirmation day arrived and we lined up to meet the bishop.

Dalziel announced he was not going on with the confirmation. The bishop asked why not.

'I am not a Christian', said Dalziel coolly. 'I don't believe in it any more.'

We thought Dalziel would be taken out and burned at the stake as a heretic, but the bishop merely took him aside and tried to turn him back to the faith. However, Dalziel never turned, not even when he was dying of cancer many years later. Bishop Riley said Dalziel was to be allowed to continue in his own way.

But I loved religion, the church, the whole ceremonial process and, particularly, the choir. As a boy soprano I enjoyed the oratorios of Handel and Haydn. Singing in *The Messiah* and *The Creation* was the most exciting experience I had known. When a boy's voice broke it was normal for him to proceed from soprano to tenor or bass. I became a bass. One afternoon I was in the house, by the notice-board, and I heard the music teacher, Mr Brazier, talking to the assistant housemaster.

'Dunstan really has a frightful voice. How do you think we can get rid of him?'

I determined they would not get rid of me. I did everything possible to make myself indispensable. I became a server at the altar and never missed a choir practice.

It was music that made school life possible. In the early 1940s musical heaven was Bing Crosby either singing 'Star Dust' or putting his full groan into 'Deep Purple'. We had a 78-r.p.m. record with 'Star Dust' on one side and 'Deep Purple' on the other. Then, on an even higher plane of heaven, there was the big band of Glenn Miller. 'In the Mood' was the revelation of the year. There was a radio in our Room Two study that would go all afternoon through to study time. Suddenly we would hear the first drum note and trumpet blast of Glenn Miller. There would be a scream, 'It's "In the Mood"'. Boys would come running from every corner of the building to crowd around the wireless, feet tapping, until it was over.

Just over the road from Francis Brown there was the music school, a large, beautifully designed building. I don't think many of us at the time realised what a priceless asset it was. There were sound-proof rooms where students could learn to play the piano, the violin or the complete range of wind instruments. I asked my father if I could learn the violin. He said 'No'. Other members of the family had tried their hand at the piano and shown no permanent interest. Unquestionably I would be exactly the same.

However, whether a boy played an instrument or not, it was still possible to listen to music. There was a special room with a record-player and a library of 78-r.p.m. records. Apart from choral music, I had never heard any great orchestral music. I have often wondered since who would be the composer, what great piece of music would be the ideal one, to lure a child away from rock and pop. For me it was Beethoven. It happened when I was 16, on a grey, dull, Sunday afternoon. Sunday afternoons at Corio always seemed duller than anywhere else on earth. I wandered into the music school alone, went into the record library and by chance put on the first of six records that made up Beethoven's Seventh Symphony. The first movement I found exciting, full of drama, but it was the second movement that brought me to the edge of my chair, haunted me then, and haunts me still. It began with a slow, majestic progression of sound – darm, dump-dump, darm dum – then went on and on, building and building, with a rhythm so relentless it seemed Beethoven had created an engine he could not stop. I sat spellbound, overcome. It was almost like the revelation of God to a pilgrim. I played through the whole symphony and was so excited I ran back to the house to tell others of my incredible discovery. No one was interested. The ratbag was out of his mind.

I went back again and again and listened to all the Beethoven that was available: the Fifth and Sixth symphonies, the 'Emperor Concerto' and, ah yes, the beautiful Fourth Piano Concerto. The school had Schubert's 'Unfinished Symphony', the Chopin preludes and mazurkas, Brahms, Rachmaninov and the voluptuous *Scheherazade* by Rimsky-Korsakov, which in 1940 was all the craze. I had been spending my spare money on model aeroplanes. From then on every penny went on gramophone records.

Australia was deep in its cultural cringe towards Britain and almost everything overseas. If it was done in Australia it couldn't be any good. Broadcasters on the Australian Broadcasting Commission spoke with an English accent. Governors and governors-general all came from Britain. The colonies provided excellent retirement posts for the British military. Sir Isaac Isaacs, appointed by a Labor government, was an exception, but what an outrage his governor-generalship was to the conservatives. The Anglican Church in Australia found only the English-born suitable material for its bishops and archbishops. It was a firm tradition at Geelong Grammar to appoint English-born headmasters, and a candidate's chances of becoming a teacher at Geelong were improved if he had a degree from Oxford or Cambridge.

James Ralph Darling was only 31 when he became headmaster at Geelong Grammar and replaced the conservative Dr Francis Brown. Darling had been assistant master at such famous schools as Charterhouse and Merchant Taylors'. He was to be one of the great headmasters in the history of Australian education. As a Christian he had enormous faith and from the pulpit he unceasingly thundered out the old-fashioned virtues. Above all he liked to see his boys pursue the professions: medicine, the church, the law, the permanent armed services. By the time I arrived he was already acknowledged as a great headmaster. He walked slightly bent, with his arms behind his back. With his billowing gown and mortarboard, he seemed a towering figure.

It wasn't that Dr Darling was a harsh authoritarian – in fact, he was very human – but he had an aura about him. Whenever we were called to a special assembly to be castigated for our behaviour at the boat race or our declining morals, it was impossible to escape a sick feeling in the stomach. To be summoned to the head's study for some frightful offence was like walking death's row. Dr Darling's memory for names and people, even when he was 90, was remarkable. Behind his back we called him 'The Boss' or, more simply, 'Ralphie'.

Dr Darling's political views were more left than right, and he seemed tortured by his social conscience. He would tell us about our privileged positions as sons of the affluent middle class or the rich. What right had we to be there? We all had a duty to repay society for our privileges. He liked to see Geelong Grammar triumph on the sporting field, and his battery of school prefects included sporting heroes, but, even so, he believed sporting heroes should remain modest and secondary to the clever boys.

The greatest sporting event in the social calendar was the boat race. It took place two times out of three on the Yarra and the rest of the time on the Barwon at Geelong. The Geelong schools came down to Melbourne on special trains decorated for the event and with the school crests on the engine fronts. In the 1930s the boat race was a huge social event, something to look forward to, second only to the Melbourne Cup. For many weeks beforehand the *Herald*, the *Age*, the *Argus* and the *Sun* commented on the progress of the crews, and to have a son in a school first eight was a social victory.

Training was so serious schoolwork was difficult, but then rowing was important. If there was the faintest possibility of a son making the first eight his parents kept him at school for another year. Everything had to be done to make sure crew-members reached maximum fitness. At Geelong Grammar and other boarding-schools first eight men, those who wore crossed oars on their blazers, were fed on steak. The rest of the school, like starving Asians, might remain on subsistence fare. But, as Henry Varley had pointed out long before, there was another factor involved in virility. Francis Brown House had a rower in the first eight and as boat race day approached the awesome thought occurred, what if he had a wet dream on boat race eve? His strength would surely be impaired. So he took necessary precautions a week before the race.

Both boys and girls went in school uniform to the boat race. If a boy had a girlfriend at Morongo, St Catherine's, the Hermitage or wherever, she wore his school badge with a metre of ribbon attached. There was a ritual. The young man might take his lady to lunch at the Wattle. Failing that it might be Sinport's, the old basement café on the Block. There she received a Schoolgirl's Dream, which was a sickly affair with a milk and ice-cream base. If she was starving she had a banana parfait, which contained banana, chocolate, ice-cream, nuts and whipped cream.

It was important to wear military boots to the boat race because much jumping had to be done. As soon as the race started there was a roar from about 90 000 people, which did not stop until the crews passed the judge's box. Rowers didn't hear any individual exhortations to pull for their school, just the roar. If your crew won, which it never did in my day, it was correct to rush to the boatshed to exult in its triumph.

'We want crew! We want crew!', its supporters cried.

Then, as the crew came in, everyone chanted, 'Well rowed bow, well rowed two, well rowed three, well rowed four . . .'

On special theatre nights, which the whole school attended, the crew, those men of almost unapproachable distinction, sat together in the place of honour in the dress circle.

There were always fights after the boat race. Flour bombs and water bombs were thrown constantly. Specially refined flour bombs were mixed with cocoa. When your team lost there was the miserable chant 'Who's going to win next year?', after which it was the tradition to drown your sorrows at Hillier's in Collins Street, next door to the Regent Theatre. Hillier's made the best malted milks, so thick they had to be eaten with a spoon.

Dr Darling never approved of the boat race in Melbourne. Nor did some of the other headmasters. It was glorification of the schoolboy and needed toning down. In 1948, because the Swan Street Bridge was going up across the Yarra, the race took place on the Barwon. The headmasters were pleased, for they felt it was quieter there. So, with one exception, from then on the boat race was always on the Barwon and as a social event it died.

At the time, James R. Darling seemed prim, but he surrounded himself with an unusual selection of teachers whose views ranged from Marxism to the irreverence of James Joyce to ideas suitable for Czar Nicholas or the Archbishop of Canterbury. Unquestionably Darling was aware of all this and saw it as part of our education.

Manning Clark, later professor of history at the Australian National University, was the senior history teacher. He taught with great verve and style and sprinkled discussions with brilliant asides. Chapel before the start of class was a daily affair and, if there were any special religious messages, boys would be late to Manning's class.

'Where have you been?', he would ask.

'We have been in chapel, Sir.'

'The Jesus racket.'

'We were praying, Sir.'

'I suppose it doesn't do you any harm', Manning would sigh. 'All that standing up, all that getting down on your knees. Very good exercise for young boys.'

Manning Clark told us, too, of the wonders of the music of Rimsky-Korsakov and the voluptuous strains of *Scheherazade*. He said that he liked to make love to his wife while he played *Scheherazade* on his record-player.

'The only trouble is', he added, 'I have to get out of bed to turn over the records'. *Scheherazade* at that time came on 78-r.p.m. acetate discs.

Our teacher of the classics was Mr P. Chauncy Masterman, later a professor at the Australian National University. Chauncy, as he was known to everyone, was ex-Charterhouse and ex-Brasenose College, Oxford, and sounded rather more splendidly English than King George himself. He had a mannerism of ending each sentence with 'phew'. His technique for teaching Latin was to play a game of musical chairs. The class was seated in order from one to thirty-two. Chauncy asked questions and, if there was one boy who succeeded over all the others, he moved straight into number one spot and everyone else went down one. There was a constant shuffling of seats. One of our favourite pranks was to fill a handkerchief with coins then pull it out of our pockets so that coins sprayed all over the room.

'Dunstan, flaunting your wealth, pheww', Chauncy would say to the delight of everyone.

My education in my final year was all science and mathematics. I was under the illusion that I should become a writer. My skills seemed to be limited entirely to English. At 16 I even wrote a full-length novel titled 'The She-devil'. I was heavily under the influence of Captain W. E. Johns, a First World War aviator who wrote adventure stories in *Chums* and *Boys' Own Paper*. The hero of my story was a fighter pilot in a Hawker Hurricane who, with dauntless courage, shot German after German out of the skies. He became involved with a raven-haired female of startling beauty who was not only wicked but also a spy: the she-devil, no less. She caused my hero's downfall. Laboriously in left-handed scrawl I filled half a dozen school exercise books with this novel, and my father was impressed. So much so that his suffering secretary had to type it and bind it.

Yet Dad was experienced. He had noted that people who wrote novels starved. The future of the world belonged to the engineers. The early 1940s might belong to the accountants, but, come the war's end, the world would need to be rebuilt and the engineers would control all. So with overwhelming determination he insisted I prepare myself for an engineering course at Melbourne University. My subjects in 1942 were four mathematics, physics and chemistry. I could score reasonably at all the humanities subjects, but trigonometry, logarithms, differential calculus, algebra and geometry were chain-gang stuff. A brave and brilliant maths teacher, H. R. McWilliam, managed to get me a pass for all those terrible subjects, and Charles Cameron, an equally brilliant science teacher, managed to push me through chemistry.

Chemistry was suffering of a special kind. The behaviour of molecules was all too strange and mysterious for me. I rose at 5 a.m., slipped down to the study room in the dark and worked for two hours before anyone else appeared. Cameron, who was lame and walked with a stick and was close to retirement, took pity on me when he discovered this.

'Boy', he said, 'come to my house at 8 o'clock tomorrow morning and we'll work at it together'.

For several weeks before the Matriculation examinations he gave me private tuition. Just before the Matric exam he looked at me with what I thought was almost affection.

'Dunstan, you are stupid. You have no brains at all. But you do have guts.'

Dr Darling had an innovative, hugely inventive brain, always dreaming up new ideas. I am sure his staff was terrified about what he would dream up next. One of his ideas was 'national service'. Wednesday afternoons, for example, were devoted not to sport but to this new, uplifting activity that was supposed to improve our skills and make us of service to Australia. Some of the activities on behalf of our nation, such as weeding greens on the golf-course and gardening, were a little strange, but we also did fire drill and learned first aid.

Wednesday was national service, Thursday was school cadets. Military training was compulsory. Our uniforms were antique, First World War. We wore heavy, khaki serge jackets with pale blue tabs and brass buttons. The buttons had to be polished with Brasso at dawn on Thursday mornings. We wore the heavy riding breeches used by motor-cycle police, boots that had to shine like the sun, and puttees just like those the Diggers wore at the Somme.

Puttees were an even bigger misery than hard collars. They came in long rolls and were wound around the calves. Maybe puttees were useful in the mud of the trenches, but to us their purpose was unclear. They had to start at the ankle and finish absolutely at a perfect spot under the knee, on the right-hand side of the leg. Everything had to look smooth, with no steps or stairs. The agony was in getting the puttees to finish at the right spot. Wind and rewind as I might, they always finished in the wrong position, at the front or the back. I then started my puttees, say, 5 centimetres further back at the ankle, but it made no difference; by some perverse magic the puttees still finished at the back. The greatest sin, almost worth a court martial, was to put a tuck in puttees. That was spotted at once when we were inspected by the searching eye of our cadet commander, Major Cartwright.

At first we carried rifles – single-shot affairs that had been used in the Boer War back at the turn of the century – then we graduated to First World War .303 Lee Enfields. We paraded. We marched. We formed fours. Once a year we went to cadet camp, which I thought a penance. It was bad enough being at boarding-school without losing good home time at cadet camp.

One year there was a mass gathering of cadet corps at Puckapunyal, which involved many schools. We had mini-wars and manoeuvres that went night and day. The grand toughening-up climax was a 25-kilometre route march. We were instructed to wear two pairs of socks and rub the insides with raw soap. I am sure that helped, but it was a hot summer's day and by the end of 20 kilometres I had endured enough. There was a cadet sergeant who could have played Lejaune in *Beau Geste*.

'Come on Dunstan, pick up your feet. Left, right, left. March! This is a route march. You are not taking your dog for a walk in the park.'

There was a tall, lean character marching in the row just in front of me. He had an eloquent nose that would have fitted him for the role of Shylock in *The Merchant of Venice*. Suddenly he left his ranks, stood in front of the sergeant and said 'Leave that little bloke alone or I'll drop you'.

The sergeant was completely taken aback. He was not aware that this was akin to mutiny. Immediately he became meek and sweet mannered. He troubled me no more. As for the man with the splendid nose, that was Adrian Benns from Camberwell Grammar School, and the incident was the start of a friendship that was to last for more than fifty years.

From army cadets I moved to the Air Training Corps. The

Second World War was becoming steadily more serious. On 17 February 1942, just after the fall of Singapore, Mr Curtin announced on the radio:

> He would be a very dull person who does not accept the fall of Singapore as involving a completely new situation . . . Our honeymoon has finished. It is now work or fight as we have never worked or fought before and there must not be a man or a woman in this Commonwealth who goes to bed at night without having related his or her period of wakefulness to the purposes of war.

Black-out crêpe went on all the school's windows, and Dr Darling had the idea that we should all build air raid shelters. Every afternoon instead of sport we dug trenches 2.5 metres deep outside Francis Brown House, supporting them with timber. Next we put in stairs and covered these graves with earth. Then we had air raid drill. Kittyhawks and Aircobras were being assembled at the International Harvester factory nearby and fighter aircraft flew daily over our heads. The war did not seem far away. In this heady atmosphere it was not easy to concentrate on education. The importance of war and getting to war over-shadowed everything.

CHAPTER FOUR

Following a VC

The Second World War brought with it a sense of obligation and duty that hung heavily, indeed. The Second World War was to us precisely like the First World War, a war between good and evil. Good was Great Britain, King George, the Queen and the unquestioned loyalty of the British Empire. Evil was the Kaiser, the terrible wickedness of Germans and, with the advent of the Second World War, Hitler and the Nazis and their aim to dominate the world. Not even faintly were there any shades of grey. The day the war was declared, 3 September 1939, I was on school holidays and we listened to the Prime Minister, Mr R. G. Menzies, intoning the news:

> It is my melancholy duty to inform you officially that, in consequence of the persistence by Germany in her invasion of Poland, Great Britain has declared war upon her, and that, as a result, Australia is also at war. No harder task can fall to the lot of a democratic leader than to make such an announcement . . .

There was no delay, no waiting period, we were not even consulted. R. G. Menzies, it seemed, wanted to be the very first to show the loyalty of the Empire. For Australia in another hemisphere, far from Europe's problems, it was purely black and white. We had to be there.

I was fascinated. Almost from that moment I started a scrapbook. I bought big Norman Brothers diaries from the stationer, and every day I cut out the war news from the *Herald*, the *Sun*, the *Age* and the *Argus*. On days when the news was insufficiently spectacular, I cut out diagrams and sketches showing intimate details of Royal Air Force aeroplanes, such as the Gloster Gladiator, the Fairey Battle and the new Hawker Hurricane. These scrapbooks I continued for nearly three years until I joined the Royal Australian Air Force.

It was inevitable as the coming of the dawn that all the family would be involved in the war. On the living-room wall there was a very large, gold-framed photograph of my father receiving the Victoria Cross. Does it ever strike you that somehow photographs were better when taken sixty, seventy, eighty years ago? This one is in sepia, superbly sharp and well composed.

Dad is on the steps at Parliament House, Melbourne, with those big, pawnbroker's-ball lamps in the background. Incredibly the same photograph could have been taken yesterday. The scene has not changed. The cast, of course, is very different. Dad is shaking hands with the Governor-General, Sir Ronald Crauford Munro Ferguson, who wears a general's uniform. Over to the left – huge moustache, classic gold-chain across waistcoat, and bowler hat – is that tough campaigner, ex-carpenter and minister for defence, Sir George Foster Pearce. Dimly in the background is a white figure, Nellie Melba. She had to be there, she was practically patron saint of Australia. All are wearing black armbands. Why? Four days earlier, on 5 June 1916, Lord Kitchener had been lost at sea. He died when his ship was struck by a mine or a torpedo on its way to Petrograd.

Oh, Lord! In this picture William Dunstan looks so round faced, clear of skin and young – far younger than any of my children now. He was just 20 years old and a corporal when he won his Victoria Cross. A columnist for *Table Talk*, 15 June 1916, reported:

> Our latest V.C. hero, Lieutenant W. Dunstan, is a modest young man, and was rather overwhelmed by the ordeal of the ceremony at Parliament House on Friday . . . There was no catching him to chair him and carry him shoulder-high, for he incontinently fled. The photographers were there with their glaring camera-eyes focused to where he should have been but was not, and they waited in vain. One more lynx-eyed than the others noted a fugitive-looking figure in uniform plunge into the Grand Hotel doorway. After some search he found the valorous one hiding in the most obscure corner of an innermost room. The hero was coaxed to venture by quiet corridors to an obscure out-door spot, where he could be snapped, but he could not be induced to face the crowd again. In spite of

what he has faced and gone through and achieved, this youth of twenty still has a great deal of the boy and the boy's shyness in him.

Undoubtedly the photographer had some success because *Table Talk* carried a whole spread of pictures, including one of the entire Dunstan family. There was William Dunstan, senior, in black bowler hat and Mrs Dunstan in a fox fur and a hat bedecked with flowers. Three brothers and two sisters were also present, and they, too, were wearing very fine hats. The reception after the ceremony was at the Grand Hotel, a very good choice for the Dunstans because it was a temperance hotel and uncontaminated by drink. The Grand did not get its licence until 20 December 1920; on that day it changed its name to the Hotel Windsor.

There are so many legends about Dad. He was born in Ballarat. His father, also William Dunstan, was a bootmaker; a surgical bootmaker, our family always emphasised. Dad was educated at the Golden Point State School, which he left at 14 to start work. He used to deliver goods by bicycle for Snow's Stores and study in his spare time at night.

Dad was always interested in the Army. When only 16 he joined the Army cadets, rose to the rank of cadet captain, then transferred to the Australian Military Forces as a lieutenant. When the First World War broke out he was in camp at Queenscliff with the 70th Infantry Regiment. You could say he was involved in the very first shot that was fired in the First World War. On 5 August 1914 the German cargo vessel *Pfalz* – so new she wasn't even on the Lloyds register – sped at high speed down Port Phillip Bay. Just as she was entering the Rip, the fort at Queenscliff opened fire and a shot plunged 50 metres astern. The *Pfalz*, very sensibly, returned to Williamstown to become the first prize for the Allies.

Lieutenant Dunstan was desperate to get into action. He resigned his commission with the Australian Military Forces, left his job as a clerk with Snow's and on 1 June 1915 enlisted in the Australian Imperial Forces as a private. He was courting my mother at the time, and she used to ride pillion behind him on a Red Indian motor-bike. This was received with little enthusiasm by her father, Harry Carnell. The Carnells felt they were definitely superior to the Dunstans. Harry Carnell was manager of Farmer's Hams and

Bacon, while Billy Dunstan was the son of a bootmaker. Legend has it that Grandmother Carnell said, 'You can marry my daughter if you come back with the VC'.

The legend went even further. When Dad did win his medal, the news boys for the Ballarat *Star* shouted, 'Ballarat boy wins the VC'. Grandmother Carnell did not buy a paper.

'Wouldn't be anyone I know', she said.

You can gauge the terror and urgency of the Gallipoli campaign by the speed with which my father was sent into action. He enlisted in the AIF on 1 June and sailed on 17 June. He went straight into action with re-enforcements to the 7th Battalion at Lone Pine. Lone Pine was the second great attempt to take the Gallipoli Peninsula and has been described as the peak of valour in Australian military history. There were seven Victoria Crosses awarded for bravery at Lone Pine, four in twenty-four hours. The 1st Australian Division lost 2000 soldiers, and the 7th Battalion was almost destroyed. It went into action with fourteen officers and 680 other ranks. At the finish only two officers were still alive, and 340 other ranks were dead.

Before the fatal day of 9 August, W. Dunstan had already been mentioned in dispatches two times and had been promoted to corporal on 6 August.

C. E. W. Bean tells the story in Volume II of *The Official History of Australia in the War of 1914–1918*. In the early morning of 9 August the Turks staged a massive counter-attack on a trench newly captured by the battalion, which went on for three days and three nights. Lieutenant F. H. Tubb had ten men at his disposal. He put eight up on the parapet, while two corporals down below had the job of catching Turkish bombs and throwing them back or smothering them with Turkish greatcoats, which were lying about the trenches. Tubb recklessly exposed himself on the parapet, firing his revolver and shouting 'Good boy', whenever a Turk was hit.

One by one the bomb catchers perished. Corporal Wright was killed when a bomb exploded in his face. Corporal Webb, an orphan from Geelong, had both his hands blown off. Several bombs landed in the trench simultaneously, killing four. Tubb, bleeding from wounds in the arm and head, continued to fight. Twice the sandbag barricade was blown down. Dunstan climbed up to build it again. Finally only Tubb, Corporal Burton from Euroa and

Corporal Dunstan were left. Dunstan and Burton were rebuilding the barricade once again when a bomb landed between them. Burton was killed and Dunstan terribly wounded by shrapnel to the head. Tubb obtained help from the next trench but by now the Turks had given up the fight and did not attack again.

All three – Tubb, Burton and Dunstan – were awarded the Victoria Cross, Burton posthumously. Tubb, rising to the rank of major, went on to France to be killed at Passchendaele in an action that could well have earned him another Victoria Cross.

Dunstan was sent back to Australia to recover. He was blind for almost a year. As he recovered in the repatriation hospital he often walked around arm in arm with another soldier. Dunstan had sight in his right eye only, his colleague had a little sight in his left. This way they did not bump into doors and chairs. On his return to Australia Bill Dunstan had been promoted to lieutenant, and on 1 February 1916 he was demobilised from the AIF, an invalid.

There is yet another legend concerning Dad's Victoria Cross. There was no greater shame in 1916 than being a non-soldier. One day, when he was wearing civilian clothes and travelling by tram in St Kilda Road, a diligent lady handed him a white feather.

He married my mother two days before Armistice and they spent their honeymoon at the St George Hotel, Fitzroy Street, St Kilda, a very fashionable watering-place in those days. They watched the Armistice celebrations from the hotel window.

Of course, it was a matter of great pride having a father who was a Victoria Cross winner. It hung over all of us, my brother, my sister and myself. Yet the First World War was something that was never mentioned in our house. I was dying to take my father aside and say, 'Dad, tell me all about it'. But I never did. We might almost have never known he had been in the Army. We just knew action in Gallipoli had been so terrible that it was something he did not wish to discuss. I have pondered many times the reasons why he did not want to talk about the war; so many others had similar experiences, but they talked. I suspect now there was a feeling of guilt. He won the Victoria Cross, he was fêted and he returned as a hero, but what about the others? Many of his mates, right there in the 7th Battalion, were just as brave. They, too, could have won the VC, yet they remained, buried in the mud at Lone Pine, unknown and unhonoured.

The VC and other medals were kept in a box in a cupboard under the stairs. Maybe on two or three occasions my mother secretly took out that box and showed them to me, and I marvelled at the rather dull medal made from the bronze of cannon captured at the Crimea.

Now it is too late and I curse myself that I did not ask for at least some of his Army experiences. He had shrapnel permanently in his brain and for the rest of his life he suffered from terrible headaches. When the headaches came there was no sleep and as children we were told to move very quietly about the house. The entire household was aware of his suffering.

There was one day when it all came back: Anzac Day. My mother dreaded it. Dad would go off to march with his friends of the 7th Battalion and have a drink. That was the only day of the year when he maybe had a little too much to drink. I have vivid memories of them all coming back to the house and sloping arms with broom sticks up and down the hall. One Anzac Day there was a huge dish of salmon for dinner and Dad dropped it on the floor. It wasn't easy salvaging salmon among the broken crockery. On another Anzac Day Peter McIntosh, my future brother-in-law, approached Dad to ask for my sister's hand in marriage. Things had to be done formally in the 1940s and late on Anzac Day could not have been a better time. It worked.

Immediately the Second World War broke out Dad contacted General Blamey. He expected to be given a command. He saw himself as a colonel, at least, in charge of a commando unit. The job would have been ideal for him. Of course, it was just a dream. He had not the faintest chance of passing his Army medical. He was disgusted when he was rejected on medical grounds.

It was taken for granted that the children of a VC winner would all join up. There was prestige to be had by joining up very early. If your mates lagged behind until 1940 or 1941 you would say, 'Bit slow to hear the bugle, weren't you mate?'. The answer to this was: 'What got you moving so early? Didn't you have a job?'.

Brother Bill heard the bugle very early, but not quite as early as he wished. On a Saturday at the beginning of September 1939, just after the outbreak of war, he went to a party at Croydon. He remembers: 'Quite a lot of people were there and I met rather an attractive girl. After the party was over I offered to give her a lift home. Unfortunately she didn't tell me where she lived, and

I found it was a place called Montrose in the foothills of the Dandenongs'. He was driving a little green open Austin tourer. On the way home at midnight he lost his way and crashed into a tree. It was after 4 a.m. and approaching dawn when he recovered consciousness. He had gone through the canvas roof of the car and was lying on the side of a dirt road. He managed to stagger to a nearby farmhouse and gave the occupant the Dunstan telephone number, so easy to remember and well-organised: Windsor 6000.

Dad rushed out in the early hours of the morning, collected his 19-year-old son and laid him in the back seat. Bill had a depressed fracture of the skull. So started a nightmare, as Dad went the round of Melbourne's public hospitals. One after another refused to do anything. They were all full, they said; they had no beds available. Dad was frightened, indeed. Bill could die from these injuries. Finally, and it was a last resort, he went to the Mercy Hospital. There the nuns said they had no room available either, but they could not turn him away. They set up a bed in a passageway and he was there for several days until a room became vacant. Altogether he was in the Mercy Hospital for six weeks.

Bill recalls: 'One of the people I met there was Lindsay Nicholas of the Aspro family. He was suffering from some form of leukemia, from which he finally recovered. He was either married or engaged to Hepzibah Menuhin, and she used to look me up from time to time when she was visiting Lindsay. She was a beautiful girl – looked about 16, with blue eyes and blonde hair. Lindsay had a suite in the hospital and had a grand piano installed so that she could play to him. I was wheeled in to attend the concerts'.

My father never forgot the Mercy Hospital. It was the start of a lifelong association, and I think he was half in love with Sister Mary Brega, who eventually became the mother superior. Dad had a number of serious illnesses and he always went to the Mercy. He used to send the nuns all sorts of little favours from the Herald and Weekly Times office, and there would be a case of champagne at Christmas. We never knew whether they drank it or not.

At the time of his accident Bill was already in the militia. He was called up in February 1940 and that April the Second AIF called for volunteers. Bill was one of just three from his militia unit who actually volunteered. He went to Puckapunyal and became an original member, a gunner, of the just-formed 2/4th Field Regiment. That day there was a photograph in the newspaper with the headline 'VC's Son Joins the Army'. It almost stated, 'We expect him to get the VC, too'. I won't say that he spent the Second World War looking for a VC, but I am sure it haunted him. He hated periods of inaction. He embarked for the Middle East on the *Mauretania* in September 1940 and transferred to another vessel, euphemistically called a troop ship, at Bombay. Actually it was a bug-ridden, cockroach-ridden tramp with decks so close together down below the troops couldn't even stand upright. Our father had travelled on exactly the same troop ship during the First World War and it had not improved. Bill was with the 2/4th Field Regiment in Syria, with the British Army at the Second Front, at the terrible action of Anzio in Italy and even in Java when almost everyone else had finished fighting.

Dad, I think, had a hand in Bill's movements. Dad was gregarious, a man with an immense number of friends and, as general manager of the Herald and Weekly Times, quite dynamic in business. He was a brilliant administrator. He had a photographic memory for facts, names and telephone numbers, and a relentless determination to get what he wanted. Melbourne was smaller then and I am sure there was not a person of importance he did not know. He belonged to all the clubs, and at some time or other he was president or on the committee of most of them. He was a member of the Australian, the Melbourne, the Athenaeum and the Naval and Military social clubs, the Royal Melbourne, Metropolitan and Barwon Heads golf clubs, the Victoria and Moonee Valley racing clubs and the Melbourne Cricket Club. It was an era when people belonged to clubs but he out-clubbed most.

No one could ever argue with Dad; he was convinced he was right, and he usually was. As children we were frightened of him but he never raised a hand to any of us. When I had even a single hair growing over one ear he would thunder: 'Get a haircut. If you came to me with hair looking like that and you wanted a job you wouldn't get one'.

When he was away touring he carefully went through all the local newspapers and magazines, took out clippings and then posted them off in dozens of letters. Asked why he did this, he said: 'That article on farm machinery will be very interesting to Chester Manifold. This piece on mining will fascinate Harold

Darling and that story on swimming I'll send to Frank Beaurepaire. This sort of thing costs me very little and it is very useful to them'. It was typical of his thoughtfulness for the needs of others.

Dad also prided himself on being a fixit, a get-things-done man. There was, for instance, the time after the war when my friend Brian Johnstone came down from Brisbane on a visit. He came to dinner and had an argument, at times extremely heated, with Dad on the military merits of the British intervention in Suez. Brian thought the British Prime Minister Anthony Eden had made a terrible mistake.

'Give me a battalion, just one battalion, and I'll clean up the whole mess', Dad thundered. He would have, too.

I thought it was the end of Brian Johnstone, but next day Dad said: 'I liked that young man, he's got a bit of spirit. I'd like to take him to the races at Moonee Valley'.

I tried to telephone Brian, but there was no answer.

'Go out to the house and contact him direct', said my father.

'I can't. I don't know the address.'

'You have the telephone number, that's all you need.'

'The PMG won't give you the address from a telephone number.'

'Why not?'

'I don't know. It's the law. We'll have to forget it.'

'I'm not going to forget it. I'll ring up the Postmaster General and get it from him.'

'You can't do that', I pleaded. 'It would be outrageous to worry the Postmaster General over a thing like that.'

'Nonsense', he replied. He went straight to the telephone, found Norman Strange, the Postmaster General, at his home and got him busy tracking down the address of the house where Brian Johnstone was staying.

I went out to the address. Brian was still not to be found. But Dad had had his triumph. He had proved a point.

Perhaps, however, my father's most remarkable fixit triumph was for Ben Chifley, immediately after the war. In 1948, as well as being general manager of the Herald and Weekly Times, Dad was a director of Newspaper Supplies, a company comprising representatives of all the metropolitan daily newspapers in Australia. Newsprint was still in very short supply worldwide in 1948, and in Australia there was strict import licensing and credit control. Prime Minister Ben Chifley was part-owner of a small country newspaper in Bathurst, the *National Advocate. National Advocate* newspaper stocks became low, indeed, and the PM asked W. Dunstan if he could help. My brother remembers Dad telephoning one of his friends at the Powell River Company office in Vancouver and telling them how important it was to help the Prime Minister. The newsprint, about 25 or 30 tonnes, was manufactured the same day and arrived in Sydney less than three weeks later. There was much embarrassment about the PM having no import licence. Undoubtedly the Herald and Weekly Times wrote it off against theirs.

So, given his temperament, it was entirely predictable that Dad would play a part in Bill's wartime movements. When Bill returned to Australia from the Middle East in 1942 he was posted to the Armoured Division. He soon became very fed up with defending Western Australia, so he applied to join the British Army. He did not really believe there was a chance that anybody would listen to him. He thought he was doomed to spend the rest of the war doing nothing. However, miraculously an order did come through. In late 1943 he was posted back to the Middle East, discharged from the AIF and enlisted in the British Army. He went almost immediately to join a regiment in Italy, where he fought on the beaches at Anzio in an action that had some of the terrible overtones of our father's battles at Gallipoli.

Bill says: 'When I left Australia Dad was overseas on business so I didn't see him. I always suspected that he had something to do with my transfer, that he pulled strings with his top-brass Army friends. Although he never admitted it, I am fairly sure he did, because I called on General Rowell at the War Office in London in June 1945. General Rowell had been sacked by Blamey in New Guinea and eventually given a job by the British Director of Plans at the War Office. When I saw him he said, "Don't ask me to get you out of the British Army, you will have to stick it out"'.

Helen joined the Women's Royal Australian Naval Service, the women's branch of the Royal Australian Navy. She worked at Monterey, near Albert Park, with a United States radio unit. Their job was intercepting messages from aircraft and ships, interpreting and decoding. The women had the same shifts as the men, eight hours on and eight hours off, round the clock. Helen suffered from exhaustion, which brought on a serious ear infection, and she had to go into hospital at the old Queen Victoria at the corner of Swanston and Lonsdale streets. Her illness gave W. Dunstan another opportunity to prove himself a man of action. Helen did not improve in hospital and Dad became increasingly impatient. He visited her every night and finally announced, 'I'm taking you home where you can be treated by our doctor'.

'You can't do that', said Helen. 'I'm in the Navy now, I'll get court-martialled.'

'Rubbish', he replied.

The next night he arrived at the hospital with a suitcase, packed her clothes, put her over his shoulder, carried her out and took her home. Then he called Dr Cyril Tonkin, his own doctor. Helen remained at home for three weeks.

Next he went to work on Commander Gos Lane, Helen's commanding officer, and the whole problem was smoothed over.

'I think Dad really believed that women had no right to be in the armed forces', Helen recalls.

Our house in the war years was actually like a camp for the combined armed forces. It was always filled with soldiers, sailors and airmen who had come to stay while on leave. My mother belonged to an organisation called Flags Fly that billeted servicemen. There was almost an air of desperation about her work. Keeping busy with war activities was one way to overcome worry; but there was another angle, too. Mum believed that if she was kind to the sons of others, someone might be kind to her sons wherever they might be. Most of the billeted soldiers were very grateful, and for years afterwards they wrote letters to her and sent pictures of their wives and children.

There were many characters among them. Norman McKinnell, in particular, was a favourite. He stood over 193 centimetres tall and had natural charm and style. He had been in the newsprint business. Every time Norman arrived on leave he had a new rank. He came home as a corporal, then a sergeant. After that it seemed no time before he was a lieutenant, then captain. He celebrated his captaincy with a party at Menzies Hotel. He was about to embark overseas for the Middle East so the whole occasion had an eve-of-battle madness to it. Just before the main course was served Norman whipped all the spoons and forks off the table and put them into the capacious pockets of his military jacket.

'You will be able to use those, Marjorie. Bit short at home aren't you?'

He called the waitress for new settings. As soon as she was gone he put all these in his pockets, called another waitress and had them replaced. He continued this with the dessert cutlery. Mum became more and more nervous. She pleaded with him to put everything back on the table. Eventually he relented.

'Aw, all right, I suppose I have to keep you honest', he said and emptied his pockets.

The party returned to Wallace Avenue and Dad opened some beer for a nightcap. Norman started emptying his pockets again; piles of knives, forks and spoons clattered to the table.

'Well, we didn't do too badly. I had a few left over.'

Mum was almost in tears. 'Norman, you shouldn't. We will have to get out the car right now and take them back.'

'Oh, no', he said. 'You have so many guests. It was the least I could do to supply you with some decent eating irons.'

Then Mum looked a little more closely. It was her own cutlery. He had stolen it out of the cupboard in the breakfast-room when she wasn't looking.

There were some disasters. There was an Army man from Malta who arrived with an enormous quantity of baggage and equipment, which he stacked all the way down the back passage. He had electric fans and he had radios. We wondered whether it had all been legally acquired. He treated everyone as his servant: clapped his hands when he wanted anything, snapped his fingers at the maid if he wanted more bacon and eggs. A United States serviceman was also there. He snapped his fingers at the Army man from Malta.

'When I do that I am saying I'd like one of your cigarettes', he said, but nothing changed the man from Malta. We couldn't get rid of him.

My mother was always tired, coping with all the hospitality. Violet, the maid, never quite approved of this strange military invasion. After servicemen departed she went over the bathrooms with Lysol. She particularly disapproved of the Navy. She had noted their 'goings on'; she had seen the way they behaved in the park. She thought it terrible to have strange soldiers and sailors in the house.

As the war proceeded it was patriotic to knit for the armed forces, so an endless stream of balaclavas, socks and sweaters poured from Mum's loyal needles. Patriotic people saved money and bought war savings certificates for 16 shillings, which in five years matured to a pound. When they did very well they earned a metal sign, stating 'This is a War Savings Street', which they could nail on a lamp-post outside their houses. Later, in the 1960s, Barry Humphries started a campaign to find out which streets still sported their old 'War Savings Street' signs; a great many did.

Patriots could also be part of the 'Fats for Britain' campaign and seal up tins of dripping to send to Britain. Mum did more than that. Her war-long personal campaign to prevent Britain from going hungry was beyond belief and must have cost the Dunstans a fortune. Every week she sent off at least eight food parcels. They contained all kinds of tinned meats, fruits, nuts, biscuits and powdered milk. The parcels themselves were a work of art. They were covered in calico and carefully hand stitched, with the address beautifully printed on top. Then there were the fruit cakes. The Aga slow-combustion stove in our large kitchen went night and day. During those war years it never seemed to stop baking for Britain. Mum's fruit cakes, packed almost solid with Mildura dried fruit and laced with brandy, were something to behold. She even learned how to handle a soldering iron, and these cakes would be soldered into the tin before being packed off to England.

Many of the parcels went to a Mr and Mrs William Surrey Dane in London. News came through that lemons were in short supply in England (in fact, they remained almost unseen for the duration of the war). The Bill and Marjorie team prepared a special food parcel. Already they had been sending eggs rubbed all over with Kepeg to preserve them. This time they packed some lemons in diatomaceous earth, the material used for filtering swimming pools and clarifying beer. The lemons arrived in perfect condition, and Mrs Surrey Dane was so overcome by this marvellous treasure that she presented them at her church fête. Parishioners were allowed to inspect the lemons for threepence a sniff.

There was sugar rationing, butter rationing, meat rationing, but somehow Mum's cakes and parcels kept coming. She used to hide spare cakes around the house. It was an era of drinking dry sherry or tawny port and my father bought his from Morris or Sutherland Smith at Rutherglen. It came by rail in 5-gallon stone jars covered in basketware. The prices were absurd, just a few shillings a gallon. Naturally after dinner it was necessary to have fruit cake with the port.

'I think possibly I could find a mouldy old cake somewhere', Mum would say.

She would disappear into the cupboard, which was like the Magic Pudding, an eternal fountain of fresh nourishment. The cake she produced was often more than a year old. It had matured beautifully like an old Grange or Lafite.

We battled eternally with ration tickets. There were tickets for meat, sugar, butter, clothing and petrol. They came in little books, and the correct number had to be cut out by the butcher or the grocer or the garage attendant. The scissoring process caused a delay with every transaction. For those good at losing things, such as car keys, spectacles and wallets, ration tickets were another dreadful item that had to be found daily.

The monster most to be feared was the gas producer. Gas producers were made in Melbourne. They looked like over-sized steel rubbish-tins and were mounted on the luggage-racks at the rear of cars. In the early days of gaslight, back in the 1860s and 1870s, before the City Gas Company provided a regular supply of gas by pipe, enterprising shopkeepers made their own gas to light their shops. They had their own retorts and made it from coal. The gas producers of the Second World War were similar, except that the gas was made from charcoal. To say that the whole system was horrid is an understatement. The charcoal had to be put into the gas producer and lit and then gas pressure had to be allowed to build up inside the tank. This could take thirty minutes or longer. Blonde females who had gas producers turned into brunettes, white-collar workers turned into black-collar workers. The idea was to start the car on petrol, then cut in the gas supply from the gas producer. God willing, the car glided along happily.

We had one extraordinary journey, using the gas producer, when Bill returned from Syria with the 7th Division, to defend our shores after the fall of Singapore, and went into camp near Adelaide. This was supposed to be top secret, vital war information, which must not leak into the hands of the enemy, but naturally Dad, with his contacts among the generals at the Naval and Military Club, found out the second they arrived. He announced that we would all drive to South Australia to see Bill. He extracted me on special leave from Geelong Grammar, and packed Mum, Helen and me into the Buick. There was no possibility of getting to Adelaide on ration tickets that did not allow petrol for even 80 kilometres a week. It had to be done with the gas producer.

Hannibal crossing the Alps by elephant could not have had a more difficult expedition. We covered the 725 kilometres to Adelaide in a single day, starting at 5 a.m. and arriving at 9 p.m., driving almost non-stop. On the morning of our departure there was the delicate operation of starting the producer. At home we used to fear starting the Aga stove when it went out. This was worse. Getting the producer going was a work of art. Nor did the Buick like its new diet. It was a big eight-cylinder car capable of over 160 kilometres per hour. Now it became a creature in the throes of emphysema and unhappy with 80 kilometres per hour. Sometimes the wheezing of the Buick got too much and we had to stop to put in more charcoal and wait until the gas pressure built up again. That was another thing. There was little room on the Buick for luggage. Running-boards had to be occupied by bags of charcoal.

We drove straight to the military camp. Dad had with him several dozen precious bottles of Victoria Bitter. This was wartime: you did not ask how a human being had happened to put his hands on two dozen bottles of Victoria Bitter. If Mum stroked the butcher's cheek to get good meat, heaven knows whose cheek Dad stroked to get the beer, but it was a wondrous, riotous reunion with Bill. It was my first excursion interstate and I still look back on it as one of the great adventures of my life.

As the war became progressively more serious, the playground of Glamorgan school next door was cut up for slit trenches. We had to put brown paper over all the windows for the black-out. We had buckets of water at the ready to put out fires after a bombing. There were pamphlets about what to do: get under tables; don't stand in doorways; listen for air raid alerts and all clears. We had air raid practice. Mum was very important. She was in charge. At our first rehearsal she instructed us all to get under the table in the hall. She looked at Violet, whose face had gone all crinkly and sunken around the mouth.

'Well, it said in the pamphlet, you put a piece of rubber between your teeth', Violet said.

She had taken out her dentures and carefully stored them with a piece of rubber between top and bottom.

I joined the Royal Australian Air Force. Dad grumbled when I chose the Air Force. That was not the Dunstan tradition, I should have joined the Army. Reluctantly he admitted that had he been my age he would have done the same thing.

The Dunstan children were photographed walking down the drive at Wallace Avenue – Army, Navy and Air Force. Once again we made the newspapers: the patriotic children of a VC winner. I must confess my motives for joining up were not so splendid. This was coming out of gaol, the release from Siberia; no more chemistry, no more calculus, no more cross-country running in the frigid Corio south wind, no more dry bacon on toast.

Then there were the aeroplanes. For years I had made model aeroplanes from kits supplied by the Central Aircraft Company, Princes Walk, Melbourne, just under Princes Bridge. Children started with the Rocket, proceeded to the Meteor, then the splendid Ibis and lastly the huge Albatross sailplane. I made them on the table-tennis table in the attic at Wallace Avenue. Strips of balsa, ribs and spars were pinned down with Mum's sewing pins, then laboriously covered with Japanese tissue, which was shrunk tight and doped. Propellers I hand-carved and the power came from long strips of rubber. Our flying-field was Como Park, but flying was a hazardous operation, with the most disastrous crash rate ever seen in aviation. Como Park, shaped like a basin, was a whirling cauldron of unpredictable winds. Models that had taken months to make rarely survived three or four flights. The experience was character building. After several appalling crashes I would return to the table-tennis table and start again.

So it had to be the Air Force. I had continued to build scrap-books of war cuttings and they always had a leaning to the activities of the Royal Air Force and the Battle of Britain. Scores of the aircraft shot down I kept like football results. RAF shootings down were always double those of the Germans. Cobber Kane, the champion British ace, was my hero. My life almost came to an end when he was killed in France, trying to loop a Spitfire at low altitude. What a great man. Wouldn't it be splendid to be another Cobber Kane.

Bob Dalziel and I were members of the Air Training Corps, which gave us priority in the call up. I could not be called up until I was 18, but I went into the Royal Australian Air Force with Bob Dalziel on my eighteenth birthday, 3 February 1943. There was a farewell lunch with Bob's father, who was a neat, handsome, but slightly awesome, figure. He was very much the old sea captain. When he gave orders he expected them to be obeyed. The farewell lunch was at the Ritz. We waited an interminable time for a waiter to bring the menu. The Captain's glare grew more pronounced as the minutes passed, until finally he brought his fist down on the table with a thump and shouted, 'Steward!'. The result was immediate. Waiters came running from all round the room. It was an interesting lesson on how to obtain service in a restaurant.

We had expected to be posted to Number 1 Initial Training School at Somers. Instead we went to 2 ITS at Bradfield Park, Sydney. We were issued with dark blue dress uniforms for wearing outside the camp and dark blue, single-piece outfits, almost like overalls, for general wear, which were known as giggle suits. For head gear we wore dark blue forage caps with a flash of white to signify we were trainee air crew. The term at Bradfield Park was to be three months and we were on 38 course.

Our group arrived on a Monday morning and received its uniforms immediately. A second group arrived in the evening. We looked in contempt at the newcomers in their miserable civilian clothing.

'Rookies!', we shouted at them.

One of the so-called rookies had a splendid check sports coat with huge shoulders.

'I believe he still has his coat-hanger in his suit', Dalziel said.

The spell at Bradfield Park was a time of lessons in theory of flight, aircraft identification, meteorology and elementary navigation, but most of all it was a period of moulding – of months of parading, jumping to attention, saluting, performing wretched menial tasks, being observed and being turned into an utterly correct model of discipline. Our orderly sergeant could not believe this man Dalziel.

'What's your name?'

'Dee-l, Sir.'

'How do you pronounce it?'

'DEE-L, Sir.'

'Oh, yes, Dee-l, eh? And how do you spell it?'

'D-A-L-Z-I-E-L, Sir.'

'And can you tell me, DAL-ZEAL, how you get Dee-l out of D-A-L-Z-I-E-L?'

'It goes back many centuries, I believe, to France, Sir. We Dee-ls have always pronounced it that way.'

'Well, so far as I'm concerned, from now on *you* are going to answer to Dal-zeal. Get it? DAL-ZEAL. So what is your name?'

'Dee-l, Sir.'

Dalziel was fearless. Although the sergeant roared, raved and bullied, Dalziel remained Dee-l and never gave in. There were other sergeants, warrant officers, even group captains who attempted to turn him into an ordinary, common Dal-zeal but, like the Normans at Agincourt, Dalziel refused to concede.

The first two months at Bradfield Park were a sorting-out period. The serious moment came with the interviews for air crew. What did I want to be?

'A pilot', I said.

Very carefully I explained my passion. I told of all the wonderful models I had built – the Rockets, the Meteors, the Scorpions, the Ibis, the Albatrosses and even the little Gladiators, Hurricanes and Spitfires that I had carved out of balsa.

'What is your second choice?', asked the assessment officer, a flight lieutenant.

'I don't have a second choice', I answered. Somebody had told me this was the way to behave. Be bold, strong and definite. This would impress them no end. So I added, 'I am only interested in being a pilot, nothing else'.

The assessment officer looked at me sourly. Clearly I was making the wrong impression. He started asking pertinent questions about my sporting prowess. Was I in the school football team? No. Cricket team? No. Crew? No. I nearly added timidly that I had been captain of the house seconds for two years in both cricket and football – positions of inestimable importance for training purposes – but thought better of it.

Several days later the results were posted. Both Dunstan and Dalziel were to be trained as wireless air gunners, or WAGs. Suddenly my entire career seemed over. I had imagined myself

being a pilot, an aviator, a Kingsford Smith even, for the rest
of my life. Now I was to be a WAG. Even the word sounded
awful.

The next two days were terrible. I telephoned my father and
told him the humiliating news, and I resigned myself to learning
about wirelesses and gunnery. I had at the time an ingenious shaving
kit, given to me by my Uncle Harry. It contained a clever device
that would sharpen razor blades. It was unnecessary because the
RAAF provided a ration of free blades, but I was fascinated with
this wonderful device. In my misery I left it behind in the wash-
room, in the bag with my tooth-brush, shaving-brush, everything.
Later I observed the awesome flight sergeant carrying my wash-
bag in the direction of the guard house. I should have rushed
forward and said: 'Hey, that's mine. I left it in the shower-room'.
But no, I was too frightened. That would be held against me.
It would be another example of my incompetence and unreliability.
Dunstan leaves things in wash-rooms.

That afternoon there was an order for Dunstan and Dalziel to
report to the commanding officer at 5 p.m. 'My God', I thought,
'they have discovered the owner of the wash-bag. Now they won't
want me on course at all. I won't even be a WAG'. The moment
we saw the group captain we knew something was terribly wrong.
He was white with rage. We stood before him at attention.

'You know somebody, don't you Dunstan?'

'No, Sir. I don't know what you mean, Sir.'

'Oh yes you do. You know how to pull strings. You have been
shifted from here. You have jumped a course, and a whole month
of training. You have been posted to 11 EFTS Benalla, and you
start there on 37 course next week.'

'Sir . . . I?'

'Get out!', he said. 'Get out!' He had decided it was better to
say no more to people who pulled strings.

What had Dad been up to? I found out later. He had gone
to his friend Air Commodore F. R. W. Scherger and arranged
for Dunstan and Dalziel to go to Number 11 Elementary Flying
Training School, Benalla, as – oh heaven! – future pilots.

CHAPTER FIVE

The sprog

Yes, heaven indeed it was to be close to real aeroplanes at last. In 1938 my father had taken me to Essendon to see the first Douglas DC2, the forerunner of the DC3. It had only one wing and I couldn't believe the enormous size of the thing. In 1942 I had my first flight in an aeroplane. This was organised for cadets in the Air Training Corps and we flew from a flying-field not far from Geelong Grammar. Now here was the opportunity to look at and feel DH82 Tiger Moths. They fitted the romantic ideal of the planes flown by Richthofen, Johns and all the heroes of the First World War. The DH82s, with canvas, two wings and open cockpits, were little different from the Camels, SE5s and Bristols of 1918.

The first month was an orientation period, with no actual flying. We were the lowest form of life on the base and known as 'erks'. Other erks on 37 course were Weston Bate, future historian and professor of history at Deakin University, and Bill Borthwick, another famous name. Bill was to become deputy premier of Victoria.

The erks' task was to assist with the starting of the Tigers. Tiger Moths, like ancient automobiles in the 1920s, had no starter mechanisms and had to be hand cranked. But instead of turning a crank handle the erk had to throw the propeller. The pilot turned on the switches, called 'Contact', then the erk had to throw the propeller. This meant standing in front of the Tiger, grabbing the propeller high, near the tip, and giving a mighty heave downwards. Ker-dunk. The motor would turn over once. Having been warned that the most dangerous place on any aerodrome was within range of a propeller this was an unnerving experience.

On cold mornings the Tigers with their four-cylinder Gypsy Major engines could be reluctant to start. I remembered my Rocket and Ibis model aircraft. So much winding had to be done to these Tigers that maybe they, too, were powered by a rubber band.

After swinging the propeller, the erk had to whip away his hand before the engine coughed into life. The biggest danger was a backfire, a kickback, when the propeller swung the other way. In my first week it did precisely that and cracked my right hand, across the metacarpals. The whole hand swelled like a small football and there was no propeller swinging for the next three weeks. I was just able to use it in time for the start of pilot training.

Flight instructors by tradition are nervous, frustrated people, brilliant at invective. In moments of crisis the student is roared at, cursed at and abused into acquiring the correct skills. My instructor was Flight Sergeant Bill Dale, a gentle man, who used an entirely different approach. He never raised his voice, never showed fear when a heavy-handed student was approaching earth at a suicide angle; he just said calmly, 'I will take over now'. His system was to coax and plead. The student, or 'sprog', sat in the back seat and the instructor in front. Both wore leather flying-helmets, which were inescapably vintage Biggles, and communicated through a speaking-tube.

I went through all the classic moments of training. There were those vivid seconds when for the first time Bill Dale turned the Tiger upside down, and we were both hanging by the straps at 1000 metres. I was startled by a gentle rain of sweets papers and cigarette butts past my nose. The next moment of middling terror came when we were chugging happily in the Benalla sunshine, looking blissfully across to the Warby Range, and Bill Dale suddenly pulled off the throttle.

'You now have a dead motor. You have, of course, been paying attention, constantly looking for emergency landing areas. Now find one!', Bill said.

There were just twenty seconds to look for a suitable paddock, put the plane in a gliding mode and try to avoid gum trees and electricity wires. Just before touch-down Bill pushed on the power again.

'Today we do spins', Bill announced, after six hours of training. We climbed and climbed to 2500 metres. He pulled the stick right back, gave it full left rudder. The Tiger stalled, then went into a violent, top-like spin. The entire world went into a mad revolution.

'You get out of this', said the calm Sergeant Dale, 'with stick right forward, full right rudder, and see, you dive out of it. Now we will do a spin to the right'.

We did this again and again and again. Soon I cared little whether we spun left, right, forwards or back. If only he would stop. The scrambled eggs and bacon we had had for breakfast were churning. Suddenly they erupted all over the dashboard and my flying suit. We kept on. 'Now you do the spin to the right.' I vomited again, and the slip stream blew the vomit back into my face. Eventually, oh mercifully, we returned to earth. Bill Dale looked at the disaster behind him.

'We have just one rule here, LAC', he said. 'When you are sick in the aircraft you clean it up yourself. Go and get a bucket of water.'

On good days the Benalla sky was filled with Tiger Moths. There was no actual airstrip. Aircraft took off from the smooth grass. Nor was there radio; pilots received a signal from the control tower and took off into the wind, indicated by a wind-sock. If there was excessive wind, junior erks held the wings and steadied the Tigers as they taxied. The DH82s had two wheels up front and a tail skid at the rear, so clear vision was to be had only by sticking a head out either side. On one bright, sunny morning two Tiger Moths took off side by side. A trainee pilot in one aircraft had his head out to the left, a trainee in the other had his head out to the right. At a height of 20 metres the two Tiger Moths collided and in a terrible tangle crashed to the ground. Both pilots were killed.

Next day there was the funeral at the Benalla cemetary, with cadets all in their best blue. We did that terrible, slow funeral march, which seemed more than ever to add to the horror of the occasion, as weeping parents looked on. I was a very good letter writer and reported almost everything to my parents. But not this. As in my boarding-school days, parents were told only what was good for them.

It was the normal custom immediately after an accident to get all pilots up in the air. The theory was that there must be no time for them to meditate or they would lose their nerve and confidence. As many as possible immediately took to the air, but my chance did not come until the next day. The time was 11 a.m. We taxied to the end of the field and parked for a moment before turning into the wind, ready for take off. My log-book stated I had received only nine hours ten minutes instruction. There was some conspicuous fumbling in the front seat. Bill Dale was throwing off his straps, he was climbing out and now he was standing beside the plane. He had his stick in his hand. (Never was it referred to as a joy stick. That was only for comics and *Boys' Own Paper* adventure stories. It was either the stick or the control column.)

'I reckon you're okay. Just carry on and fly the way you have been flying. But this time you're on your own. Do a couple of circuits, land and come back. I'll wait here. Good luck.'

It is not easy to recapture those exact moments in your life when you are convinced that you are completely happy, approaching perfect nirvana. There was my first visit to Luna Park, my wedding, my first byline article in a newspaper, my first home-grown, flawless dahlia and – ah, yes – going solo. Oddly enough there were no nerves, no terror. Taking off is always the most thrilling moment in an aeroplane; just the act of pushing the throttle right forward to give maximum power is extraordinary. We had one pilot on the course who said: 'When I get a chance I'm going to fly a dirty big bastard, a Liberator or a Lancaster. I want to push four throttles – you know, in a bunch together, all held in my hand at the one time – all the way'. One throttle was sufficient for me. How marvellous it was to feel the pressure in the middle of my back, see the scenery moving faster and faster.

'Look at the speed. Forty . . . Fifty . . . Lift the tail. Sixty . . . Sixty-six . . . Lift off. Climb away. Steady now. Keep her straight on course. Five hundred feet, turning left . . . Climb on.'

My state of ecstasy was beyond belief. I was free. I was a bird.

'I'M FREE! I'M FREE! I'M GOING SOLO', I shouted at the top of my voice, with no one to hear me.

I did two circuits, made a last careful approach and in my euphoria hit the ground with a most indelicate bump. There was one hop, another and I was down.

After the first solo there was another and another and another. There were even solo cross-country exercises, with visits to

Shepparton and Tocumwal. One day when I was flying at 600 metres I spotted the crack Victorian streamlined train, the *Spirit of Progress*.

'This is Cobber Kane, DFC, swinging to the attack!'

I peeled off in the best Spitfire manner, went into a shallow dive on the *Spirit*'s tail and dived and dived and dived. The *Spirit* was moving at over 110 kilometres per hour. There was a headwind of at least 50 kilometres per hour. Slowly the *Spirit* pulled away, the easy victor. My DH82 never had a chance. It was another of my little flying humiliations.

Training proceeded. Next on the list were aerobatics, stall turns, loops and rolls. Barrel rolls were just fine but, being left-handed, I found slow rolls the very devil. Rolls to the left were also fine, but rolls to the right against the torque of the propeller required extra strength and much co-ordination. The problem was always to keep the nose up, left rudder, over on the back, stick forward, over side-on again, right rudder, then back up again. I found I had to use both hands on the stick.

Night flying was worse. It seemed impossible to judge height just by two rows of dim lights on either side of the strip. Night flying took place by turns and the durk-a-durk sound of Tigers went on right through to midnight. Nights at Benalla were inevitably cold, clear and beautiful, and with the black-out there was the glow of a million stars, but flying after dark had its perils. One night very early in our training all flying was suddenly cancelled after 9 o'clock. There had been a mysterious and never adequately explained accident. A Tiger Moth containing an instructor and a student pilot had crashed right in the circuit area. The DH82 had hit the ground vertically, engines and wings leaving a deep imprint in the earth. Both men had died instantly. What happened will never be known, but the theory was that the student had frozen on the controls. All instructors held a fear that a student would become so frightened that his hands would become rigid on the control column. In many modern trainer aeroplanes the instructor and the trainee pilot sit side by side. In the Tiger Moth, instructor and student were well separated, so there was little a teacher could do beyond shouting.

There was another funeral at the Benalla cemetery, another slow march, more tortured parents. The Australian public never knew how many air crew died long before they ever met the enemy.

On our course it was at least 15 per cent. The public did not know because accidents in training were not reported in the newspapers. Such information would not have been good for morale or conducive to the war effort.

If 15 per cent died by their own hands, maybe another 20 per cent failed to complete the course. Either they failed academically or their flying and navigation skills did not reach the required standards. Trainees had regular tests, not with their instructors, but with a more august official, a senior pilot or the chief flying instructor. If a trainee failed to pass his test a dreaded shift resulted, maybe to air gunner, navigator or ground staff.

We had just a week to go before completing our elementary training when Bob Dalziel received word that his father, the redoubtable sea captain, had died suddenly. Perhaps in a more civilised time, when there was room for a little compassion, he would have received a month's leave. All Bob received was a day's leave for the funeral. He lost all concentration and found himself unco-ordinated when he went for his flying tests. There was a word for it: he was scrubbed. We were both devastated by the news. He shifted to ground staff, and I saw little of him until the war's end.

Before leaving Benalla, trainees had to make another choice: whether to do their future training on multi-engines, which meant almost inevitably twin-engined Avro Ansons, or on single-engined Wirraways. I told my new assessment officer how I had always dreamed of single-engined fighters, how I had watched Kittyhawks and Aircobras flying overhead at Geelong. I was convinced I would be better at this kind of flying than on multi-engines. But I had a fear that I dared not mention. If I was a bomber pilot, making nightly air raids over Europe, could I drop bombs on German cities? Could I drop bombs, possibly on domestic houses, not knowing what I was doing, whom I was killing? My thoughts no doubt were illogical. German bombers had already caused terrible destruction and death in London. The pilotless buzz bombs were still operating. But it seemed that if I flew single engines at least I would have a better idea of whom and what I was shooting at. This time I was lucky. The posting was to Number 7 Senior Flying Training School at Deniliquin, to fly Wirraways.

The Wirraway was Australian-made, a development of the United States Harvard. It had a 650-horsepower Wasp engine and a cruising speed of 225 kilometres per hour. Absurdly in 1941 it was our front-line aircraft, and a squadron of Australian pilots had the suicidal task of defending Rabaul with Wirraways, against the Japanese Zeros. However, it was good for training. It handled splendidly in aerobatics, its only failing a tendency to ground loop in a cross-wind on landing.

We had several more accidents. Two Wirraways collided during formation flying, one coming down on the top of the other. The pilot in the lower aircraft was decapitated by the propeller of the other. Another accident was the result of a cross-country flying exercise at night.

There were all sorts of cross-country trips. Some were conducted at low level, the entire route being flown at less than 150 metres. This made navigation difficult. The smart thing for the pilot to do was to find out where he was by reading the signs on railway stations. Some stations, however, removed their signs to confuse any invading Japanese. Their hypothetical confusion was nothing compared with the confusion experienced by train travellers and lost Australian pilots.

Low-level flying was tricky, but much more difficult was the night cross-country. At the time it seemed madness. The Wirraways provided only one form of navigation, a compass aided by map reading. There were no radio aids. Our course was a triangular affair, done solo: Deniliquin to Moulamein, Moulamein to Jerilderie and Jerilderie back to Deniliquin. It was a time of black-out, but by agreement a light was left on in both Moulamein and Jerilderie. Then, of course, the runway lights were left on back in Deniliquin. What happened when clouds came down or you missed a single light, nobody explained. Presumably you just kept on flying into the arid northern wastes, back of Bourke.

Mercifully, on my night cross-country flight, I found those two lonely lights and returned safely, but one pilot lost his way. Or did he go to sleep? A week later a sheep farmer found the crashed Wirraway, called the RAAF and asked to have it removed from his paddock. At Deniliquin headquarters they had a board with photographs of every trainee pilot. If a trainee was scrubbed off course, a big X was put over his photograph. If a trainee died in an accident, his photograph was marked with a cross. Now we had three crosses on our SFTS course.

One of the Wirraways I flew on training at Deniliquin, 1943.

The graveyard of Liberators, Marauders and Bostons at the end of the airstrip at Morotai, Indonesia: an awesome reminder of the perils of take-off there.

Landing ship at Labuan beach: troops barely had to get their feet wet.

Air Commodore Scherger and Major-General Wootten on Labuan Island: face to face at last. (Australian War Memorial)

Just some of the hardware I brought ashore at Labuan Island, towards the end of the war. (La Trobe Collection, State Library of Victoria)

Sir Keith Murdoch. (Herald and Weekly Times Limited)

Marie Rose McFadyen, on her graduation day, 1948.

Wedding day, 5 September 1949.

Sir Keith Murdoch (left) and Marie's father,
Charles McFadyen, at the wedding.

Groomsman Bob Dalziel and bridesmaid Anne Cornwell.

Marie Rose with our son, David, New York, 1950.

Brian Johnstone, the Brisbane gallery owner, with one of his greatest paintings by Robert Dickerson. (Brisbane *Courier-Mail*)

Marjorie Johnstone. (Brisbane *Courier-Mail*)

My mother and father at their favourite stopping place, Honolulu, 1954.

The Herald and Weekly Times building in Flinders Street, floodlit for the Melbourne Centenary celebrations, 1934. (Herald and Weekly Times Limited)

I graduated in November, just eight months after I started. The thrill of having wings pinned on my left breast was something better than a baronetcy, Order of Merit or anything else the King could bestow. My wings had to be sewn on my tunics and on all the summer rig shirts. What a pity they could not also be worn on pyjamas. For a week there was a tendency to walk with the left breast slightly in front of the right. On graduation night there was a party, with furniture being broken and elated, super-excited pilots fighting it out with hoses on the parade ground. It was all a failure for me. Alcohol instead of inducing courage and euphoria had the opposite effect on me. While this mayhem was taking place I was curled up in the corner of my hut, asleep. Our commanding officer, the group captain, reacted precisely like Dr Darling after a boat race. We were all a disgrace to the RAAF and our leave was cancelled for twenty-four hours.

My pleasure at graduating did not subside easily. I needed the family car to celebrate properly, but up to then I had not acquired a driving licence. My father asked a Herald and Weekly Times driver, Bill Dixey, to take me to the Motor Registration Branch for a driving test. A large policeman told me to drive round the city. That was reasonable enough. Next he put me through a routine of hill starts and complex backing manoeuvres. I was hopeless. My backing finished metres from the kerb. The policeman scratched his head.

'I dunno. I don't think you're good enough.'

'You know, he's a pilot', Bill Dixey said. 'He already has a flying licence.'

'You don't say?', replied the cop. 'Can he do the loop-the-loop?'

'Easy', said Bill. 'Slow rolls, any aerobatics you like.'

The cop was impressed.

'Crikey. If he can fly a plane he must be able to drive a car. I had better give him his licence.'

I was posted to Army Co-operation and became Pilot Officer Dunstan. The percentage of officer pilots to sergeant pilots was maybe one in three. I had no merit over any of the other pilots, probably less, but being posted to Army Co-operation meant automatic officer rank. This was an RAAF ploy, in the face of having to deal with the Army. The RAAF felt its representatives should have the advantage of the King's commission. A very odd, pink-cheeked officer I was, too. My training had been shortened by a month, I had jumped from 38 course to 37, so for a brief period I was the youngest, rawest, most inexperienced officer in the RAAF, aged only 18 years 8 months.

No Army Co-operation course was available, so to fill in time I received a posting to a wireless air gunnery school at Maryborough, Queensland. My job there was to fly trainee WAGs in Wackett Trainers. The Wackett Trainer was another product from Wing Commander Wackett. It was like a poor person's Wirraway: similar in shape but hideously underpowered and with a most unreliable United States engine.

My ambitions were great, but my flying skills singularly unremarkable. The Wackett Trainer was so heavy and so lacking in power that we were warned never, repeat never, to attempt to go round again just before landing. I had been at Maryborough only a week when, only 70 metres from the ground and just about to touch down, I found another aeroplane fully occupying the strip. I had no choice, I had to do the dreaded impossible. So I pushed the throttle right forward and limped on, trying to go round again. I had full flap and, had I raised the flaps, in one move the Wackett would have dropped out of the sky. Wackett Trainers had a fixed undercarriage, so I could gain no advantage by pulling up the wheels. I inched up a small flap, but we sank a little. Inched up a little more, but we sank further. In, out and round the trees, close to church steeples, just over telegraph wires, I brought up those flaps millimetre by millimetre until I was eventually able to climb safely away. Never was I closer to death in the Air Force and never was I more terrified. I landed safely on the strip and had difficulty in standing I was so frightened. In the process I had forgotten all about my sprog WAG in the rear seat. He came up and took me by the arm.

'Gee thanks, Sir. That was marvellous. I have never been in a beat-up like that before', he said, beaming.

I did not explain how close he had been to death.

WAGs were not the only inmates of Maryborough. There was a group of pilots who were waiting for re-posting to other duties. They were sergeants, flight sergeants and warrant officers who had performed with a Vultee Vengeance squadron in New Guinea and the Indonesian islands. The Vultees were dive bombers, huge single-engined aircraft with ugly, cranked wings. Pilots who flew them peeled off like a string of sausages and went down in a vertical dive to attack the enemy. Those who flew them were heroes, indeed. They deserved kind treatment. The Air Force owned a holiday house at Pialba, which was the lovely tropical seaside resort just a few kilometres down the road. One day the commanding officer called me in and said the visiting pilots, plus some Women's Auxiliary Australian Air Force personnel, were going to the house for the weekend. I would be in command.

'Dunstan', he said, 'I don't want the place wrecked. I expect you to maintain good order and discipline'.

I was almost as frightened as I had been in the powerless Wackett. How was I going to handle these sergeant pilots? Some were even senior sergeants. Some were nearly 30, for heaven's sake. They were experienced, veterans of real war. How could I, 18 years 8 months, order them around?

The house at Pialba was one of those rambling Queensland houses, raised on stilts. It had a splendid verandah all around. I immediately established good order and discipline. Males would sleep in bedrooms at one end, females at the other. Lights would go out at 10.30 p.m., reveille would be at 7 a.m.

The party was in full cry by 6 p.m. The Vultee boys not only had beer but case after case of Bundaberg rum. By 11 o'clock lights were off, okay, but everyone had paired off – WAAAFs and male sergeants all bedded in together. Not only could I imagine what they were doing, I could hear the squeals of delight and all the other accompanying noises of sexual union.

What could I do? I had no WAAAF. Could I go in there and scream 'Stop it! This is immoral. All get back to your own beds!'? I sat, lonely and miserable, on the verandah and didn't go to bed. Actually there was no longer a bed available for me. I looked out on the still, moonlit waters of the Pacific and had the most wretched night of my life.

'You've failed. You're not an officer at all. There's no discipline in there. They're all sleeping together. Unmarried. Those WAAAFs will get pregnant, have babies, and it will be your fault. When the CO finds out, you'll get court-martialled. Dunstan, the incompetent officer who ran the RAAF bawdy house.'

There was one other young officer at Maryborough, although not quite as young as I was. He was 21 years old. In this sex-charged atmosphere at Pialba he suggested the only way to beat the thing was to join it. We went to a dance down at the local hall. There was dancing both inside and outside. The dancing outside was bare foot, almost on the sand, to lots of 'In the Mood', 'Deep Purple' and 'Moonlight Becomes You'. It was not long before we had moved from bare-foot dancing to the beach.

After forty-five minutes of remarkable cuddling it was singularly clear that my colleague was doing all those things skilfully perpetrated by the sergeant pilots. My WAAAF had shirt off, bra off, and bliss seemed at hand. Her name was Wendy. She was a brunette, with a turned-up nose, and very slim. She told me her brother was in the RAAF and flying with a bomber squadron in England. Suddenly I thought, 'What do I do now?'. Women always become pregnant when they get into bed with men. The two sexy books by Messrs Cronin and Roberts that I had managed to read under cover in the school library had made this perfectly clear. It took precisely one night, one copulation, to get a woman pregnant. There I was about to do this to a fellow officer's sister while he was fighting for his country in England. Enough! I suggested it was time to return to the camp.

Wendy had been very nice, very friendly, indeed. The following afternoon I suggested we go to a movie. There was a good show on with Greer Garson and Walter Pigeon. She did not answer. She just looked at some distant object over my left shoulder. That night she was with Jack Humphrey, one of the more aggressive Vultee pilots.

Despite my forebodings the Pialba weekend was without repercussions. No one cried 'Rape!', no one had an unwanted pregnancy and no questions were ever asked. Dunstan had escaped court martial for the time being.

Flying at Maryborough continued to be alarming. The Warner Scarab engines in the Wacketts had a habit of losing power. I had two forced landings in twenty hours, one on the beach not far from our love-nest. The other was directly on the airport at Maryborough; my engine expired at 1000 metres – fortunately over Maryborough – and I was able to glide down to the airstrip.

At last my posting came to Army Co-operation headquarters at Canberra. There I did a course on how to co-operate with the Army and did exercises in spotting for the artillery. We flew Wirraways and yet another of Wing Commander Wackett's creations, the Boomerang. The Boomerang was Australia's single-seater fighter. It cruised at about 180 knots. Theoretically it had a top speed over 480 kilometres per hour. Maybe it did if it was put into a vertical dive. It was light, manoeuvrable and had a good rate of climb, but it was no contest for almost any front-line enemy fighter, so the RAAF used it for Army Co-operation.

At the end of the course there was no position for Dunstan in any Army Co-operation squadron. At just 19 years he was considered too young for overseas service, so there was yet another posting, this time to a wireless air gunnery school at Sale. The job was to fly Fairey Battles and tow drogues. The Fairey Battle, like the Spitfire, had a Rolls-Royce Merlin engine, but there the similarity ended. At the beginning of the Second World War the RAF used Fairey Battles as light bombers on extremely hazardous raids over Europe, but even then they were obsolete. They flew like a truck, a large reliable truck, and were long, commodious and single engined. At Sale we used them to tow drogues, a type of wind-sock. The drogues were dragged behind on a long cable. Air gunners in Avro Ansons had gunnery practice shooting at the drogues. We flew over Bass Strait for periods of up to three hours, flying A to B, B back to A, then A to B again. It was very monotonous flying. There was a song well known in the operations hut. It went like this:

> I joined the Air Force keen to be,
> A fighter pilot, DFC.
> Do you want to know what happened to me?
> I finished towing drogues from A to B.

As time passed it was obvious to us all that the RAAF had far too many trained pilots. The Empire Air Training Scheme was continuing to produce pilots by the thousand, but insufficient squadrons were available to accommodate them. At Sale there was a mess full of pilots, more than twice the number needed to operate the Fairey Battles and Avro Ansons. Pilots had to manoeuvre, connive and plead just to get their hands on an aeroplane.

There was a little Ryan at Sale, a United States aircraft kept for the pleasure of the CO. How it got there, I don't know. It was designed in the 1930s, ahead of its time. It was a low-winged two-seater, very clean, almost like a junior Spitfire. It took weeks and weeks of nagging to get permission to fly the Ryan. The CO put me in the book to take it up at 1 p.m. on a certain day. A colleague had it for 12 noon. He flew all over the sky doing aerobatics. The Ryan had supporting spars that braced the wings from the top of the fuselage. After he pulled out of a dive, a bolt that held one of the wings sheared off. The wing folded upwards and hit him on the head, knocking him out. He never had a chance to use his parachute. He went down with the Ryan and was killed. So I did not fly at 1 p.m.

There were many days with little to do. I filled in my time playing music. I had a small electric turntable with pick-up, which plugged into an AWA mantel-radio set, plus my large collection of Beethoven, Mozart, Tchaikovsky and Rachmaninov. By this time my devotion to Russian composers ran deep. Tchaikovsky's Sixth Symphony, with all its moody crying and warlike declamations, suited my gloom. Steel- and diamond-tipped needles were disastrous for acetate records. Fibre needles, which came with a special fibre sharpener, had to be used. I went one better. I used cactus needles that I plucked from cactus in the rock garden at Wallace Avenue. I sharpened the needles on emery boards purloined from Mum. Cactus needles did not stay sharp for longer than a side and a half, so Tchaikovsky and the agony of the retreat from Moscow, or whatever was taking place, would become dimmer and dimmer, scratchier and scratchier. Therefore, while listening, it was important to keep sharpening needles for the next side. It kept one occupied.

The RAAF came up with a new idea to resolve the problem of surplus pilots: a special course at Deniliquin where all spare pilots could be sorted out and only the best, the most skilled, picked for squadrons in the Pacific. It was known as the 'scrubbo' course, the course designed specifically to get rid of excess labour.

Ahead I saw doom. The dreaded posting to the scrubbo course duly arrived. Flights at Sale had become even harder to get and I had not flown for a month. I felt like a cricketer chosen to play a Test without having bowled all season. Once again my father came to the rescue. He spoke to his friends at the Naval and Military Club and arranged for some special instruction at Point Cook. A somewhat bewildered flying instructor gave me several hours, flying circuits and landing in a Wirraway, until he considered all wrinkles gained from flying heavy Fairey Battles had been removed.

So I went to Deniliquin. There were nigh on 130 pilots waiting for execution. The day for my big test came. I waited on the tarmac. One pilot would get out of a Wirraway and another get in. When it was my turn, the instructor told me to take off, fly a circuit and do some aerobatics. I was pleased, all seemed to be going perfectly. The instructor told me to land. It seemed to me that our circuit was a little high and our approach steep, but the landing was mercifully smooth, with no dreaded crunching of the under-carriage. Then a sour voice came over the intercom.

'Flying Officer, will you please check your altimeter.'

He wanted me to check the barometric pressure on the altimeter. Oh God, it was reading 70 metres too high. It should have been set to zero when I got into the cockpit.

'Did you check it when you got into the aircraft?'

'I think I forgot that one, Sir.'

'Shouldn't it be part of your cockpit drill?'

'Yes, Sir, but I presumed that it had been done by the previous pilot.'

'Dunstan, you don't presume anything. Aeroplanes are dangerous vehicles. Get out!'

It had all been a carefully planned trick. He had told the previous pilot to give the altimeter knob a quick turn. So I had a false reading, and I did my circuit at 370 metres instead of 300 as ordered.

Of the 130 pilots tested only ten passed and went on to fly Mustangs with squadrons in the Pacific. I was scrubbed, remustered to ground staff. I lost my flying allowance of 6 shillings a day. That was unimportant compared with the humiliation. It was almost like being cashiered in classic fashion from the French Army – slapped in the face, stripped of regimental insignia and marched off the parade ground.

The next move was to Number 1 Personnel Depot, at the Melbourne Cricket Ground. The trip back by train to Melbourne was the longest I could remember. It was barely a year since the previous trip on the same train. Then I had been triumphant, with a glorious flying future ahead. Now I was grounded, wings clipped, the prospect of ever flying again remote. Suddenly the entire world seemed to have come to an end and I could visualise no future.

CHAPTER SIX

The stevedore

The Melbourne Cricket Ground was cold and cheerless. I was becoming used to it now. Every posting had meant a few days – and sometimes weeks or months – at the MCG, waiting, waiting for something to happen. The armed forces were always a very good lesson in patience. You learned very early not to question, that you were an object waiting to be moved.

The Melbourne Cricket Ground was now a very curious place. The Crown took it over on 7 April 1942. For a short period it was home to the United States Air Force. They called it Camp Murphy. Then the United States Marines moved in. They changed the name to Camp Ransford, in honour of Vernon Ransford, the Melbourne Cricket Club secretary. The officers took over the Members' Long Room and the sergeants were on the floor above. Stands were boarded up to make tiered dormitories and the Americans installed hundreds of tent heaters, little fuel stoves on slabs of concrete. The Melbourne Football Club gymnasium was the medical centre and the number one outer dressing-room was the lock-up. The cricketers' changing-room in the Grey Smith Stand was the armoury and the Grey Smith bar was the PX. In 1942 this was the best shop in Melbourne. An American who could bring a young woman a gift from the PX was really a creature to know. The PX sold beautiful white towels, superior quality cotton shirts and trousers, watches, tinned foods, bowie knives, chocolate, tinned nuts, boots, shoes, raincoats and the very latest thing, which women would die for – well almost – nylon stockings. Lucky Strike, Camel and Chesterfield cigarettes were 5 shillings a carton.

Taxi drivers went to the MCG in a never-ending rush. It was the latest version of the gold-rush. Women went there, too. They waited all around the ground from early morning until late at night. The Americans hung out of the windows high up in the stands and waved to the women and the women waved back. On one or two occasions women were even smuggled inside and up into the grandstands. The officers, on the other hand, held dances every Saturday night in the Long Room.

The Americans moved out of the MCG in 1943, the RAAF moved in and so Camp Ransford became Number 1 Personnel Depot. All airmen who were moving interstate, going overseas or returning from overseas passed through the MCG. When they approached the orderly room to file their papers they always entered through two doors marked 'Members Only'. The Grey Smith Stand became the quartermaster's store. Here many thousands of airmen received their shirts and ties and boots. Tailors, too, worked here, shaping uniforms to fit. The RAAF took over the ground much as the Americans had left it, except that the new lock-up was the Americans' old security room, the place where the pass out tickets had been kept. Nor was the ground so comfortable. The cosy tent heaters had gone and the RAAF officers certainly did not hold dances every Saturday night in the Long Room.

I had three enforced stays at 1 PD. The long tunnel underneath the Southern Stand became known as Pneumonia Alley. Winds, damp and penetrating, swept around there, and it seemed the coldest place on the globe next to the Antarctic. At times I was on guard duty or orderly officer. At 1 a.m. or 2 a.m. I would sit in the moonlight and gaze at what was once the centre wicket. I remembered Bill O'Reilly, Alan Kippax, Clarrie Grimmett. I recalled that astonishing day when my father took me to the MCG and Bill Bowes got Bradman for a duck. Dad was so upset he didn't speak for half an hour. Now Hedley Verity was dead, killed leading an attack in Italy. Ross Gregory was dead. Farnes died in flying operations in 1941. Bill Bowes was a prisoner of war. I meditated on these things and even seemed to see visions of the players out on the ground. The stands, with their fronts all boarded up, were like creatures that had been blinded. The old ground was devastated, and I wondered if we would ever see players out there again.

At last a posting came through. It was to Number 9 Transport and Movement Office, stationed on the Indonesian island of Morotai. I was to leave within a week. Even if I could fly no more at least some of my humiliation was relieved. For the first time I was leaving Australia and venturing into an area where something was happening. I was so elated, I felt I had to contact Marie Rose McFadyen.

Marie Rose was the niece of my mother's best friend, Doris McFadyen. Doris had blue eyes and a smile of such charm it was always said she could melt any creature from a chairman of directors to a flinty-eyed Toorak matron. Doris left school when she was 13, started work as a sales assistant at Georges and very quickly worked her way up the fashion ladder. In her twenties she went to Myer's, where Sidney Myer soon discovered her talent and put her in charge of the fashion department. Doris had a disarming, fey, almost Billie Burke manner of guileless simplicity. But behind this there was a shrewd business brain, and rich matrons from Heyington Place, Toorak, to Canterbury Road, Camberwell, were helpless in her hands. She spent three to six months a year travelling to Paris, Berlin, Rome and New York, buying for Mr Myer.

In 1942 Dad invited a group of famous war correspondents to dinner. They were from the big United States newspapers, the *New York Times*, the Hearst Press and the *New York Herald-Tribune*. Mother needed an ally so she invited Doris to help break up the party. The war was at its most serious stage, and General MacArthur was in Melbourne, with headquarters at the Hotel Australia. The dinner-table talk centred on the survival of Darwin, the power of the United States Fleet against the kamikaze Japanese bombers, and the skill of General MacArthur as a strategist. The discussion went on through the fish, the roast chicken and the dessert, strawberry tart. The women had no chance. Just as the correspondents were dealing with the Fall of Singapore and the sinking of the battleships the *Prince of Wales* and *Repulse*, Doris burst out.

'I bought an umbrella today.'

The foolish war correspondents did not realise the magnitude of this statement. In wartime Melbourne umbrellas were considered a non-essential product. Anyone who could find an umbrella, let alone buy one, had scored a celebrated shopping triumph. After her statement there was a long, mystified silence, with correspondents wondering how a mere umbrella fitted in with the sinking of Britain's two finest ships of the line. But, after that, 'I bought an umbrella today' went permanently into the Dunstan vocabulary. It was useful when anyone wanted to break up a conversation.

Doris was in her forties when she married John McKeddie, MC and Bar, who served in the Middle East and New Guinea. She had no children of her own, but she was almost a mother to her niece, Marie Rose McFadyen. Marie had been casually brought around to our house one afternoon and I had immediately thought she was the most beautiful girl I had ever seen.

Now, euphoric with the news of my overseas posting, I felt there was no time for delay. Marie Rose must be contacted absolutely at once, immediately. Perhaps we could play tennis that very afternoon. However, Marie Rose was now doing her final year at the Presbyterian Ladies College and young men do not find it easy to get to Presbyterian ladies during class. Nevertheless, I had a plan. It was wartime and every citizen had to possess an identity card. Identity cards had to be kept up to date at all times. Perhaps if I just made a simple telephone call to PLC and announced that I was John Robinson, an identity card inspector, and that I wished to check a few details on Miss McFadyen's card I would be able to speak to her. So I rang PLC and put my case. I had not realised the commotion it would cause. Miss McFadyen was summoned to the office of the headmistress, a revered sanctum where girls seldom set foot. The headmistress was Miss Mary F. B. Neilson, a dour Scottish lady equally as grand as Dr Darling. Beside her was Miss Helen Hailes, the senior vice-principal, who was almost as formidable, and there were other female knights present, ready to do battle against the terrible invasion of bureaucracy. Miss Neilson handed Marie the telephone.

'Hello, Marie', I said cheerfully. 'It's Keith here. Do you think you could slip away for tennis after school?'

At first there was a startled silence, then Marie said, 'I am unable to speak to you now'.

Our conversation was brief and Marie showed a singular lack of interest in tennis that afternoon. As delicately as possible afterwards, Marie explained to the headmistress that the identity card inspector was not someone to be feared.

At the Melbourne Cricket Ground I received my tropical greens, broad hat for tropical wear and Atebrin tablets to ward off malaria, then I caught a troop train north. First we went to Brisbane, then to Townsville, sitting up or sleeping in luggage racks at night. The trip continued by RAAF DC3 to Darwin, Port Moresby, Lae, Biak and finally Morotai, an island that seemed at the time virtually to sink under its load of aircraft, particularly United States Liberators, Marauders, Mitchell B25s and endless DC3s, Commandos and other freighters.

Nine TMO was close to the end of the airstrip and all day long Liberators with heavy bomb loads almost staggered into the air. Between the end of the strip and the sea was a graveyard of twisted wings and bent fuselages, the wreckage of aircraft that had failed to make it. Everything was expendable in 1944–1945.

Not far from the strip there was an open-air cinema where we had movies three times a week. The films were the latest releases, flown directly from the United States. Even better was the arrival of an entertainment unit. The greatest occasion was the arrival of Gracie Fields, the almost legendary Gracie, the most loved singer of her day. We went to the ground, armed with camp-stools or empty 5-gallon drums to sit on. But it was the wet season and as soon as we reached the cinema site the monsoonal rains came down, centimetres and centimetres in an hour. Nobody moved, nobody went home, and Gracie arrived right on schedule. She, too, was soaked. Hour after hour she sang all her famous songs, 'On the Isle of Capri', 'The Biggest Aspidistra in the World' and that great tear-jerker 'Wish Me Luck', while water ran down her face.

Nine TMO had only three officers: Flight Lieutenant Jim McKenzie, Flying Officer Keith Cramp and myself. Its job was to control the movements of Air Force men and supplies throughout the First Tactical Air Force. Morotai was the staging point for strikes further north and the invasion of Borneo, first at Tarakan, then at Labuan and later at Balikpapen. I arrived in time for the TMO detachment to take part in the assault on Labuan. We embarked on United States LSTs (landing ship tanks), which were large, comfortable ships. Fully loaded trucks could be driven straight out of doors that opened at the bow, onto the beach. The United States Fleet bombarded Labuan for several days, then the LSTs hit the beach on 10 June 1945.

We had five or six days travelling with the United States Navy and we rather wished we could have travelled with them until the end of the war. Our diet in the RAAF, although never as bad as that of boarding-school, had played variations on the theme of bully beef, tinned meat and vegetables, dehydrated potatoes and tinned peaches. The Americans had unlimited quantities of fresh beef, chicken, turkey and fruit. Breakfast always consisted of scrambled eggs, bacon, hot cakes and the most delicious tinned grapefruit. There was no alcohol, but there were always quantities of ice-cold Coca-Cola and those on board could help themselves from Coke machines, no charge. We were on our way to do battle with the Japanese, but how comfortable it all was. As a tropical cruise we had everything but deck tennis.

The LSTs landed on the beach and Army vehicles drove straight into action. There were some brief and quite violent encounters. Altogether 389 Japanese were killed on Labuan Island and eleven prisoners taken. The 24th Brigade of the AIF lost thirty-four killed and ninety-three wounded. My job was Air Force representative with the Army, Number 1 Australian Beach Group, Ninth Division, which was responsible for the landing. On day one I had to study the map references and find the camp for our headquarters. The in-fighting for the best campsites was rather sharper and more clearly defined than the battle against the Japanese. The Army stole our site, so I promptly reported the news to the RAAF Commander, Air Commodore F. R. W. Scherger, the very man who had manipulated me back into pilot training.

'Sir', I said, 'the Army has taken our site'.

Scherger never used two words when only one was sufficient.

'Dunstan, tell General Wootten to go and get fucked.'

The verb 'to fuck' in 1945 did not get the generous use it does now, and I was startled to hear it from an air commodore.

'Sir, I can't tell General Wootten to go and get fucked.'

The Air Commodore was a small man but ferocious when aroused.

'Yes you can, and that's an order. Tell General Wootten to go and get fucked.'

Major-General G. F. Wootten, a successful commander of Australian campaigns in the Middle East, was as formidable as Air Commodore Scherger. He was immense around the girth but wore regulation khaki shorts. Legend had it that he was nigh on

130 kilograms and it was a matter of considerable wonder that he was able to fit into a jeep.

I saluted Air Commodore Scherger, wandered off into the jungle and pondered what to do next. What style would I use? – 'Sir, Air Commodore Scherger sends his compliments and you are to go and get fucked'? My courage failed. I did not even visit Army headquarters. I went back to my plans. Maybe we didn't need quite that much space. If we shifted our area a little over here, we might get away with it. That is precisely what happened.

There was one raid by Japanese bombers, and a week after we landed a group of Japanese filtered back into Australian lines and attempted a suicidal massacre. They were caught, gunned down and laid out on the road near the beach. It was the first time I had actually seen dead bodies. They were not a pretty sight. Australians had tried to kick out their teeth, looking for gold fillings.

My tent in the jungle was lonely, and that night I had all sorts of nightmares. What if the Japanese should come back? At 2 a.m. there was no doubt about it: the Japanese were stealthily moving towards me. I could hear their feet softly plodding through the long grass. My God! What now? I pulled out a Colt .45 automatic. It was large, so large it had been an embarrassment to carry about. In Morotai, a United States Army officer, desperate for a drink, had given it to me in exchange for a bottle of Scotch. So I sat on my bed, Colt .45 in my hand, finger on the trigger, sweat running off my head. I waited for the end. The strange footsteps outside kept coming and coming. At times it seemed as if the whole tent was surrounded. At dawn I was brave enough to creep outside. The noises that had exactly mimicked footsteps were ripe mangoes plopping off a tree just behind the tent.

The unit, 9 TMO, was, in effect, an air and shipping agent. I was the shipping officer and it was my job to bring supplies ashore. Supplies included a great parade of jeeps and trucks, airfield construction equipment, crate after crate of Rolls-Royce Merlin engines, spares for the Mustang squadrons of 81 Wing and, what really astonished me, large quantities of kerosene-operated refrigerators. The RAAF preferred to move in comfort.

Cranes for lifting the engines were too light for the job, so often, in driving monsoonal rains, we had to push a truck into position, place skids at the end of the tray, then, in hair-raising manner, allow gravity to move the engine from truck to ground. The people at Rolls-Royce who built these engines would have been horrified, but there was nothing else we could do. I was really a non-union stevedore. Liberty ships would arrive, sometimes six at a time, many of them with thousands of tonnes of bombs and .50-calibre ammunition. I would work round the clock, not going to bed for three days. Then there would be a lull until the next convoy arrived.

Labuan is an island off the north-west coast of Borneo. It has lovely sandy beaches, palm trees, paddy-fields, bananas and an agreeable climate. To us it was almost a paradise, and it has since become a cherished Malaysian holiday resort.

Yes, it was an easy war. One day I was sitting in my tent when a great tip-truck arrived – not your normal truck, but a huge United States six-wheel drive, used for carting coral in the construction of the airstrip for the Mustang squadrons. It appeared with such shattering force I thought my guy ropes would go and the tent would come down on my head. Out stepped a sun-tanned, incredibly untidy airman: digger hat, no shirt, ragged shorts and big boots. It was Adrian Benns, the same character who had rescued me at cadet camp, some years before.

After that Adrian was an almost daily visitor, embarrassing at times. But he was still capable of getting me out of trouble. Jeeps were a floating commodity, a currency like rum during the Rum Rebellion of early New South Wales. If the stealing of cars is a problem in Melbourne, Sydney or London, it is nothing compared with the wave of car thefts on Morotai, Labuan and other occupied islands at that time. Jeeps were fair game because they did not have a key. A driver's only hope of preserving a jeep was to take out the distributor and even remove the steering-wheel. It was possible to take off the steering-wheel just by removing a central nut, and it was common on movie nights to see characters going into the open-air theatre carrying their seat in one hand and their steering-wheel in the other. I had an Army friend who was a nigh-unbearable back-seat driver. One day I carefully loosened the steering-wheel nut, then, just when he began to hand out his usual advice, I lifted off the steering-wheel, handed it to him and said, 'Okay, you drive the bloody thing'. He did not complain again.

Yet, despite the precaution of removing steering-wheel and distributor, I had my jeep stolen. My plight, with ships to unload, was serious, indeed. When Adrian made his regular visit that day I told him of my difficulty.

'Don't worry about it, little Keith', said he. 'I might just happen to find you one.'

Which he did, three hours later. I was careful not to ask where he had found it.

We had been at Labuan less than a month when I got a call to report to Air Commodore Scherger. 'Oh Lord, what have I done now? Maybe they have identified my jeep. Probably it belonged to an American general and I'll be ruined.'

I went to First Tactical Air Force headquarters and was ushered straight in to the great man. He was much more friendly than at our last meeting.

'Hello, Keith', he said. 'I saw your father at the Naval and Military Club in Melbourne last week. He asked me to bring you this parcel.'

It was one of my mother's famous hampers, filled with priceless items: fruit cake, precious tinned delicacies and a couple of bottles of Foster's. From then on parcels started to arrive regularly. Couriers were Army colonels, RAAF senior officers, including Air Commodore McCauley and Air Vice-Marshal Bladin. The contents of the parcels were astonishing: the daily newspapers from Melbourne, chocolate, nuts, cake and eventually, as Mum became more and more daring, fresh oranges and fresh eggs. We had bacon and eggs for breakfast on tropical Labuan.

What a comfortable war. I had installed 44-gallon drums at the corner of my tent and put guttering under the fly, so I had my own water supply and, with a little complex piping, even my own shower. At the corner of the tent there was a kerosene refrigerator. Next, Mum sent by special courier ice-cream mix, powdered milk and condensed milk. We made our own ice-cream. My tent became notorious around Labuan. Visitors, including Adrian Benns, would arrive, enter uninvited, sit down on the bed, reach underneath for the inevitable box filled with unobtainable treasure and say, 'Well, what has Keith's mum sent him today?'.

Dunstan, VC, was shameless. In 1946 my brother, Bill, now a captain in the British Army, was serving with his unit in Java. My father was president of the Naval and Military Club, and he played host to Admiral Lord Louis Mountbatten when he visited Melbourne. Mountbatten was on his way to Batavia so Dad said, 'My goodness, you must look up my son'.

Just at that time Bill had met in Batavia an old friend, Alfred Brooks. They celebrated in Batavia, drank too much and stayed out half the night, with the result that Bill was absent without leave getting back to his unit. A furious commanding officer sent him on jungle patrol as punishment. When Admiral Lord Louis Mountbatten arrived shortly after Bill's departure and asked to see young Dunstan, Bill's commanding officer could not believe what was going on.

Labuan was to be the supply centre, the springboard for the next mighty leap by the Australian and Allied forces: the assault on Singapore and the Malay peninsula. It all became unnecessary. The United States dropped the atom bomb on Hiroshima and Nagasaki, and the war was over.

The news reached us on 15 August 1945. I had been up all night, unloading bombs from a Liberty ship, bombs that would never be needed. At 4 a.m. I pulled out four bottles of beer and a bottle of sherry I had been saving for this special occasion. Out in the harbour there were frigates, cruisers, Liberty ships, vessels of every kind, all firing rockets, flares, tracer bullets and Very lights and setting the sea and sky ablaze with colours. Searchlights were waving about the sky and their accompanying anti-aircraft batteries were firing. There was even some lightning and tropical thunder to add to the celebration. Henley Regatta was a side-show compared with this demonstration. We opened our beer, thought of home and wondered, 'What next?'.

Labuan became a staging-camp, a movement area for prisoners of war returning from mainland Borneo, Burma and surrounding areas. On 16 September I wrote home:

> Labuan is the centre of many moving and tragic events. The hospitals are full of wrecks of human beings left by the Japanese. I have seen them coming off boats and aircraft – just skeletons covered with tissue. They look about with big, unnatural eyes from their thin faces, too weak to raise their heads. Most of them have lost 6 stone.
>
> When they saw sisters in the hospital, they all wept. 'Just like home', they said.
>
> One POW came off the ship, walked up to a digger and said, 'Christ, you wouldn't read about it'. The digger looked at him, embarrassed, not knowing what to say. He let out a yell. It was his own brother. The POW started crying.

There was a major leaning on a thick stick. I asked him about it, thinking it was some souvenir he had picked up. 'No lad, that's a stick with which the Japs beat me every day I was in captivity.'

The commanding officer of the Beach Group here is a full colonel, DSO and Bar. He went to Sandakan on the mainland to take over from the Japanese and to see the POWs. Later his unit was to follow and ship the POWs back to Labuan. But he found there was no need for the others – the 2000 POWs were dead. He told the Jap commander to clean up the place. If it wasn't done by a certain date he would be shot.

The Ninth Division held war crime trials, and on 11 December 1945, I wrote:

The court was made up of a grim array of majors and colonels. The defending officer was a Japanese colonel and the prosecuting officer was a young Australian lieutenant. The accused was a Japanese sergeant-major who admitted to the killing of forty-six Australians. His clothes were dirty and torn, his hair was cropped close to his head, a grisly moustache trailed from his upper lip. His face was an expression of contempt. Only the Japanese colonel spoke English, so everything took place through interpreters.

This was the story: on 10 June 1945, the Ninth Division landed at Brunei and Labuan. At Miri, 50 miles down the coast, were forty-six Australian POWs, held in a Chinese house. The Japanese sergeant-major, becoming worried, decided to shoot them. Many of them were too sick to move, but those who could walk he marched outside. Five suddenly realised what was happening and they made a dash for it, but they were mowed down by rifle fire. The sergeant-major immediately gave orders for the rest to be shot and, if still living, to be bayoneted. Even then some of the Australians were still alive when thrown into a common grave.

The court sentenced the Japanese sergeant-major to be shot, providing the Governor-General is agreeable.

After bringing huge stocks of equipment into Labuan, now I had to send them home again. Nobody wanted to stay. Almost everyone who could lift a pen was applying for home leave and discharge. Labour for loading the ships was short so daily I collected detachments of Japanese POWs. They were ragged and thin and many of them were ill-equipped to work as wharf labourers. I found them compliant and prepared to work for astonishingly long hours. Some were clumsy and fell down hatches, but they seemed to feel no pain.

I had a Japanese batman. He did everything for me, even before I could think of it. He cleaned my boots, mended and washed my clothes, scrubbed out the tent and washed my jeep. He came from the prison camp every morning to report for duty. He would march up to the tent, stand stiffly to attention, salute three or four times and, with a big grin on his face, say, 'Washy, washy'. He would then pick up the washing from the floor, run to the wash tub and work with furious activity. I could not change my clothes fast enough to keep up with him. He was young, clean and, like his colleagues, perfectly honest.

We also had Japanese working in our transport section, making major repairs on the heavy trucks. They were clever technicians, more skilled than our own fitters. They worked solidly for long hours without supervision.

I wrote home, very puzzled:

> I can't understand these Japanese at all. I even like them. They work hard and are so anxious to please. I don't understand it at all. A few weeks ago they were acting like barbarians. At the British Sergeants' Mess they had a Japanese working for them, a happy intelligent boy, who didn't have to be told what to do. One day a civilian POW walked into the canteen. He complained bitterly to the authorities because here was the Japanese who had almost beaten him to death, while making a road, right here on Labuan.

There was a distribution of spoils. Officers of the Army and Air Force each received an official gift of a Japanese officer's samurai sword. I was so disturbed by what I had seen and heard that I felt I did not want a Japanese sword or any part of the business. I arranged a camp table-tennis tournament and offered my sword as a prize for the winner. I did not enter the contest.

Thousands of soldiers and airmen left for home and we were left with their campsites and equipment. Our unit, once nigh on sixty strong, became smaller and smaller. Jim McKenzie had gone, and our CO now was Flying Officer Jack Williams. We were so short of staff and so short of trained drivers that I had to learn to drive everything from six-wheel-drive trucks to the largest bulldozers and airfield construction equipment. There was a certain feeling of freedom, even dominance, when flying a Wirraway or a Fairey Battle, a noble feeling of aggression when at the wheel of a 6-tonne tip-truck, but nothing could equal the feeling of arrogance when manoeuvring a bulldozer. Maybe it was the experience of two levers, one in either hand. One operated the left track, the other the right track, thus providing jerky, very direct steering. Ah yes, the road was mine, every creature had to get out of my way. My greatest pleasure was driving the RAAF's biggest bulldozer. It was a mighty thing and weighed over 20 tonnes. The bulldozer was so big that it was a task even to climb into the seat. To get it going the driver had to start a small motor, which in turn started the big diesel. It was a joy driving the bulldozer the 10 or 12 kilometres from the airstrip to the wharf.

One day I drove the largest bulldozer right up to the wharf's edge in preparation for loading, got out of the saddle, stepped back to admire my handiwork and the rest was like the Keystone Kops or other hilarious silent movies. There was a terrible groaning and splintering of wood, a portion of the wharf collapsed and my wonderful bulldozer went down into the water.

What to do now? There was no crane anywhere between Labuan and Darwin that could lift it. No ship's captain was prepared to tackle the job with his gear. I just quietly adjusted the papers so that the bulldozer was lost in action and no longer existed. As far as I know it is still there, deep in the sand under the waters of Labuan: a twentieth century wreck to be compared with the famous wrecks left behind by the Dutch, the Spanish and the Portuguese in the sixteenth and seventeenth centuries.

Months went by. There were several thousand tonnes of bombs to be returned to Australia, but it was a difficult task persuading civilian captains of ships to take them. I waited and waited. Boredom set in. On long Labuan evenings I played a little wind-up gramophone, a treasure souvenired from others who had gone home before me. Adrian Benns, too, was one of the last to go. We had one 10-inch record. It had 'Mean to Me' on one side and 'Girl of My Dreams' on the other, songs permanently etched on my memory. We also had a perfect set of Max Bruch's First Violin Concerto. The wind-up gramophone did not have sufficient spring power to last for an entire 12-inch record, so we had to give it extra turns half-way through each side to keep it going. It was a matter of great delicacy to prevent the needle from jumping on the grooves. I suppose the reproduction was appalling, but it is amazing how hi-fi is often only a state of mind. The better the hi-fi the more you worry whether you are getting your money's-worth. The luscious, extravagant music of Max Bruch and the savage thrusts of the violin seemed especially exhilarating, those nights in the Labuan jungle. We played it so often it was etched perfectly in our memories. We played games. There I was, Sir Thomas Beecham, conducting, with Fritz Kreisler and the London Symphony Orchestra. Going through the music in my mind, I could start with the first beat of the baton and finish precisely at the right second.

It was mid-April 1946 before I finally had my release from lovely Labuan Island. Now, whenever I hear Max Bruch, usually on ABC FM, I think of Labuan.

CHAPTER SEVEN

Byline dreamer

At last it was back to Australia and 1 PD at the Melbourne Cricket Ground. Within days I was discharged. The farewell gesture from the RAAF was an appalling Victory suit, one of those austerity suits invented by Mr Dedman, Minister for Post War Reconstruction. It was cuffless, narrow of lapel and free of lining and had no shape whatever. My father thought differently. He had a cousin, J. Dunstan Lewis, who had a business in the T & G Building, Collins Street. Mr Lewis was a tailor, a kindly gentleman of great patience. A suit was something that had to be constructed with great patience. It took at least a month, in which time there had to be at least three fittings.

'On which side do you dress, Keith?', Mr Lewis asked.

I had no idea what he was talking about. People never referred to the penis in 1946. He explained further.

'On which side do you place your personal equipment?'

I was still not sure what he was talking about but slowly things began to dawn.

Australians still had to provide clothing coupons, and for a time I was in deep trouble. Mr Lewis had definite ideas.

'A gentleman needs a different suit for every working day of the week. I suggest you think of having five suits. A suit always needs several days to recover and come back to the right shape.'

Eventually he did make five suits, and they all lasted at least twenty years, a profound and sensible investment. They were the first and last handmade suits I ever owned. By the time I needed to buy another, J. D. Lewis was no longer there.

Bill, Helen and I settled back into civilian life. Brother Bill, after battling in Java, ultimately managed to get a discharge from the

British Army. An office desk looked anything but inviting to him. What could he do? For a time he even contemplated crocodile shooting in the Northern Territory. He was talked out of that, and went into the newsprint business with Gollan and Company. He had a long, successful career and became a director of the Tasman Pulp and Paper Company.

Helen became a journalist, worked for the *Herald* and wrote a column titled 'Nan Heard Today'. In one of her early columns she gave readers advice on how to organise their clothes: 'Keep your cupboard like a filing cabinet'. When Helen returned home that day Mum in triumph led us all into her room and announced, 'I want you to see Nan's filing cabinet'. Mum threw open doors to reveal chaos. Helen's cupboards looked as if the place had been raided by the CIA. Helen was a good journalist, but marriage and three children halted her career.

Dad still wanted me to be an engineer. That was the path to power and a prosperous future. The thought of slide rules, mathematics and chemistry, all over again, filled me with dread.

'I want to be a journalist, a writer', I said.

'Yes, I understand that', he replied. 'Journalism and newspapers are our business. You can still be *associated* with journalism. You can do both. You can be a newspaper engineer, the man who prints the newspaper, the man who installs and runs the presses. Fascinating. I would love to do that. You would make much more money.'

'I don't care about money', I replied, in the classic style of the 21-year-old. 'It's what you do that's important.'

'You go into journalism and you will end up a hack', he thundered. 'Think of me when you are an underpaid sub-editor with three kids to keep, slaving over tired copy at three in the morning. Don't do it.'

Next morning I went into the Herald and Weekly Times building, saw Archer Thomas, Editor of the *Herald*, and asked him for a job. I pleaded with him not to tell anyone, and it was three days before Dad discovered I was one of his employees. He did not complain, and never again did he accuse me of being a potential hack.

At that time cadets were alternated between the *Herald* and the *Sun* to give them experience. Cadet training was four years, and I observed that it was similar to pilot training: the trainee could be scrubbed off course within days, months or the first year. My spelling was wretched – so bad that in the *Herald* sub-editors' room I was known as Chaucer. Spelling remained a great mystery for years. Several sub-editors suggested it might be better if I found a different occupation. Archer Thomas saved me. He was a great extrovert of a man, Hollywood handsome. He was not a great thinker, but he would become excited over big stories, and when he did he was capable of inspiring every member of his staff.

'I think just possibly the boy can write', he said. 'We have lots of people who can spell, but not many who can write. Let's keep him.'

So I was saved. I noticed early that the best chance for a young reporter to get a story in the newspaper was on police rounds. There was a range of rounds and cadets had to do them all by turn to gain full experience. There was the shipping round. There were good stories to be had here, meeting all the P & O and Orient ships and interviewing the passengers who had just arrived from that magical place, 'overseas'. There was the western round, covering the Board of Works, the railways and the tramways. There were good stories to be had here, too, given the frequent strikes of the trams and trains. The famous communist secretaries of the Australian Railways Union and the tramways union, Mr J. J. Brown and Mr Clarrie O'Shea, were considered monsters of evil by our editors and by Sir Keith Murdoch in particular. I became fond of both men, who were always courteous and understanding – much more so than the Minister for Railways, Mr Kent Hughes, who had the abruptness and incivility of an ex-colonel, which he was.

The next was the Town Hall round, covering the often sinister machinations of the Melbourne City Council. I hated that. The most illustrious rounds were Victorian Parliament and Federal Parliament, Canberra. However, I always angled for police rounds. The others were mostly in the grip of the old hands, the senior journalists, so the best hope for a cadet to make the front page was picking up a quick horror story, and these were to be had on police rounds.

There were two shifts for *Sun* reporters: 10 a.m. to 6 p.m., or 6 p.m. to 2 a.m. or later. The Press rooms, at the northern end of police headquarters, were dingy and dun coloured. There were a number of famous police reporters, such as Geoff Sparrow, who with immense patience took me everywhere, introducing me to all their contacts. There were others, such as Alan Dower, who were highly skilled but jealous of their beats and so introduced me to no one.

Official relations between Press and police were generally poor. There were times when the police believed it best to tell the Press nothing. Then we had to listen to police radio, D24. The police used numbers to describe various events; for example, twenty for robbery, seventeen for indecent behaviour, ten for fire, twelve for armed assault, fifteen for rape and thirty for murder. Frequently D24 changed the code to confuse the Press. When this happened, reporters had to depend on a mate inside to slip them the latest code. Reporters virtually had to be Reilly, Ace of Spies.

There were long, dreary hours, sitting at night just waiting for things to happen. At 2 a.m. after a terrible, eventless night we consoled ourselves at the George Inn, a Greek cafe in Russell Street inhabited by police and reporters, which went all night. There customers ordered the classic culinary triumph: rump steak, two eggs, onions, chip potatoes, a slice of tomato, lettuce cut into streamers and razor-thin slices of stale white bread and butter.

A dozen steak and eggs would go by and I would think my career was getting nowhere; only a miserable assault here, on page seventeen, a traffic accident there, four paragraphs (always called pars) on page twenty-five, or a robbery in Heyington Place, Toorak, a third of a column on page twelve. Not even a decent bashing. I didn't wish anybody harm, but a satisfactory throat cutting on St Kilda Beach would have been a great help.

My greatest dream was a fire in the Exhibition Building. That great domed edifice, built for the International Exhibition of 1880, was unloved and unprofitable in the 1940s. Most of us knew it only as the cold and draughty building where we had suffered when we did our Matriculation examinations. It had not become the national treasure that it is now. I knew it was made of wood. I knew it was very nearly the biggest wooden structure in the Southern Hemisphere, with quite appalling fire precautions. I wanted it to burn down after the *Herald*'s deadline. That meant later than 5 p.m. But then for a really super front page spread, with pictures, I wanted my article to catch the *Sun*'s first edition to the country and that went to the railways by midnight. It would be perfect if the Exhibition Building could ignite, say, between 7 p.m. and 9 p.m. on any night except Saturday. Saturday night would be awful because we had no Sunday newspaper. There were a few false alarms, but the Exhibition Building remained intact, regrettably.

Reporters on the police round sat and waited and waited, always within earshot of the D24 radio. If a number came up that sounded promising, we called pictorial and dashed to the spot with a photographer. Photographers got cars; reporters did not. One night at 1 a.m. I heard the D24 signal: 'Twelve at 15 Fortescue Street, West Preston. Could be a bad one'.

'Ahhhh, twelve: armed assault', I said to myself. It was too late for a photographer. I didn't wait for anyone but grabbed a taxi and got the driver to drive at high speed to Fortescue Street. There was not a car on the road, we made brilliant progress. Lights were on in the house, but nothing seemed to be happening. I knocked on the door and it flew open. A woman grabbed me by the coat lapels.

'Thank God, you've arrived', she said.

'What do you mean?', I asked.

'My husband!', she screamed. 'He's out there with a Japanese sword, and he's coming back to kill me.'

'But . . . but . . .', I said. 'I'm just a reporter.'

'Aren't you a policeman?', she moaned.

I explained the terrible truth and immediately started putting up barricades. I was even more terrified than she was. The police arrived ten minutes later and were very amused. It was the longest ten minutes I could remember. The husband meekly surrendered an hour later, and the story was too dull to make the late editions.

Another night the longed-for number, ten, came on air.

'Ten at Chitty's Wood Yard, Dandenong Road, East Malvern.'

'I see, a fire. Better get onto that one', I thought.

Again it was after midnight, right on edition time. I called a taxi, hoping beyond hope that the fire was big enough and disastrous enough to replace other stories and make the late editions of the *Sun*. It was indeed a splendid blaze, and a house next door was also on fire. I had my notebook and pencil in hand, ready to interview what I quickly discovered were fairly desperate people.

'Excuse me, Sir. Is this your house? Could you please tell me how the fire started?'

'Of course it's my house, you bloody idiot. Help me get the furniture out.'

Suddenly I was assisting, carrying out beds, a piano and sofas and putting them in the front garden while fire took over the rest of the house. By the time I had done my fire-battling duties it was all too late and I had missed the late editions.

That was a serious matter. Competition was ruthless. Fire, murder and disaster were more useful in the 1940s for selling newspapers than they are now. The *Age*, *Argus*, *Herald*, *Sun* and *Truth* all had their full-time teams at Russell Street police headquarters. Some reporters were so keen that, if they got to the scene first, they would even pay witnesses of crime and accident to keep quiet and not speak to other reporters. We were convinced *Argus* reporters were distributing 5–pound notes. But if you were first with a story it was usually a question not so much of 5 pounds as of whom you knew in the police, who in the Homicide Squad could tip you off. I had just one or two friends. My best was Senior Constable Cec Hughes, a veteran, working in D24. Cec Hughes would meet me in the hotel and relate stories of the old days. He often told me of the days when he was an original member of the wireless patrol back in the early 1930s.

'The patrol cars were Lancias', he said. 'You know, the old Lancia – huge, very long, like a coffin, with an engine that would fire at every second lamp-post. The wireless gear was so heavy it took up the entire back seat. Brakes? Sort of. You'd get arrested now for having brakes like we had. One early morning we were involved in a car chase. We were doing about 90 in Swanston Street, up there beyond the City Baths. Our brakes failed and we couldn't stop until we were across Princes Bridge down near Wirth's Circus.'

Cec Hughes gave me the tip about most things, but he could not be on duty twenty-four hours a day. The most spectacular crime during my time was a Chinese murder at an illegal baccarat school in Little Bourke Street. I went home at 3 a.m. convinced it was a quiet night, nothing happening. The next morning I picked up the *Argus*. Oh horror, there were banner headlines: 'Murder in Little Bourke Street'. I had been beaten hopelessly. I have often thought that if ever I came down to earth again I would try to be the curator of the Botanic Gardens. At least with the planting of trees if you make an error people take twenty years to find you out. In the newspaper business your errors, your failures to achieve are all too evident the following morning. I looked at the *Sun*, miserable, close to tears. The sensational story was all over the front page of the *Argus*, complete with pictures of the baccarat den and diagrams of where police had found the body. In the *Sun* nothing – just a humble story on proposed improvements to the Hume Highway. Dare I even go into the office? Perhaps I should resign at once and look for a job at a bank or as a grocer's clerk?

That afternoon I stood in the office of the Chief of Staff, Rod Travis, a big man with a Henry Lawson moustache, a former lieutenant-colonel. He had the *Argus* in front of him.

'Why?'

I explained that the Homicide Squad tipped off the *Argus* and the *Argus* alone.

'I'll get them for this. I'll take our complaint right up to the Chief Commissioner. We're the biggest circulation newspaper and, by God, they need us. You make sure it doesn't happen again.'

He was a very kindly person, which was unusual in a chief of staff, but there was a threat in his voice. Never again did I feel comfortable on police rounds. Every morning I rushed to see the rival papers, the *Age* and the *Argus*, which I read first to see whether I had been ruined.

The Herald and Weekly Times was like an all-embracing mother. It was very different in Sydney. Frank Packer's *Daily Telegraph* and Ezra Norton's *Daily Mirror* had reputations for terrorising journalists and there were constant tales of sackings for lack of performance. Reporters were rarely fired on the *Sun* and the *Herald*. However, the Herald and Weekly Times had a reputation for care and parsimony. The company did not use regulation toilet rolls in the staff lavatories, it used carefully cut squares of copy paper. Our typewriters were vintage, nigh-antique Remingtons. They screwed to the tops of the desks. The tops were on a hinge and could be folded underneath.

Sun staff started mostly at 2 p.m. and finished at 11 p.m. After 8 p.m. it was often boredom waiting for things to happen. Rod

Travis tried to keep us busy. A favourite method was to have us all write letters to the *Sun*. I wonder how many people realised then that often letters to the Editor came from the staff. Rod Travis would walk into the reporters' room at 9 p.m. and say: 'Okay, I want a letter from you, a letter from you and a letter from you. Don't make them too dull'.

One time I wrote this letter:

Sir,

I think it is disgraceful how Myer's, Buckley and Nunn's and Foy's frequently leave dummy models in their shop windows, unclad. The sight of the naked form like this can have a very dangerous effect on impressionable youths. To make matters worse I have noticed that some of these dummy models are black.

Would the proprietors of these stores please make sure their models are clothed at all times.

Yours etc.,

'Shocked', East Malvern.

The result was splendid. The 'Letters to the Editor' column rocked for weeks with charges and counter-charges full of moral indignation.

Cadet training was diligent. Osmar White, who had been a famous war correspondent, officially had the task of training cadets. His methods were very direct: bludgeon cadets into action.

'You're all no good', he would say, glaring at us. 'If I had my way I'd sack the lot of you.'

There was a sub-editor on the *Sun* called Lyle Cousland who was relentless. Almost every night I was hailed to his desk. An old gentleman who delivered messages would give the dreaded call, 'Dunstan, you are wanted in the subs' room'.

Lyle Cousland was small, barely more than 150 centimetres tall. He had a large, soft, black pencil. There would be line after line through my copy.

'Why do you always use the passive voice?', he would demand. 'It's just an excuse for avoiding what really happened, and you take all the punch out of the copy.'

'You've got "it was said". That's no good to me. I want to know who actually said it.'

'The accident took place in Hawthorn? All right, which street and which corner? And what time?'

'What on earth are you trying to say here? Get that sentence down to twenty words.'

'Oh Lord, what are you trying to be? Alfred, Lord Tennyson? You don't need all those adjectives.'

'Why do you take so long to get into the story? Nobody's going to take the trouble to read all that garbage. You know the rules: How? Why? When? and Where? In a news story you've got a fiftieth of a second to attract your reader, then he's gone.'

It was painful, but I learned more in six months about English from sub-editors on the *Sun News-Pictorial*, than in a dozen years of school and academic training.

The editor of the *Sun* was J. C. Waters, a large, ebullient man. 'Promising Jack' he was called because Jack Waters was always promising a sublime and glorious future to every member of his staff. Jack's ideal was London's *Daily Mirror*: short news stories and every day something different. The theory was that even the Second Coming of Christ would be worth only three days' coverage. Average readers were scanners, Jack argued. Their eyes hopped quickly over the headlines; few had the concentration to go beyond seven or eight sentences. Only news stories of vast moment required more than that. Therefore the information, exactly what happened, had to be provided instantly, starting from the first paragraph and working in descending order of importance. He believed in good pictures, very large, and he frequently ran a picture right across the front page. The *Sun* photographers were unquestionably the best in the land. Journalists were nomads, creatures of movement and ambition, who would stay a few years then move elsewhere. The photographers were the backbone of the *Sun News-Pictorial*.

Good pictures, short, precise stories and simple Anglo-Saxon words – that was the recipe. John Williams, who was to be editor-in-chief and chairman, used to give a warning about the typical reader. This reader lived in a triple-fronted brick veneer in Moorabbin, was married, with two children, and was struggling on a mortgage. He had a radio and a mental age of 14, so we must never attempt to use fancy Latin derivatives, which he and his wife would not understand. Furthermore, this couple was conservative in outlook and easily shocked. We were always to remember that the *Sun* was a family newspaper. It was this philosophy, coupled with brilliant sub-editing, that gave the *Sun* almost double the circulation of any newspaper in Australia.

It was an era when news stories appeared without a byline. Only the very great reporters like Clive Turnbull or Rohan Rivett ever scored a byline. After the 1970s bylines became the common practice. Even a tale that was really only a hand-out from a public relations firm or a blurb from some politician seeking publicity could merit a reporter's name. But in the 1940s the byline was almost unknown.

There was an exception. If a journalist could get a feature article into the then-illustrious *Herald* weekend magazine, this would earn the wonder of wonders, his or her name in the paper. My school-days were unfortunate, my Air Force career lacked glory and my father had warned me that I would become a 3 a.m. sub-editing hack – surely writing feature articles was the one way left to get on, to be noticed? I made a resolution. I would write a feature article in my spare time every week.

I was already doing an arts course part-time at Melbourne University, but I showered the features editor with article after article. The features editor was Fred Aldridge, a former war correspondent and a brilliant journalist. He was patient, indeed. He would go through my copy, suggest different leads or a new approach, but would always end with the words: 'I don't know, Keith. It just doesn't quite ring the bell'. Months went by. In despair I asked myself, 'When is that damned bell going to ring?'.

But I kept on trying. On a round-Australia tour with Sir Keith Murdoch I made an investigation into United States ex-servicemen who had decided to settle in New South Wales, Queensland and Victoria. Fred Aldridge did not comment on the article this time. I kept wondering whether he would use it. The *Herald* weekend magazine was put together on Thursdays. If one walked up to the fourth floor it was possible to see the pages already made up in metal on the stone. Three weeks went by. Every Thursday and Friday I surreptitiously crept up there just in the hope that Fred might have relented. On the fourth week I went up late on Thursday night. The light was dim, but it was possible to see page two of the magazine all made up in metal. There in reverse type was my article and, oh joy, back to front, the line:

By Keith Dunstan

It was a moment of pure happiness, like flying solo. I purred. I had broken through. Getting an article into the paper was never quite so difficult after that. My success was all due to Fred Aldridge.

The awesome figure who towered over us all was Sir Keith Murdoch, father of Rupert. Sir Keith was editor-in-chief of the Herald and Weekly Times Limited, a supreme commander, an old-fashioned newspaper proprietor. He liked to impress his personality not only on the *Herald* and the *Sun* but also on Australian politics. Never did the *Herald* deviate from the conservative line. Never was there such a thing as a justified claim by trade unions for more pay. And never was there such a thing as a justified strike. As for Labor politicians, if they were not all communists, their policy of socialism made them just as bad, a lighter shade of red.

I was studying politics part-time at Melbourne University where lecturers pointed out the imbalance in the *Herald*'s coverage of the Canberra and the Spring Street political scenes. They would go over the newspapers with a ruler and announce the copious inches, even feet, devoted to the conservatives and the sparse treatment given to Labor. Resentment against the *Herald* and the *Sun* was all too obvious when as a reporter I tried to cover the Trades Hall scene. I even noted it as a police reporter. In Fitzroy one day, when I was trying to gain information on a simple robbery, an angry character slammed a door in my face.

'I won't speak to any Murdoch cunt.'

That was a shock. All the way home in the tram that night I worried: 'What do I do now? I'm a Murdoch cunt'.

But Murdoch, always determined to be a king-maker in politics, was unlike any newspaper proprietor that I ever encountered. He was the omnipotent, even ruthless, chief, but at the same time he wanted to be the benevolent, paternal father of us all. His father had been a clergyman and Sir Keith liked a display of old-fashioned Christian ethics. He believed his reporters should always look well bred. Male journalists had to have short hair, and, unlike in the 1970s or 1980s, suits and hats were compulsory.

One day soon after I joined the staff I met him in the lift.

'Dunstan', he said, 'where's your hat?'.

'I haven't got one, Sir Keith.'

'GET ONE!', he thundered.

And I did, half an hour after that moment.

Murdoch insisted on interviewing every cadet before he or she was hired, then worked hard at remembering names. He had a beautiful 'humble' line. When asked to describe his profession or craft, no he was not a journalist, he was a 'reporter'. Daily he would go on a grand parade through the reporters' room, determined to make friendly conversation. It was always an embarrassment because Sir Keith was ungifted at small talk.

'Well, Dunstan, what are your reading?', was a favourite opening gambit.

I had to think quickly of something appropriate and splendid.

'Um . . . *Crime and Punishment*, Sir Keith.'

Only Frank Murphy, *Herald* Chief of Staff, showed no fear.

'The *Sporting Globe*, Sir Keith', he replied when Sir Keith asked him the inevitable question.

My life moved closer to Sir Keith Murdoch's than I had anticipated. My skills were singularly few, but I was good at shorthand. While still in the RAAF I had taken a course in Pitman's Shorthand. I would practise while listening to a radio, and love songs were particularly useful. I could write 'I love you' faster than anyone else on earth. By the time I started as a cadet I already had over a hundred words a minute. This was another crafty method for getting on: those with good shorthand got the major court cases. But there was a disadvantage I had not anticipated: the Sunday round of the churches. Religion received much better treatment in the 1940s than now. Monday's *Sun* always had a round-up of the best and most fiery sermons. I would telephone the clergy on Friday, get the exact times they were giving their sermons, then on Sunday sprint from church to church, taking in shorthand at least six sermons: those of the Reverend Crichton Barr, the Reverend Gordon Powell, the Reverend Dr Irving Benson, the Reverend Dr A. H. Wood . . . Fortunately some of the more publicity-hungry gentlemen had their sermons already printed for me when I arrived.

Sir Keith was always making business trips to Sydney, Brisbane and Adelaide and frequently visited his big property, Wantabadgery, near Canberra. He needed someone to act as secretary, to write his letters. Seeing that I was competent at typing and shorthand, he often took me with him.

One must understand this was a delicate era. Sir Keith kept his newspapers pure of anything faintly related to sex. Rape was indecent assault or, in extreme cases, an outrage committed against a woman. Brothels were houses of ill fame, and prostitutes – how could you mention such a word? – were women of ill repute. Homosexuals almost did not exist. The best you could do was point to indecent or unnatural behaviour. Sir Keith not only had to be pure, he had to appear to be pure. It would have been improper for him to travel with a female secretary. Far better to have a young man to take his letters. Thirty years later it might have been considered normal and proper to travel with a female, whatever shape, size and marital condition, rather than tour with a young man.

Yet there was more to it than that. He believed young reporters should be educated. They could learn by travelling with him interstate. In the aeroplane he would hand over voluminous accounts and annual reports of the Herald and Weekly Times.

'Here, study these. See how they work. You will need to understand all this before long.'

He was good, indeed, at watching the pennies. There were no wild extravagances on his trips. He indulged in all sorts of Presbyterian economies. On one trip we lunched at the elegant Hotel South Australia in Adelaide. The lunch was almost over when I was called to the telephone. I returned, looked at the bill and put down a 10-shilling note. I was expected to look after minor details, such as the paying of accounts.

'What's that for?', Sir Keith asked.

'That's the tip for the waiter, Sir Keith.'

'I've already paid the tip.' He picked up the 10 shillings and put it in his pocket.

Sir Keith's secretary, Miss Demello, told me he had an old-fashioned attitude to economies. Often when he was writing cheques he made a mistake. There was threepence duty, pre-paid, on every cheque.

'Miss Demello, I've mucked up this one', he would say, coming out of his office. 'When you go to the bank get a refund.'

I asked her what she did.

'I would tear it up, of course', she said.

Sir Keith's Christian conscience went further. He believed in cultivating young people, getting to know them. He made new cadets presents of books about great editors, biographies of such people as Horace Greeley, founder of the *New York Tribune*, who had invented the line 'Go west, young man'.

Sometimes Murdoch's grand ideas went awry. He would meet journalists, writers, even diplomats, and in a moment of largesse say, 'You must come and work for me in Australia'. Then he would forget he had ever made the offer. When these candidates arrived on his doorstep, he would honour the promise, but often they had no journalistic training and were the despair of chiefs of staff.

One man who impressed Murdoch was a diplomat, an expert on Indonesian affairs. He was given an office and told to write. Indeed he produced a number of weighty articles on the Pacific scene. The prose was so turgid that fewer and fewer appeared in the paper. He became disillusioned, packed up his things and, without telling anyone, left. Three months later there was a call from the pay office. What were they to do with this man's money? It was all there, uncollected. The Editor had forgotten him and no one had noticed his departure.

In late July 1949, almost at the end of my cadet training, I received a message to report to Sir Keith Murdoch 'at my convenience'. This was a euphemism for 'immediately'. I went into his splendid, walnut-panelled office with the elegant pictures on the walls by Rupert Bunny. He took on a lofty, fatherly tone. He said that he approved of my work and that now it was time for me to move on to other things.

'We need a new staff member in our New York office. Would you like to go to New York?'

It was like offering a place in the Australian Eleven to a cricketer, a sainthood to a priest, the job of prime minister to a back bencher.

Half gasping, I said: 'Yes, Sir Keith. I would love to go to New York'.

'How old are you?'

'I'm 24, Sir Keith.'

'I need someone in New York a month from now, but you're far too young. We don't approve of sending away young, single men.'

He looked out the window across the Jolimont railway yards, and I could see him pondering the terrible fate that overcame unattached males in libidinous, far-off cities.

'You really want to go?'

'Oh yes.'

'I'll tell you what I'll do. If you can find yourself a young lady and get yourself married in that time, it's on. You are not engaged or anything like that?'

'No, Sir.'

'Do you have anyone in mind?'

'Ye-es, I think I do.'

'Well, go to it then.'

The young lady I had in mind was Marie Rose McFadyen, and she had been on my mind for at least four years. Our romance had quietened while I was in Labuan, and there had been little correspondence, but it started again once I was home in Melbourne.

Marie was a brunette with one dimple and a smile so dazzling I thought it could melt the Manchester Unity building. She had a lovely sense of humour, a keen eye for the absurd and a love of music, but there was something in particular we shared: a shyness, even a terror, created by the wowser society we lived in. Her aunts used to say that as a child she tried to sit as far away as possible when a man entered a tram. We were victims of our background. Her father many times said he disapproved of even hand holding in public. Geelong Grammar's monastic society had created in me a fumbling ineptitude with women, which took years to overcome. Recognition of each other's nervousness drew us together, and even as early as 1947 I found it hard to imagine life with anyone else.

Marie's father, Charles Hector McFadyen, was a senior public servant, who became department head of the Department of Shipping and Transport. A sporting champion, he had played cricket and football for Essendon. In the First AIF he had played for his division in both Australian Rules football and rugby. Furthermore he was a boxer. All the McFadyens were good at sport. Marie's brother Alan was a sprinter so good he was on the verge of Olympic selection for the 400 metres. Her elder brother,

Ken, could also run and was an outstanding footballer. Marie, too, was good at all sports. She could beat me easily at tennis, she was good at basketball and her smooth style across the pool was something to behold. She had been a champion swimmer. All this was disturbing for young Dunstan, who had no sporting gifts whatever and in the year 1942 was credited with being Geelong Grammar's slowest creature in the 100 yards sprint. Any sort of Hitlerian selection committee would have banned the liaison at once.

Charles McFadyen, known as Chub, adored horse racing and was a gregarious man, but his standards were high, and he thought also that young people should be chaperoned. Dunstan had to take care. Yet in the years after my return from overseas service there were opportunities for romance, and Marie and I had many interests in common. How wonderful it was on a summer evening to get up on the cast-iron balcony of the old mansion at 20 Wallace Avenue when the azaleas and the rhododendrons were in bloom and we could hear the shriek of the cicadas. Many people condemn that violent noise, but to us it was the most Melburnian of all noises – the signal that at last this was summer. I ran an extension cord up the narrow stairs from the attic to the roof so that we could play my turntable, which operated through an AWA mantel radio and used cactus needles.

'Why do you want to take all those rugs and things upstairs?', asked my mother. Why, indeed.

We played *Scheherazade*, so splendidly recommended by Manning Clark, we played Schubert's Unfinished Symphony and the piano concertos of Rachmaninov, our passion at the time, but we were also deeply moved by Bing Crosby. We had a 10-inch HMV record with 'Star Dust' on one side and 'Deep Purple' on the other. So the turntable turned, the music poured out over the cicadas below and the air was soft. The steel deck underneath tended to be slightly hard, but our eyrie up there, looking down on Toorak, was very close to heaven.

Marie was a nurse at the Royal Melbourne Hospital, and after graduation she assisted in the operating theatre. She worked with such famous names as Mr Albert Coates and the celebrated prisoner-of-war surgeon 'Weary' Dunlop. Hours in the theatre were long and hard. Even after operations were over the young nurses had to wash down the theatre themselves; floor and walls had to be washed seven times with antiseptic. It seemed I spent a lifetime waiting outside the Nurses' Home at the Royal Melbourne. However, waiting was not as arduous as it might have been because I could wait in a Holden, an FX Holden.

Holdens were launched on 29 November 1948. The *Sun News-Pictorial* first became excited about the Holden a few months before the launch. General Motors-Holden had four or five of these snub-nosed models – windscreen divided down the centre, grill that looked like a shark trying to smile and mudguards all smoothed into the body – at their test course at Lang Lang, near Melbourne. Newspaper photographers carried out all sorts of espionage. They hid behind bushes, took furtive shots, then published the pictures with captions that read 'Is this the new Holden?'. And, of course, it was.

Dad knew everybody on the Board at GM-H. He adored anything new, any new gadget. He had to have a Holden, and his wangling skills were so great that he managed to buy number twenty off the production line, even though the waiting list was as large as that of the Melbourne Cricket Club. Everybody stared at our new Holden. I thought it better than a Rolls-Royce, so I did not mind sitting there, waiting hour after hour for Sister McFadyen. One night when we were coming home at midnight from a dance at Kew, I failed to see a car approaching from the right at the corner of Barkers Road and Auburn Road. Nobody was hurt, but the beloved Holden received a huge dent in the side and had to be towed away. Shock, terror, guilt. How could I face my father? He loved the new Holden as much as I did. He looked at the damage and never said a word.

Marie and I loved to dance. We danced at the Power House at Albert Park or at Number Nine Darling Street. My very smart mother always worded me up correctly.

'When you take out a girl always make sure that you have a single gardenia for her.'

Expensive things gardenias: 5 shillings or even 7 and 6 each. The gardenia was always delivered with ribbon attached and in a Cellophane box.

At all dance places there was inevitably Dennis Farrington and his band. Dennis had the mysterious skill of being able to appear everywhere. We danced to 'Star Dust', 'Moonlight Becomes You',

'How I Love the Kisses of Dolores', 'Lovely to Look At, Delightful To Know', 'Alone' and 'Alone With the Light of Romance'.

If we could get away with it and we had the loan of the family car we detoured before we went home: over the MacRobertson Bridge and down the Boulevard along the Yarra. Sustenance workers – men on the dole – built the Boulevard during the Great Depression of the 1930s; the dole was 5 shillings a week for men living away from home, 1 shilling and 6 pence for those living with a relative. At the time the workers could not possibly have realised they were building the perfect love-nest for future generations. Always, after 10 p.m., there was a line of cars at two favourite spots along the Boulevard. One spot looked across the water to Toorak, the other to Hawthorn and Scotch College. There was always a blur of white faces in the back seats of the cars.

When I tried to creep into the house after midnight, the light in my parents' room would be on. Never would they go to sleep before Helen or I had reported in. There was always a debriefing. Mum and Dad had to know everything.

'I can't imagine what you've been doing that would keep you up to this hour', my father would growl. I think he had a fair idea.

The Murdoch offer was one sent from heaven. Marie and I had been dreaming of and angling for marriage for six months, but flats in the 1940s were even harder to find than cases of Scotch. After scanning the real estate advertisements and finding a possibility, a chance, not only was the rent exorbitant, but there was the extra touch of blackmail, key money, and that palm greaser for the key could be 500 pounds. Ah, but in New York we would not have to find a flat. The Herald and Weekly Times would see to it.

After my historic interview with Sir Keith Murdoch I hurried home in a state of euphoria. There was just one way to do this. I needed a car. This time the Holden was not available and I did not have the courage to ask my father directly for his beautiful Buick. Craftily I negotiated through my mother.

'Of course, Billy, he must have the car', she told my father.

That evening I drove round the Yarra Boulevard to our favourite spot, the love line-up with the view across to St Kevin's and Lansell

Road. I formally asked Marie if she would marry me and come to New York. Marie said 'Yes'. The future looked limitless.

Next came the ultimate honour. Sir Keith invited Marie and me to dinner with Lady Murdoch at their stately mansion in Albany Road, Toorak. He invited several other cadets. This was part of his policy: a chief executive should know the young members on his staff. Murdoch received much criticism for his political tactics and ruthlessness but, in my experience, no executive since has tried so hard to help young journalists.

'Whatever you do, don't outstay your welcome', was my father's solemn advice. 'At 10 o'clock you announce you must be gone.'

The dinner was very grand, with servants and a butler. Drinks were exquisitely served. The main course was chicken, which Sir Keith carved himself from a small side table. He was just severing a drumstick when the chicken skidded off the tray, shot through the air and landed on the floor. We looked in wonder, hushed, not daring to comment or, heaven forbid, laugh. What would he do now? Discard the chicken and order another from the kitchen? No, indeed. He stepped forward, picked up the offending chicken and, saying nothing, went on with the carving.

After dinner we were shown the house, the antiques and art treasures and the superb Murdoch collection of Georgian glass. At 9.30 p.m. Sir Keith announced, 'I suppose you will be needing your coats'. He beat Dad's darg by half an hour.

True to Sir Keith Murdoch's orders, our wedding took place in less than four weeks. It was set for 5 September 1949, which helped to inspire a little gossip. It was the custom in the 1940s for parents to promulgate an engagement formally in the newspapers. There was none of that. The speed was almost indecent.

Just two weeks before the wedding Dad had his first heart attack. He was only 54 but it virtually put an end to his full-time working career. There was just one treatment for cardiac problems, total rest, lying in bed utterly motionless, so that the strained heart could cure itself. It seemed logical that the wedding should be postponed, but the very thought of that just raised his blood pressure. The wedding had to go on. After all, he had organised the whole event and he had even created a little book, all bound, with the names and addresses of all his overseas friends, for us to look up in Honolulu, San Francisco, Los Angeles, Chicago, Vancouver, Montreal, New York and London.

The wedding took place at Scots Presbyterian Church, Toorak. My brother, Bill, was best man, Bob Dalziel was groomsman, my sister, Helen, was matron of honour and Anne Cornwell was bridesmaid. Glenda Raymond, later Glenda Crawford, sang 'Angels Guard Thee', and how she sang. Those angels have been guarding us ever since. It was an unforgettable event, but Dad was home in bed.

Our first night was to be at the Hotel Australia in Collins Street. At midnight we called in to say goodbye to Dad. He noted that I had a bottle of champagne.

'Where are you going with that?', he asked.

'I thought I would take it back to the hotel.'

'Why?'

'To drink with Marie.'

He erupted.

'Leave it here you damned fool. There's chicken sandwiches and champagne waiting for you in your hotel room. My father did it for me in 1918 and I've done it for you.'

In later years I realised our marriage had been plotted entirely by my mother and Marie's Aunt Doris. Very carefully and with great design they brought us together.

'Marie is a nice girl, I wouldn't take anyone else out if I were you', my mother would say.

It was a marriage similar to those of the Chinese or medieval nobility, arranged entirely by the parents. Our marriage subsequently was such a success, improving year by year, that I have wondered often ever since whether marriage is not a problem too serious to be left to the young.

CHAPTER EIGHT

Correspondent

Of course, as a honeymoon, it was beyond most people's dreams: a flight across the Pacific in a Boeing Stratocruiser. This was a large, four-engine, propeller-driven aircraft. Journalists by order of the Australian Journalists' Association had to travel first class. The Stratocruisers actually had beds – very narrow ones, but beds nevertheless, with curtains like railway Pullmans. So we slept together at an altitude of 4500 to 6000 metres, across the Pacific.

There were several days at the Royal Hawaiian in Honolulu, days in San Francisco, days in Los Angeles, where we met cowboy star Roy Rogers, then further days crossing the United States via the Santa Fe Railroad. Manhattan was far too expensive for anyone on an Australian salary so our first home was a single-bedroom apartment in Forest Hills, Long Island, not far from the famous tennis club. It was a six-storey apartment building on busy Queens Boulevard, and the Seventh Avenue subway ran right under our kitchen. Every time a train went by it rattled the kitchen cups. The subway was safe, regular, clean, efficient and the best way to come home, particularly late at night. Thirty years later people would not dare step foot in it at any time, day or night.

The colours of our apartment were bizarre hectic blues and pinks so we immediately set about painting it from end to end. Our neighbours, too, were different; we noticed that everyone in the building except us was Jewish. The owner of the building was also a Jew, Theodore R. Racoosin. He was a rich financier. He had a passion for opera and Persian rugs. His apartment off Fifth Avenue looked like a Persian market. It was not enough just to have them on the floor, Ted Racoosin also covered the walls with rare and beautiful rugs. We did not realise their value, we just thought it a very strange hobby. Ted was a wise and kindly man. Marie and I pointed out to him that we were the only non-Jewish people in the apartment block. We asked him what the others were like.

'I will tell you a story', he said. 'Back in the last century – oh, it must have been in the 1820s, something like that – a German and his family moved out West in their covered wagon. After travelling for many, many months they came to a spot in the Mid West that looked very beautiful. They decided this could be the place to settle down. Way over yonder they noticed a settlement. They went over to it and sought out the head man. "We are thinking of staying. What are the people like around here?", they asked him. The head man replied, "How did you find the people back home?". "Oh, fine", they answered. "The people back home are very good, decent people." "Well", said the head man, "if you found them good back home, then you will find them good here".'

Of course he was right.

The whole district was cosmopolitan. Around the corner was Bruno, who ran the Italian delicatessen. Bruno was inquisitive and wanted to know everything that was going on. One day we were in his shop when a Central European lady came in. Bruno introduced us to her.

'Do you speak German?', she asked.

No!

'Do you speak Russian?'

No.

'Do you speak Italian?'

No.

'Greek, Swedish, Finnish, French, Dutch?'

No. No. No. No. No.

She turned to Bruno. 'Ignorant. They don't speak anything.'

'Do you speak Australian?', Bruno replied.

He jerked his thumb at us. 'They do.'

Marie was hostess to a constant stream of visitors. There were Donald and Bunty Cochrane. Donald became professor of commerce at Monash University and chairman of the State Bank of Victoria. Bunty was Margaret Schofield the concert pianist. There were Peter Parkin, who was to be an executive with Mobil, and Lyle Turnbull, later to be editor-in-chief of the Herald and Weekly Times. And we saw, too, a very young Rupert Murdoch.

A shy, diffident young man. We couldn't see him becoming a great newspaper executive like his father.

The New York office of the Herald and Weekly Times was curious, indeed. The bureau chief was Randal Heymanson, a graduate of the London School of Economics and a former academic. Sir Keith Murdoch had found him in London. Randal Heymanson had a fine brain but no great skills as a writer or a journalist. Indeed, he had never been trained as a journalist. His assistant was Bill Noble, a New Zealander, a Presbyterian and a highly experienced, hard-working journalist of the old school, accurate, fast and a real news getter. Noble tended to find the stories and Heymanson to write them.

Then there was Justine Gordon, the secretary. Justine was the daughter of a well-to-do Jewish family, and she worked for as little as 40 dollars a week. She was a warm, witty, amusing young woman. Her typing was awful and her shorthand did not exist. Frequently she sent Heymanson into rages, but labour was scarce and he was frightened he could get no other secretary for the money. Soon after I arrived he spent an hour dictating to Justine. She typed up the notes and gave them to him. A few minutes later Heymanson stormed out of his office. He tore up the letters in front of her.

'You're incompetent, you're stupid, you can't do anything.'

He turned on his heel and went back into his office again. Justine started to giggle and stuck out her tongue in the direction of the departing Heymanson.

Another time Sir Keith Murdoch was visiting and he announced: 'Justine I have about twenty letters to do. Would you be available at 2 o'clock?'.

'What on earth am I going to do?', she asked me. 'He's going to find out I can't do shorthand and that will be the end.'

'I have an idea', I said. Our offices in the *New York Times* building were divided by 2-metre high partitions. 'When Sir Keith is dictating his letters, I'm sure he will sit in Heymanson's office. I will sit on the other side of the partition, with my ear against the frosted glass, and take it all down.'

'Oh, will you?', she said.

That's precisely what I did. It was like old times, taking Sir Keith's letters, but he didn't know I was there.

When I arrived Heymanson and Noble were like Stalin and President Truman. Actual hostilities had not been declared but there was an ugly case of cold war. They did not speak to each other. This was not easy in a small office, but they managed. Heymanson did a day shift, Noble a night shift, starting at 5 p.m. Noble in the evenings watched all the wire services and the early editions of the morning newspapers and provided what was called the Melbourne Herald Cable Service. Heymanson looked after events during the day and made sure he was gone by 4.30 p.m. It was all right to exchange notes, but not to speak to each other. I wondered why there was not an explosion, given the tension. Why wasn't either Heymanson or Noble removed? The answer was they were both indispensable. Heymanson was more than a journalist. He ran the Australian American Association, and he had contacts in New York and Washington. He could arrange meetings with important people for Murdoch and others. Noble, on the other hand, was a ceaseless fountain of usable copy. So the situation continued.

This sort of atmosphere was not unusual for an overseas office. Fifteen thousand kilometres from home it is very easy to develop a persecution complex, a sense of not being wanted. Many a story that seems brilliant, vital, even of world importance, in New York, Paris or London, fades terribly when it lands on a desk in Melbourne, Sydney or Brisbane. How can it compare with four dead in a crash on the Hume Highway or the star full-forward who has just been suspended at the Monday night tribunal?

Work varied. Often it was very mundane and involved sitting up late at night. Australian Associated Press provided the basic news service to Australian newspapers. We went through out-of-town newspapers and studied the American wire services, looking for items that AAP might have missed. We cabled these to the *Herald* in Melbourne, the *Courier-Mail* in Brisbane, the *Advertiser* in Adelaide and the *West Australian* in Perth.

Yet there were other opportunities, such as being the first to see the stage production of *South Pacific* and write of its marvels or being able to attend sessions of the United Nations and wonder at the Soviet Union foreign minister haranguing the West. There were chances to interview entertainment stars, such as Johnnie Ray and Frank Sinatra. Oh yes, I interviewed a young, sallow-faced

Frank Sinatra, in a theatre off Times Square. It was a dull time for Frankie, his audiences were fading and he was grateful in 1951 to get an interview with a journalist even from far-off Melbourne. There was an interview, too, with another singing star, Margaret Truman, daughter of the President of the United States. Miss Truman ceased to draw crowds after her father ceased to be president.

The Australian Press were all housed on the one floor of the *New York Times* building in West 43rd Street by Times Square. There were journalists of outstanding brilliance. Gavan Souter was there for the *Sydney Morning Herald*, John Yeomans for Sydney's *Sun*, and Sydney's *Daily Telegraph* had Peter Hastings, the journalist with the best brain I ever encountered.

Hastings had, and still has, a remarkable memory, a gift for foreign affairs and a marvellous, eclectic knowledge of literature. Our offices were next door to each other, and we put in lonely Sunday night vigils together. The Herald and Weekly Times owned a black and white television set, to us a rare and wonderful thing. Television did not come to Australia until 1956. Hastings and I would eat our evening sandwiches together, watching Sid Caesar and Imogen Coca on television and drinking a bottle of wine. Wine was a commodity that raised little interest in New York, and the only wines we could get were Chilean and South African rieslings for a dollar a bottle.

I had spent years trying to major in English literature at Melbourne University, but Hastings was shocked at my lack of knowledge. Had I read Thomas Mann? - *The Magic Mountain*, *Buddenbrooks*? No. Had I read D. H. Lawrence? - *The Rainbow*, *Kangaroo*? No. Had I read George Orwell? - *Down and Out in Paris and London*? No. How about James Joyce? *Ulysses*, of course, was on the banned list in Australia. In 1941 the Minister for Customs, Mr Harrison, had proclaimed: 'This book holds up to ridicule the Creator and the Church. It ridicules the whole moral standard of civilisation, citizenship and decency'. Some reporters pointed out to him that many critics thought *Ulysses* was the outstanding novel of the twentieth century. Mr Harrison admitted he had heard such comments, but he challenged newspapers to print a few selected extracts if they did not agree the book was obscene. None did.

In a surge of excitement I now read all of James Joyce: *Dubliners*, *A Portrait of the Artist as a Young Man*, *Ulysses* and *Finnegan's*

Wake. Finnegan's Wake, however, was a sad disappointment. I tried and tried but could not understand a word of it. I bought a copy of *The Skeleton Key to Finnegan's Wake*, which took readers through the great tome line by a line. I still did not understand *Finnegan's Wake*. I couldn't even understand the skeleton key.

The biggest impact came from *A Portrait of the Artist as a Young Man*. My faith, after reading Samuel Butler's *The Way of All Flesh*, was wavering when I studied this autobiographical novel. There are thirty pages that I think are among the most startling and graphic in English literature. Stephen Dedalus, aged 16, has bedded with a prostitute and is overcome with terrible guilt. He goes to chapel and the preacher gives a sermon on the nature of hell. Hell he describes in the most awful and intimate detail. Hell, we are told, not only has brimstone, it also has a nauseous, intolerable stench. Imagine the stench from a millionfold fetid carcasses massed together in the darkness. But what about the fire? Put your finger in the flame of even a candle and you will feel the pain. To bear the sting of an insect for a second is terrible – imagine it for all eternity. How fine are the grains on a seashore? There are millions, trillions. The years of eternity are the same. The agony is for ever.

He is inexorable, this preacher. He goes on and on. How terrible is the lot of those in hell. The blood seethes and boils in the veins, the brain boils in the skull, the heart in the breast glows and bursts, the bowels are a red-hot mass of burning pulp and the tender eyes flame like molten balls. Devils mock and cheer. Why did you sin? Why did you not listen to the counsels of your confessor? Why did you not, even after you had fallen the first or the second or the third or the fourth or the hundredth time, repent of your evil ways and turn to God? After about an hour of this poor Stephen Dedalus is on his knees, shrieking:

- O my God! -
- O my God! -
- I am heartily sorry -
- I am heartily sorry -
- for having offended Thee -
- for having offended Thee -
- and I detest my sins -
- and I detest my sins -

After reaching a peak of religious fervour Stephen Dedalus goes through a series of doubts. No longer can he believe in the Eucharist, no longer can he believe in the reincarnation. He admits he is frightened of many things – dogs, horses, firearms, the sea, thunderstorms, machinery and country roads – but he is prepared to take a risk on hell-fire, even if it is for all eternity. His friend Cranly tells him not to do anything drastic, even the most religious have doubts, and to take the Eucharist for the sake of his mother. Not he. He will not approach the altar. Dedalus is prepared to sacrifice even his mother. He is seeking 'unfettered freedom' in which to discover his own way of life and art.

Ernest Pontifex, the young clergyman in *The Way of All Flesh*, reads some of the heretical books in the library of the British Museum, suffers a terrible loss of faith and goes berserk. He mistakes a certain Miss Maitland for a prostitute, assaults her and finishes up in gaol. In contrast, Dedalus prides himself on the fact that the change in his beliefs makes no difference whatever to his morals. It just leaves him with the freedom to think. I was fascinated by all this, I couldn't read enough, and it was six years before I set foot again in a church.

In 1950 Marie became pregnant. Every time she went into the delicatessen Bruno commented. He would note the size of the swelling and say, 'Ah yes, the little fellow is coming along well'. Marie went to Dr Arthur V. Greeley in Manhattan. He was very advanced in his thinking and onto a new idea, launched by Grantley Dick Reid. Drugs were not necessary. If only mothers took care, did their exercises and learned how to breathe, childbirth would be easier, less painful. He called it 'natural childbirth'. There was even another revolutionary idea that fathers could be present at the birth to give strength and support to their wives.

My father and mother came to New York for the arrival of their new grandchild. The date for the birth passed, another ten days went by and still the child had not arrived. My father's return to Melbourne was long overdue. When it seemed he could stay no longer, Dr Greeley induced the birth.

The date was 1 December 1950. I went into the hospital and dutifully sat by Marie. This was not a great success. I was four times more nervous and agitated than she was. I have learned since that it is a common occurrence for fathers to become casualties during the transition stage of labour. It seemed that for the moment my work was over, and Marie just wanted to get the job done herself.

'Please, go home', she moaned.

Whether the natural childbirth Marie experienced was any easier or more comfortable than any other style of birth is problematical. It took place at the great Cornell Hospital on the East River. I waited and waited in the foyer. Eventually a message came down.

'A baby has been born', a nurse told me.

'What is it? What is it?', I shouted.

'Dr Greeley wants to tell you about it himself', the nurse answered.

The wait for Dr Greeley was the longest ten minutes of my life. I thought: 'I know why he wants to tell me himself. Something has gone wrong. The baby is ill. Perhaps it has two heads. Perhaps it is dead'. However, this was just Dr Greeley's style. He always liked to tell fathers personally.

He eventually stepped out of the lift, beaming, shook my hand and said, 'Congratulations, you have a fine little son'.

Soon my parents were at the hospital, and we were all standing around a happy, triumphant Marie.

The birth of our son, David, was also a lesson in economics. We had not been in the United States long enough to get maternity benefits under the Blue Cross scheme. When the day came for Marie to go home I was told to report first to the office at Cornell. There the manager told me to produce a cheque for 500 dollars. In 1950 this seemed an enormous sum of money, almost my entire bank account. The manager said firmly that I must first pass over the money then we could get the baby. The inference was obvious: no money, no baby.

It was interesting to observe the contrasts between the births of our four children. Jane was born in London two years later, under the kindly benefits of the British health scheme. By the time we arrived in England Marie was six months pregnant. There was the problem of a new country and getting into a new house. Marie's extraordinary calm was overwhelming. I kept saying, 'How about seeing a doctor?'. Maybe it was all that nursing experience, but she did not think doctors were necessary at this stage. By the time nigh on eight months had passed I was thoroughly alarmed.

I told Marie we were going out to a movie. In reality I had pre-arranged a visit to the doctor. I pulled up outside his waiting-rooms, opened the door and pushed her in. At last, I thought, everything is organised.

Marie had the birth at home, with the aid of a midwife. The birth cost us nothing. Indeed, with all the bonuses, there was a 5-pound profit. Yet the United States system, with a week in a good hospital, was a much better arrangement. The week at home, with a new baby and another child in the house, was a big strain on Marie.

The doctor should have been at the birth but he arrived late. I did not get there at all. On that day, 9 October 1952, Trevor Smith, the bureau head, assigned me to cover a rail disaster. Except for a crash at Gretna Green it was the worst in the history of British rail. It took place at the height of the morning rush, at Harrow, 17 kilometres from the heart of London. The night express from Scotland crashed into a suburban train. Then another express bound for northern England hit the wreckage. A foot bridge over the station was carried away and fell down on the station platforms. At the time there were hundreds of people on the platforms, some waiting for an underground train. The crash created an astonishing mountain of awful, twisted metal. At one point three carriages were mounted on top of each other to a height of over 15 metres. There were 108 dead and another 100 went off to hospital.

When I arrived there were still people trapped inside the carriages, screaming, moaning. Rescuers were trying to hack them free with oxy-acetylene cutters. I remember talking to a Mr William Ingham, who was travelling in the fourth carriage of the London–Manchester express.

'It just fell to pieces all around us. The carriage seemed to float up into the air. Then there was a crash, and our carriage was on the platform or what was left of it', he said.

All day long I watched rescue workers carrying away the dead and the injured. I got to the office just after 5 p.m. and Trevor Smith, a man not addicted to great emotion, huskily said: 'I have a message for you. You have a daughter. All is well'.

It was a strange, happy, exquisitely relieved feeling. Amid all that death, there was life.

Our next child, Kate, was born in Brisbane in May 1956. That famous and immensely wise person Lady Cilento brought her into the world. Sarah was born at the Mercy Hospital in Melbourne in 1958. So Marie had four children in four widely separated cities.

The three years in New York could hardly have been more exciting, but there were frustrations. There were no out-of-town assignments. Postwar reconstruction was still going, the Marshall Plan was in action in Europe and the United States dollar was the ultimate hard currency before which all countries paid homage. In 1949 Australia had a serious balance of payments problem. Economics in the 1940s were conducted according to a simple rule: what you did not have you did not spend. The Prime Minister, R. G. Menzies, imposed drastic import restrictions, which included currency, therefore only very limited supplies of dollars were available for those who wished to travel. As a consequence the only travelling we did in North America was in holidays at our own expense.

In 1952 Sir Keith Murdoch told us that we were to move to London. He believed my training would have a dreadful imbalance if I came back with only an American view of journalism. It was also the eve of the Coronation, and all staff were needed in London to cover the momentous event. So we crossed the Atlantic aboard the Cunard liner *Arcadia*. In later years I formed an organisation, the Anti Progress Society, on the grounds that things rarely improved. Ship travel was the perfect example. In the 1950s, only if people were in a desperate hurry were they tempted to take to the air, because there were all those splendid ocean liners operated by such people as P & O, Orient and Cunard. Mr Menzies usually managed to time his overseas trips just precisely when the Australian team was playing cricket in England. There was no dreadful urgency about world affairs. He travelled by ship, both there and back. He would be away for three months.

Ship travel had such beautiful, charming rituals. Cabin trunks went down to the boat. Travellers did not have flimsy fibre cases containing two drip-dry shirts. These were proper trunks, with ribs along the top and pull-out drawers inside. There were farewells aboard – drinks in your cabin with your friends before you departed. Then you met your steward, who showed you round the boat and how to handle the bath and adjust the ventilation on the porthole.

Marie had to make sure she had sufficient evening dresses because passengers dressed for dinner every night, except Sunday. Fancy dress was on the third day out. It took our ship seven days to cross the Atlantic – a blissful experience – and with a young baby we were the centre of attention.

London was a city that had not yet recovered from war. There was still food and petrol rationing, and accommodation of all kinds was desperately short. We went way out of the city to stay in a country inn at Ockley. On the first day I walked across the fields to the railway station to catch a train to London. I stepped into the train – and went off in the wrong direction. I was so used to the United States I expected the train to come up on the right-hand track. I did not get to London until noon and hence made a brilliant impression on my new chief, Trevor Smith.

After much difficulty we managed to rent a house in the depths of suburbia, at Wallington in Surrey. It was large, two storied and the coldest house we can ever remember. It had eleven different heating devices, ranging from coal and gas through to electric bar-heaters, none of which were effective. Mr Schmutzer, the owner, had filled his house with rare, ornate and quite hideous Austrian furniture. He was terrified it would come to harm in the hands of these strange Australians.

David was already articulate and very mobile. We were heavily under the influence of the new theories of Dr Spock. Parents should not check their children too much because this was likely to bruise their flowering personalities. David was flowering very well. One day he had a hammer poised above a glass-topped coffee table.

'You wouldn't do that, would you, David?'

He would, indeed. He brought down his hammer and smashed the glass. So thereafter we had a standard saying: 'David you must not do that. Mr Schmutzer will be very angry with you'. There is no question that this sank in and made an impression. We had been at Wallington six months when Mr Schmutzer made a surprise call.

'David, this is Mr Schmutzer, whom we have been telling you about', said Marie kindly.

David promptly ran across the room and started kicking Mr Schmutzer's bird's-eye-walnut, roly-poly-fronted sideboard.

The Wallington house was a special kind of prison for Marie. She was trapped there when she should have been out enjoying

the sights of Coronation-year London. She did not see the
Coronation, and my view of it was curious. England had television,
Australia did not. Large-screen television was installed in theatres
throughout Britain so that those who did not have sets of their
own could watch England's grandest production live, just down
the street. Dunstan, the most junior member of the staff, had to
write what it was like to see the Coronation on television. The
important writers, such as Trevor Smith and Douglas Brass, were
much closer to the action. My story was given only a few lines
in the paper.

Marie's lonely time became worse because of cricket. Archer
Thomas, the *Herald* Editor, wanted a journalist to cover the
Australians' 1953 tour of England. He wanted somebody apart
from the regular cricket writer, a reporter who could provide colour
and chatty items about what the players were doing, somebody
to relieve the monotony of mere run making. Dunstan was to
cover all the county and all the Test matches. Selfishly I saw it
as a dream come true, a five months, all-expenses-paid tour of
England, doing nothing but what I liked best, watching cricket.
As it turned out, even before two months were over, I was crying
for mercy. Cricket has to be played where the crowds are. England
was still rundown and dreary after the war and most of the tour
took part in the most depressed areas of England: Stoke, Sheffield,
Bradford, Manchester and all the black towns of the north. To
make matters worse it was a classic cold, wet English summer,
with one in three days of play washed out by rain. Hour after
hour I spent in grandstands, just waiting for play to start.

But what great names there were on that tour: Lindsay Hassett
(captain), Keith Miller (vice-captain), Arthur Morris, Colin
McDonald, Ray Lindwall, Bill Johnston, Ian Johnson, Doug Ring,
Neil Harvey, Richie Benaud and the very junior Ian Craig. The
man I revered and adored was Keith Miller. I was too timid and
shy even to talk to him. At Manchester he caught me in a lift.

'Hello, my name's Keith Miller. What's yours?'

Euphoria! As if I didn't know his name.

Australian cricketers were a happy-go-lucky lot, known to drink
their beer into the early hours of the morning even before a Test
match. Their leisure was in marked contrast to that of the young
team of Australian tennis players Harry Hopman was running at
Wimbledon. The tennis players were lucky if they were allowed

up after 9 p.m. and fined if they stayed out later, and their strongest drink was orangeade. R. S. Whitington in *The Quiet Australian* tells how Prince Philip asked to meet the Australian cricket team. Keith Miller had a black eye. Prince Philip immediately asked, 'How's her husband?'. Oh no, the husband was not a problem at all. Miller insisted it happened when he fell down the stairs.

The first four Test matches were all drawn. In one of the county matches, at Edgbaston, we saw a new fast bowler, Fred Trueman. The English Press nicknamed him Fiery Fred, Ferocious Fred and even Frightening Fred. In their classic, eloquent style they called him the new Harold Larwood. The Australian journalists who observed Freddie at Edgbaston also wrote about him: too erratic, and where was all this speed he was supposed to have? Just an apology for Larwood, they said, and not fast at all. England selectors are always cautious. They prefer that a player be virtually a grandfather and ready for his testimonial before he gets into a Test side. So Ferocious Fred was ignored for the first four Tests. He came into the side for the fifth. He was fast all right. He dismissed Neil Harvey for thirty-six, Graeme Hole for thirty-seven, Jimmy de Courcy for five and Ray Lindwall for sixty-two. There at the Oval Australia lost its one and only Test. Lindsay Hassett, always a charming and good-humoured captain, bowled the last ball of his last Test, the Test that lost the Ashes for Australia. He surrendered with very good grace and eloquence. There was one mad, final gesture. He threw a bottle of champagne at the clock in the dressing-room.

It was not easy covering this Test series. There was the regular *Herald* cricket writer, P. J. Millard, to do the job. He was efficient and knowledgeable, and I, as the junior reporter, had to be careful not to get in his way. He used to carry an exercise book with all his favourite adjectives and phrases written down in it. As he used them he crossed them off so that he never doubled up during a match. He told me that while he was away on a cricket tour he did not like his wife using his car.

'Percy, how can you stop her?', I asked.

'I take the battery out and put it up in the top of the garage. She can never understand why the car won't start', he said.

Percy did the full descriptions of the cricket. I had to find other things, colourful incidents, crowd reactions. Often the cricket was so dull this was hard, indeed. The English batsman Trevor Bailey was capable of being at the crease for an hour without scoring. He gave a whole new meaning to the word tedium. At Leeds in the fourth Test, which became the fourth consecutive draw, Bailey took four hours and twenty-two minutes to make thirty-eight runs. The Australians called him the Boil because he was such an irritant. His regular name was the Barnacle because he would stick without doing anything. In moments of extreme irony he was Darling Trevor. He also managed to manoeuvre the match to a draw with his bowling. He had a majestical, unnecessarily long run to the wicket. Furthermore almost every over he had to alter his run, measure it, put down a new marker. Actually Trevor was a remarkable help. He gave me a villain to write about.

I had to become an expert on meteorology. What with the eternal rain, days would go by with no cricket at all. I learned eventually to write about everything but the cricket: the behaviour of the crowds, the English towns and villages and, above all, the wonderful vagaries of the weather. Australians love to hear about the English suffering from bad weather.

At least it worked with one reader. A letter arrived from Colin Bednall, Managing Director of the *Courier-Mail* in Brisbane. Bednall was already something of a legend. He went to St Peter's College in Adelaide, joined the Adelaide *News*, then went to London. During the Second World War he was a war correspondent for the London *Daily Mail*, so good that he won the OBE for his services. In 1946 Keith Murdoch brought him back from London to be editor-in-chief of Brisbane's *Courier-Mail* and *Sunday Mail*. He was only 33 years old. Bednall, who was never given to half statements, claimed he would make the *Courier-Mail* the best newspaper in Australia. All those who worked for Bednall claim it was a restless, remarkable experience. Not only did he have half a dozen ideas a day, he had also learned some tricks from the *Daily Mail*. On Tuesday he would send a memo: 'Marvellous job this morning, John. I look upon you as the most valuable man on my paper'. On Thursday there would be another: 'I can't imagine why you handled the story on the Premier the way you did. Sloppy writing. Please do better tomorrow'.

I was excited by the letter I received from the brilliant young editor. He pointed out that the *Courier-Mail* had been receiving my copy, both from the United States and England. He said anybody who could write about something as odd as cricket must be able to write a column. He offered me a good salary, a house of my choice and a column on the front page of the *Courier-Mail* if only I would come to Brisbane.

There was one problem. In 1953 both the *Courier-Mail* in Brisbane and the *News* in Adelaide were owned personally by Sir Keith Murdoch, but were not part of the Herald and Weekly Times. If I accepted this offer I had to resign my job. However, it was not a difficult decision. Never in the reporters' room at the *Herald* or the *Sun* had I heard the charge that I was getting favoured treatment because my father was general manager, but I sensed such a feeling might exist. There was the case of my good friend Keith Murdoch. Keith was Sir Keith's nephew and named in his honour. He had served in the infantry in some of New Guinea's toughest battles. Just as I did, when the war ended, he joined the *Herald* as a reporter. He was intelligent and capable but with that name his career in journalism quickly became impossible. He had been on the staff only a few weeks when an insensitive chief of staff sent him to the Trades Hall. There Keith had to interview the tough old left-winger Patrick John Kennelly, organising secretary of the Australian Labor Party. Pat Kennelly was not only the spokesman for the ALP, he was the mouth of the trade union movement. If reporters needed a comment on the basic wage, a rise in prices or the next strike, they went to him. When Keith introduced himself as Keith Murdoch from the *Herald*, Kennelly began to laugh.

'And you wouldn't believe it now, would you? They have sent the great Keith Murdoch himself to interview me', he said.

Keith suffered so much of that that he left journalism to run his own public relations business in Brisbane.

No, this was the time for me to get far away, also. It was a chance to join Keith in Brisbane. I accepted the Bednall offer.

CHAPTER NINE

Walking the tightrope

On 5 October 1952 Sir Keith Murdoch died in his sleep at Cruden Farm, Victoria, aged 66 years. He had been into hospital for his second prostate operation the previous April, and his heart gave out. My father thought this event so climactic that he telephoned me in Wallington to give me the news immediately. International telephone calls were not overcommon in 1952. I had sent Dad a photograph of myself near the telephone in our Wallington house and he had craftily read the number on the handset, using a magnifying glass.

To us it was like the death of Caesar and contained almost equal drama. For years my father had come home raging about Keith Murdoch. Sir Keith in his later years sold all his personal interest in the Herald and Weekly Times, but while still chairman he gained control of the *Courier-Mail* in Brisbane and the *News* in Adelaide. Dad thought this was outrageous. Not only did Sir Keith own these newspapers but he used the Herald and Weekly Times to get them favoured treatment, particularly with newsprint. I would agree with Dad whenever he voiced his view.

'Yes, that's shocking behaviour. He shouldn't be allowed to do that.'

'You keep out of this', Dad would reply. 'It's none of your business. You don't realise what a great man he is.'

Desmond Zwar in his biography *In Search of Keith Murdoch* says that Murdoch before he died was plotting a new venture that would have dismayed the Australian newspaper industry. He was plotting to leave the Herald and Weekly Times entirely to buy the *Argus* and run it in opposition to the empire he had created. The *Argus* had been Melbourne's greatest newspaper. The London

Daily Mirror took it over in 1949 and made it sensational. The *Daily Mirror* entirely misjudged the staid Melbourne market and in 1952 the *Argus* was close to death. Keith Murdoch obviously saw an opportunity.

But there were other forces at play in the death of Caesar. The next in line to Sir Keith at the Herald and Weekly Times was John Francis Williams, a very complex man and almost the complete opposite to Murdoch himself. J. F. Williams had been editor of the *Barrier Miner* in Broken Hill and managing director of the *Courier-Mail* in Brisbane before Bednall and was now managing editor of the Herald and Weekly Times. Murdoch was gregarious. He liked to be seen as a king-maker, a patron of the arts and a lover of good paintings and glass. He possessed three country properties, Wantabadgery and Booroomba in New South Wales and Cruden Farm near Frankston, Victoria. Williams never wished to mix with people, he showed no interest in the arts and he had a country house once but could not bear it. His *Who's Who* entry ran to only five lines, as brief as he could possibly make it. He listed no hobbies. The newspaper business was his entire life, seven days a week. He was to be seen wandering the nigh-deserted corridors of the Flinders Street building even on Sunday mornings. When he eventually retired, that elegant *Herald* writer Geoffrey Tebbutt wrote:

> Williams: difficult, prickly, unpredictable, demanding, moody, capricious, impatient – yes, all these things might from time to time be said of John Williams. And just as truly that he is helpful, considerate, amiable, tolerant, practical, resilient, understanding and, above all, human and generous, judging people as individuals and not by their ideologies and associations.

I can't think of anyone Williams ever harmed, but his staff feared him. His comments could be short, cutting and devastatingly sarcastic, yet he was also capable of extraordinary kindnesses and generosity to his staff. In the 1940s he must have suffered torture trying to get on with Murdoch and keep up with his whims and plans.

In 1948 there was a call to our Wallace Avenue house at 1 a.m. We all leaped out of bed, thinking maybe a grandparent had died. It was the *Sun* police roundsman, Jerry Bergin. The police had arrested J. F. Williams and charged him with offensive behaviour.

The crime? Police had caught him urinating in the street at the back of Alfred Place. Dad drove into the city immediately. How he did it I don't know, but he got Williams off the charge.

My friend Bob Dalziel, who by then was a stock broker, also had an encounter with Williams. One day over lunch Dalziel commented: 'There's a character up at the University Club called Williams. He reckons he's the editor-in-chief at the *Herald*. Nobody believes him. He's drunk every night. Couldn't be true, could it?'.

My father thought it was true. He claimed that Keith Murdoch was so concerned about Williams's drinking he was planning to fire him. Had Murdoch lived another week Williams would have gone. My father thought it was the concern about Williams, the agonising over whether he should fire him, that gave Murdoch a heart attack.

Bednall in Brisbane, not Williams, was the Murdoch protégé, the young man Murdoch had made. Rohan Rivett, Editor of the Adelaide *News*, was another Murdoch favourite. He was later fired by Rupert, so neither of Murdoch's protégés survived to be leaders of the next Herald and Weekly Times generation. Murdoch almost on the day he died told Bednall he expected him to be his successor. He even suggested to Bednall that he would be his executor.

None of this seemed to impinge on the Herald and Weekly Times board. J. F. Williams took over in October 1952 and became managing director and eventually chairman of the Herald and Weekly Times. He did not have the grand aspirations of Murdoch, but he had other qualities. He restored honesty to the *Herald* and the *Sun*. To my mind he rid both newspapers of any suggestion of political bias, and the departure of Murdoch must have relieved all kinds of pressure. I never saw or heard of Williams's being drunk, after 1952.

Ah, but with Caesar's death there was the problem of Caesar's spoils. There was the problem of probate. The properties in New South Wales had to go. Furthermore Rupert, Sir Keith's son, did not have the cash to hang onto both the *Courier-Mail* in Brisbane and the *News* in Adelaide. He had to make a choice. He chose the *News* and so News Limited ultimately became the launching pad for the great publishing empire he developed around the world. Under the terms of Sir Keith's will the Herald and Weekly Times had first option to buy the controlling interest in the *Courier-Mail*.

When the Herald and Weekly Times took up the option, Colin Bednall saw no future in his newspaper career. No longer could his dream of becoming leader of the Herald and Weekly Times empire come true. He did not believe he could work under Williams so he resigned. It was a mistake. Almost certainly Williams would not have been vindictive, and there was just a chance that Bednall might even have outlasted him to become managing director himself.

In late 1953 Marie and I sailed home with two children, aboard the P & O liner *Strathmore*. It was a glorious, happy five weeks on the water. I arrived in Melbourne to learn that Bednall had resigned from the *Courier-Mail* and it was very likely that I was out of a job or, if not out of a job, forced to beg a return to the Herald and Weekly Times. I rang the new editor-in-chief of the *Courier-Mail*, Ted Bray, later Sir Theodore Bray.

'Mr Bray, a lot has happened', I said. 'Mr Bednall has gone. Do you still want me to come to Brisbane?'

Mr Bray was very direct, very honest.

'Mr Dunstan, if you don't come, we'll sue you.'

What's more he wanted me to come in a hurry.

Brisbane in January 1954 was a city of 500 000 people and very different from what it is now. It had an inferiority complex that ran deep. Nearly all its manufacturing businesses, retail houses and newspapers were owned by the south, particularly Melbourne. It was the custom for a business to send young managers to Brisbane for training before returning them to Melbourne for grander things. Newspapers were no exception.

Anyone from the south was looked upon with suspicion. Brisbane people had a way of spitting out the word 'southerner' that left no uncertainty about how they felt. The entire world was divided between Queenslanders and southerners. The citizens of Brisbane always considered that the finest weather ever granted to humankind was eternally in Brisbane. This was only slightly true. Brisbane in the wet season from December to March was humid and vile. The rest of the year it almost lived up to its claims.

In 1954 Brisbane had no dashing skyline. The largest building was the City Hall, with its splendid tower that tried to ape the campanile in St Mark's Square, Venice. The City Hall stood in St George's Square, where the main feature was an extraordinary statue of King George V on horseback, dressed in quite impossible gear for that tropical climate.

I went on ahead to Brisbane as advance guard, stayed at the Imperial Services Club and looked for a house. Stan Sherman, the General Manager, told me that the offer of a house was typical of Bednall's extravagant behaviour, but that, given I had it in writing, they would stick to the agreement. I found a lovely wooden house with a big verandah, at the top of the hill in Crescent Road, Hamilton.

I wrote to Marie and told her not to expect too much. Brisbane was a very curious place. The children tended to go to school in bare feet. The favourite pastime in the evening was to sit on the front porch in the warm air, with a glass of beer, and take in the sunset. The houses were all very different, made of timber and incredibly up on stilts, and nobody used paint much. There was little in the way of sewerage; in fact, some people thought it indecent to have a lavatory inside the house. In summer there would be plenty of mosquitoes so, for heaven's sake, get some mosquito nets from war disposals, I told Marie. Possibly I overdid it. I picked her up with the children at the airport and drove down Queen Street in the city. She looked round slowly and carefully and said: 'How nice. They've got electric light'.

The first thing I had to do was show her the house in Crescent Road. At this stage it had no carpets and no furniture. It was half past eight in the evening, and I had not bargained on the result. I turned on the lights and cockroaches ran everywhere across the bare boards. I tried to explain that the cockroach is very clean and very nearly the oldest insect known to humankind, with a very distinguished history, but it was not a good start.

As soon as we moved in the neighbours called. The lady next door, Lillian Dowling, insisted on lending us an ice chest. Another came in with a basket of pawpaws. Within forty-eight hours we knew half the people in the street. In London after two years we still had not known our next-door neighbours.

All Brisbane was like this. We were fascinated how people, no matter what their status, were on first-name terms. In England Christian names barely existed. Anyone who called on the manager or the top executive of a firm in Brisbane went straight through and Christian names prevailed. Most extraordinary of all, the

Premier of Queensland, Vincent Clair Gair, known to everyone as Vince, had his name and suburban address in the telephone book. Brisbane was really an amiable country town, but a real town for all that. Queensland was the only Australian State with a proper city–country ratio. The population of Brisbane was only a third that of the rest of the State.

My job was to take over the 'Day by Day' column on the front page of the *Courier-Mail*, almost immediately after my twenty-ninth birthday. The previous incumbent was Arthur Richards, who had done it for four years and was now suffering from stomach ulcers. Richards was a very amiable man, smoked a pipe, liked to drink a glass of Bundaberg rum, knew all the important people from the Premier down and every weekend liked to go 'down the bay' fishing. 'Down the bay' was a sort of generic term for anywhere from Moreton Bay to as far south as Coolangatta. A third of the town seemed to go fishing at the weekend.

Richards, the columnist, had become a statewide institution much loved by everybody. He had gained great experience in journalism, both in Sydney and London, and he had a rare gift as a writer. He was a born communicator. No matter what he wrote I had the desire to go on reading to the last word on the page. His column was gentle, whimsical and managed to distil the essence of the Queensland character. The very thought of taking over from him left me unnerved. However, I studied everything he wrote and listened to all he said. The sub-editors on the Melbourne *Sun* taught me journalism but my debt to Richards in learning how to write was enormous.

The *Courier-Mail* was an interesting place and there were some great characters on the staff. There was V. J. Carroll, who played Rugby Union for Queensland and was the finance editor. Later he was editor of the *Financial Review*, editor of the *Sydney Morning Herald* and editor-in-chief of James Fairfax and Son. There was Roger Covell, who became the distinguished critic on the *Sydney Morning Herald*. There was Denis O'Brien, writer and critic, and David Rowbotham, poet. Above all there was Mr John Holmes. I loved Mr Holmes. Behind his back everyone called him Jackie, but he was so distinguished, so erudite, he was the one person in Brisbane no one could ever address by Christian name. Mr Holmes was the leader writer and a walking encyclopaedia. He was English born, over 60 and a gentleman who always had the answer to every query. He was one of the last of those who had a true classical education. He knew most languages. Ask him for a phrase in German and he would say in his high-pitched voice, 'Would you like it in classical German or colloquial German?'.

Every night before we went home he said, 'Keith, I think it is time for our little reviver'.

I provided the coffee and he the silver flask filled with Amity white rum. I can't tell you what a help that rum was to the coffee.

When Brisbane acquired its first espresso coffee lounge we decided that should be the place for our reviver. Espresso was absolutely the new rage and this lounge had the grandest new Gaggia, all silver, twiddly bits, dials, tubes and flashing lights. As it produced the coffee it panted like a suburban steam train.

Mr Holmes said to the person serving, 'Could we have *due cappucini*?'

'Eh?', she said.

I interjected, 'We want two coffees please'.

'Sorry, I didn't get you. Hey Bill, they want two cappa-cheen-ohs.'

Just before my first Christmas on the paper a message arrived from Canberra. The Governor-General asked if Mr Holmes would come to Canberra for Christmas. If he accepted, Field Marshal Sir William Slim would send his aircraft to pick him up. We were agog. It was the talk of the *Courier-Mail*. Why on earth would the great Sir William be doing this? That night over our reviver I delicately broached the subject.

'Oh, you must understand', said Mr Holmes, 'Billy Slim and I were at school together. He always does this'.

Soon after my arrival Arthur Richards took me aside and told me how to write a column.

'Now Keith, you have to be brief. You might have to write a paragraph five times to get it down to the right length. Every extra word you put into a paragraph the more brilliant it has to be to retain the attention of your reader. The beauty about being a columnist is that you can write what you like. Well, almost. But remember, never try to be too clever. Don't try to be smarter than your audience. Never be a smart-arse. Always *you* have to be the fall guy. That way your reader feels a little bit superior and gets a laugh. Make Brisbane absolutely the centre of the universe and you won't go wrong. And, oh yes, the weather. Write plenty of gags about the weather. They adore weather in Brisbane.'

My problem was we did not know anybody in Brisbane apart from Robin and Keith Murdoch, who introduced us to all their friends in a hurry. Otherwise it was a completely cold start.

Red Smith, the famous sporting columnist who once wrote for the *New York Herald-Tribune*, put the agony of writing a column very well:

> I always say that writing a daily column is the simplest thing in the world. All you have to do is saddle up at your typewriter every day, no matter where you are or where you've been the night before, and start tap, tap, tapping away – every word a drop of blood. And when you've filled the space waiting there to be filled every day as inevitable as death, you say to yourself, 'There goes another chip off your brain, Smith, but you've gotta eat'.

Kirwan Ward, who was a fine columnist on Perth's *Daily News*, also had a line for it: 'It's just like walking a tightrope across Niagara Falls – a little scary until you get used to it'.

Scary? I was terrified. This was the most difficult time in my career as a journalist. Brisbane was never quite big enough. It is hard to believe it now. Today Brisbane is a city where everything happens. In 1954 it was pleasantly sepulchral. My day started at 2 p.m. and finished at 11 p.m. or midnight. By 10 or 10.30 p.m. that column should have been finished, and it was my job to show it in proof form to the Editor-in-Chief, T. C. Bray.

Bray was a little man with a rasping voice. He was efficient and extremely well-informed and had an excellent memory for facts and detail. He read the entire newspaper before it got into print, even the classified ads. T. C. Bray missed nothing. I had to hand him the column, sit in front of him and watch while he read it. This was like having your detention essay read by the housemaster.

Ted Bray read my copy without emotion, and sometimes if it was not too good he sighed: 'Mr Dunstan' – he had a mock way of doing this with the emphasis on the 'Mister' – 'Mr Dunstan, is this really your column for tomorrow?'.

The first few days, even the first week, were easy enough because I had material stored, but then it became desperately hard. I complained to Mr Bray about the difficulties.

'Ahh, Mr Dunstan, you don't see enough of the town. You should carouse. Get around the bars and soon you will pick up plenty of stories.'

I took his advice and checked out all the bars. I picked up plenty of stories all right, but none that Mr Bray would think were fit to use in his newspaper.

Arthur Richards said that whenever he had got into trouble he had written a little story about his children. He lived in Clayfield and he had called his children the Clayfield Cowboys or the Clayfield Cowhands in his column. He did it so deftly that Brisbane looked forward to the next tale about the cowhands. Richards suggested I should make use of the cowhands at Crescent Road, Hamilton. Our eldest was David, 4 going on five. We called him Steamboat because he had so much steam and as a baby had pushed himself around like a boat. So maybe once a week I threw in a paragraph about Steamboat. I am ashamed to say in arid times I watched him avidly, waiting for some new brilliant activity. Steamboat became quite famous and he was a running serial for nearly eight years. When I dropped him, the Editor-in-Chief of the Herald and Weekly Times even called me in and said Steamboat should continue.

A typical Steamboat paragraph went like this:

> Water pistols like all forms of armament have improved tremendously in the past twenty years. The latest water pistol is shaped like a Luger and made of plastic. It works by compression and holds a vast store of water. Some even have an auxiliary tank attached to the waist. The skilful operator can obtain fifty to 150 shots at one filling, depending on storage capacity.
>
> Steamboat though has a marvellous refinement. He fills his Luger with soft drink and pulls the trigger. Pure joy. This, very likely, is the finest invention since the flask on the hip.

Many years later, during the Vietnam War, David was up on a charge of assaulting a policeman at a demonstration in Williamstown. Before the trial we had a discussion with our barrister. The barrister looked at me, looked at David and smiled.

'Before I start I just want to know one thing. Tell me, is this Steamboat?'

I had to say 'Yes, it is', regretting I had ever done this thing to my son. David could have killed him.

The daily correspondence to the *Courier-Mail* was astonishing. People who write letters to newspapers are capable of remarkable rudeness and savagery. It is one way of easing tension. There was a Brisbane poet who wrote almost daily. He was a little too accurate in explaining my lack of style, my lack of originality and how I could not match the personality and skill of my predecessor. I took this desperately to heart. I had been a failure at school, a failure in the Air Force, and now I was a failure in journalism. There was another character who wrote weekly threatening, sometimes homicidal, letters. This went on for nearly two years. One day there was a telephone call and I sensed it was the person who had been writing the letters. He said an R. Robinson had been killed half an hour ago in Paradise Valley. I called the police but nobody had been killed in the Valley. I never heard from that man again. However, I did learn something. Never again did I worry about angry letters. If you are in that sort of business and do not irritate somebody you are doing a poor job.

Peter Carey has described writing as hard work, like walking up to your knees in thick mud. Column writing is a little like that. Many a column depends on one idea, an incident pulled out of a newspaper, a new invention on the market or a new miracle cure perhaps. Then the columnist has slowly to work out all the angles, all the possible ramifications. (That is something I usually do at four in the morning, before getting up an hour later.) When the column is written it should look as if it has been tossed off with ease, in one blinding shaft of inspiration.

My inspiration for my writing was, and still is, that constant purveyor of ideas and help, my wife, Marie. I could not have survived those early column-writing days without her. She was eternally patient and understanding when I came with the complaint that there was no column for the next day. What now? She would add her wits to mine and we would think of something together.

My column writing on the *Courier-Mail* went in cycles. For weeks, even months, it would seem easy. Then would come the deadly troughs when there were no ideas, when absolutely nothing seemed to happen. I would go home to dinner at 6 p.m., with not a paragraph, not a thought in sight but with the prospect of having to return to the office in Queen Street to fill what still remained a white space on the front page. I would pray – pray desperately – and it was extraordinary how the inspiration for the story would come at the last moment. Begging his or her pardon, I was sometimes critical of our Maker. Sometimes the thought did not arrive until only half an hour before the presses started moving.

Yes, there was a return to religion. Perhaps it had never been very far away, but it came soon after our arrival in Brisbane. The catalyst oddly enough was Field Marshal Viscount Wavell. English generals were different: frequently they could be erudite and very well educated. Field Marshal Wavell, while still active in the Second World War, produced a book titled *Other Men's Flowers*. The flowers were all the poetry, all the verse, he loved best – Hardy, Browning, Blake, Chesterton, Burns, Kipling, Hopkins, Belloc. Reading those flowers one day, I came across 'The Hound of Heaven' by Francis Thompson. It seemed to say everything to me, to express the whole story of humanity's struggle with religion and God. The poem begins:

> *I fled Him, down the nights and down the days;*
> *I fled Him, down the arches of the years;*
> *I fled Him, down the Labyrinthine ways*
> *Of my own mind; and in the mist of tears*
> *I hid from Him, and under running laughter*
> *Up vistaed hopes I sped;*
> *And shot, precipitated,*
> *Adown Titanic glooms of chasmed fears,*
> *From these strong feet that followed, followed after.*

It goes on:

> *My mangled youth lies dead beneath the heap.*
> *My days have crackled and gone up in smoke,*
> *Have puffed and burst as sun-starts on a stream.*
> *Yea, faileth now even dream*
> *The dreamer, and the lute the lutanist.*

And finishes:

> *Halts by me that footfall:*
> *Is my gloom, after all,*
> *Shade of His hand, outstretched caressingly?*
> *'Ah, fondest, blindest, weakest,*
> *I am He whom thou seekest!*
> *Thou dravest love from thee, who dravest Me.'*

Was it possible to believe in the Eucharist? In the Virgin Birth? In the Resurrection? And what about all the stuff on Who Moved the Stone? Faith it seemed to me was entirely a subjective thing. There was something in you; either you believed or you did not believe. And there were delicate shades of believing. Could there be a creature on earth who did not have doubts? St Peter had plenty of them. Would even the most devout cardinal ever do better than 98 per cent certainty? Or your local archbishop, did he rate better than 92 per cent? Or some of the vicars I knew – very good men but some days they seemed low, indeed. And what about me? – 80, 85 per cent sure. Some days belief, and God, seemed very close, indeed. Other times, belief was nowhere to be had. The Hound of Heaven: that is why the words of Francis Thompson appealed so much.

While I was thrashing around I thought maybe the answer lay in the style of religion. I began attending St Augustine's Church in Hamilton, Brisbane. It seemed so bland. I could not stand the ineffectual sermons. Every Sunday the preacher quoted the gospel of the day and gave us a little lecture on theology. We heard nothing on the great issues of the day. Even now I think this is the problem with the Anglican Church. Go to a suburban church and it seems insulated from things that desperately worry people, particularly young people: drugs, AIDS, poverty, political corruption, racism and the dreadful materialism of all of us. No wonder the church pews are only half full.

I thought the Roman Catholic Church must be the answer. The Catholics I knew seemed more dedicated, more disciplined than Protestants. There seemed to be entirely more guts and devotion in the Catholic Church. One evening, at a dinner party, I was talking to a Brisbane lawyer, Rex King.

'Of course, I'm an agnostic', he said. 'I don't think any intelligent person really can be otherwise.' (This is an arrogant presumption always made by those who don't believe.) 'But I do love the Anglican Church', he continued. 'I love little choirboys singing. And do you know what really turns me on, why I go about once a month? I adore the ceilings. Have you ever noticed what marvellous ceilings our churches have? When the vicar is making his sermon I study them intimately.'

For some reason Rex King was terribly shocked that I contemplated becoming a Roman Catholic. He would not have minded my becoming an atheist or an agnostic, but becoming a Catholic was really shocking, like reviling one's club in public or turning on one's old school.

'I will talk to my friend Peter Bennie', he said.

The Reverend A. P. B. Bennie was the vicar at All Saints' Church, Wickham Terrace, Brisbane. Bennie was a graduate of Trinity College, Melbourne, a poet, a former archdeacon on Thursday Island and the future warden at St Paul's College in Sydney. A genuine intellectual, he was often frustrated with not only his parishioners, but also his staid superiors in the Anglican Church. Peter Bennie liked to shock; he adored to throw bricks through windows.

Almost immediately after my conversation with Rex there was a telephone call from Father Bennie. Yes, he always called himself Father Bennie. He even sounded Roman Catholic.

'Rex King tells me you want to be a Roman Catholic. Why don't you come and see me? I could spare you time on Tuesday afternoons. Oh, it won't take as long as that. I'll fix you up in five minutes.'

So there were discussions with Peter Bennie on a number of Tuesdays.

'First', he said, 'I want you to go home and read right through the Gospel According to St John. This is the most splendid, profound piece of writing in the entire Bible. After reading St John, you must believe'.

That night I took out my long-disused Bible and began. How could anyone not be fascinated with those rhythmical phrases?

> In the beginning was the Word, and the Word was with God, and the Word was God.
>
> The same was in the beginning with God.
>
> All things were made by him; and without him was not any thing made that was made.
>
> In him was life; and the life was the light of men.
>
> And the light shineth in darkness; and the darkness comprehended it not.
>
> There was a man sent from God, whose name *was* John.

Bennie was true to his promise, and within months I was serving at his altar. All Saints' was the centre of High Church Anglicanism in Brisbane, with one of those ceilings so much admired by Rex

King. Bennie went through the full bit: bells, incense, rich vestments, Stations of the Cross and the congregation crawling all the way up the aisle to the altar on their knees on Good Friday. I explained to Arthur Richards how High things were at All Saints', so High it would have to be the envy of the Catholics over yonder.

'You ought to come over to our church, we're so Low we had to have the stumps removed', he laughed.

Over several Sundays Marie and I noticed some very formal-looking gentlemen in the back pew of All Saints'. They did not appear to be taking a great part in the service but rather were making notes. We soon found out what they were up to. They were lawyers and they attacked Peter Bennie for indulging in papist practices. Bennie, who would have made a great barrister himself, was brilliant at Synod. He poured scorn on the barristers. He called them the Three Monkeys.

'They see nothing', he cried, 'hear nothing and know nothing'.

There was so much laughter he was never troubled again.

It took me months to learn the complicated movements at altar during Mass. Oh yes, he called Holy Communion Mass. Some parishioners were repelled by all this. But I loved it. I loved the ceremony, the dress ups, the whole sense of theatre. Marie, brought up as a Presbyterian, was not nearly as impressed. Coming from a church where there was no need even to kneel, to a church where the congregation crossed themselves and popped up and down even during the Creed, she found something faintly evil about it. But I thought all the movement kept the mind alive and was an aid to concentration. Other churches after All Saints' were pallid by comparison.

We had some of our happiest days in Brisbane. It was just the right size for a city. There is an old saying about Berlin and Vienna: in Berlin things are often serious but nothing is hopeless; in Vienna everything is hopeless but nothing is ever serious. To me, Melbourne or Sydney was Berlin and Brisbane was Vienna. The hunt for the almighty dollar was not so important then; nor was it so important to other people if you did not take part in the hunt.

I found out why our house was built on stilts. Just in case you have ever wondered why Queensland houses have stilts, these are the reasons: (1) they allow you to catch the breezes (and the cyclones); (2) they provide a marvellous place underneath the house, where you can put stuff like old pianos; (3) they also provide a ready-made garage, plus a space where you can hang the washing during the wet season; (4) they are needed because most Brisbane houses are built on precipitous hills; (5) when the white ants begin to chew away the foundations it is easy to see them in action.

The years passed and our love affair with Brisbane became complete. It was the easy-going nature of the place that appealed. I liked the way that almost any day of the year I could wander out into the garden in bare feet to check whether the pawpaws were ripening and how the custard apples were progressing. Then there were those marvellous sub-tropical evenings, when we could sit out on the verandah. Everything would be so still and quiet that we could hear a person cough a kilometre away.

Things were unhurried. When the young Queen Elizabeth and Prince Philip came on their first visit, Brisbane was determined to show the south what it could do. The City Council urged a vast painting and clean-up campaign, particularly along the route from the airport. One character who had his garden just metres from the Royal Progress failed to paint his house; nor did he fix up his garden. But on the morning of the big arrival he did the decent thing. He got out his lawnmower and cut a great E II R in the long grass.

Brisbane was also stimulating mentally. There were so many fascinating characters. Magda and Igor Vollner ran a restaurant in a basement off Queen Street called Two Seasons. This was the gathering place for talkers, poets, writers, architects and musicians, such as Rudolf Pekarek, the conductor of the Queensland Symphony Orchestra.

Next door to the Two Seasons, and also in a basement, was the Johnstone Gallery. Brian Johnstone was married to Marjorie Mant, an actress and a very good one: a gorgeous extrovert of a lady, addicted to long, flowing gowns. She suffered from asthma, and I remember her walking into Her Majesty's Theatre on opening night, when the stalls were filled with expensively clad women, and saying, in her superbly projected voice, 'What I can't stand is all these women who come here drenched in Fly Tox'. Brian was educated at St Peter's College, Adelaide, and graduated as an Army officer from Duntroon. He became disillusioned with the Army and bravely turned to art. The Army should never have let him out of its hands. Intellectually he was another Wavell.

Brian worked away in his underground gallery in the Brisbane Arcade until it gave him tuberculosis. After he recovered he never returned to the city. He needed more room, more style, better air. So the new Johnstone Gallery was their house at 6 Cintra Road, Bowen Hills. It was just below Cloudland, that vast old dance hall, reception house, call it what you will, that was so beloved by Americans during the Second World War. Cloudland was on the marvellous pimple of Bowen Hills, sitting astride all Brisbane. Cloudland, barbarously destroyed at dawn by the Sir Joh Bjelke-Petersen Government, was a classic building of old Brisbane.

The Johnstones' weatherboard house was Brisbane in its purest form: on stilts, verandahs to catch the breezes, galvanised-iron roof to record the shattering artillery of the December–January rains and at every turn, every glance, a thing of beauty, a breath-taking work of art. The Johnstones bought the house next door, connected the two and added further accommodation for visiting artists and friends. The gallery rambled, and steadily Marjorie and Brian gathered a collection of great Australian art, which by comparison made the Queensland National Gallery holdings look like a pathetic, starving relative. The walls were covered with Arthur Boyds, Charles Blackmans, Ray Crookes, Jon Molvigs, Sidney Nolans, Donald Friends, Robert Dickersons – not just ordinary examples, but great pictures painted when these artists were at their peak.

Brian Johnstone had an extraordinary, a matchless eye for talent in an artist. At a time when they were virtually unknown he was putting on exhibitions by Boyd, Dickerson, Blackman, Crooke, Molvig, David Boyd, Milton Moon, David Strachan, Keith Looby, Lawrence Daws, Max Hurley, Kevin Connor, Kenneth Jack, Charles Bush, Phil Waterhouse . . . Brisbane artistically was low on the scale in the early 1950s, but the Johnstones were putting on exhibitions by Sidney Nolan and their great friend Russell Drysdale. Brian Johnstone has never been given credit for the profound effect he had on this great renaissance period of Australian art. He was a teacher, and his enthusiasm was such that, when he was selling a picture, he was overwhelming – so much so that during the 1950s and 1960s Brisbane people spent more on art than anyone else in Australia.

It was not just selling for the sake of selling. Both Brian and Marjorie were noble, emotional characters. Brian was fierce in his likes and dislikes. He had a contempt for the creature, the barbarian, who bought just for investment. He was likely to refuse to sell a picture to a 'swine' who did not deserve it. Swine was his favourite word. 'Filthy swine, they're all swine', he would exclaim. The swine might be an art director he believed was dishonest – 'The swine's a crook' – or perhaps a government official holding down an art position. Invariably the swine had their own sty.

The Johnstones were passionate in their belief in the importance of art. Their art openings were famous. They were not merely openings, but splendid Brisbane parties, conducted in the warm night air. They were not like the art openings of old, with dreadful cream sherry or wine that could only be described as carbonated fizz. The Johnstone bath-tub was filled with ice and unlimited quantities of good wine.

The gallery was set in a leafy, tropical garden of frangipani, poincianas, stag horns and umbrella trees. Under every tree, beside every shrub, there was a lovely sculpture, many by Len and Kath Shillam. My favourite was by Arthur Boyd. It was a play on Nolan's Ned Kelly astride a horse. However, the man on the horse was not really Kelly, he was a judge, and if you looked carefully this judge was really a sheep. Or was he an ass? Oh yes, the law was an ass.

Donald Friend and Margaret Olley were always in and out of the gallery at Cintra Road. Brian teed up a special project, the painting of a great mural in the lounge at Lennon's Hotel, which Donald and Margaret did together. They worked while the guests slept through the long midnight hours. They used standard Taubman paints, and the result was a mad, triumphant *mélange*, an evocation of everything that is Queensland: cane fields, little steam trains, cane toads, taipans, goats, weird old Queensland houses, cactus, jungle, ratbags, graziers . . . The result was priceless and should have been preserved for ever. When the hotel was renovated and changed hands the Philistine owners just painted it over. If only somebody had been smart enough to tell them the mural was worth money it might have been saved.

Brian Johnstone retired in 1972. Without question, had there been more recognition from the officials who controlled art in Brisbane, he would have continued. The closure of the gallery was a cultural disaster for Queensland. He died in 1988.

We went down to Melbourne for four weeks every Christmas by courtesy of my father. There was no nonsense about modern Christmas dinners at our house. Even if the temperature was 40 degrees Celsius it had to be done properly.

The dinner began with cold mangoes, very hard to get in the 1950s. There was only one fruit shop in Melbourne that had them: Mr Jonas's. Mr Jonas was at Melbourne Mansions in Collins Street. Rich graziers from the Western District who kept town houses in Melbourne for events in the social calendar, such as the Spring Racing Carnival, always shopped there. The fruit at Mr Jonas's establishment was always perfect, often rare and always expensive. Melbourne Mansions came down to make way for the horrid CRA building, which itself became the first of the modern towers or filing cabinets to be replaced.

After mangoes from Mr Jonas came turkey, splendidly stuffed and accompanied by bread sauce, followed triumphantly by the plum pudding made months before. Dad would personally heat the brandy in a saucepan – far too much so that we always had a conflagration – pour it, flaming, over the pudding, then bear the blazing pudding into the darkened dining-room. There was always money in the pudding. My mother used to cheat. She would put extra 2-shilling pieces under the serves for the grandchildren to make sure they didn't miss out.

Christmas 1956 was particularly joyous, with Dad in his grandest, most eloquent style, carving the turkey. Several weeks after the dinner, Dad said to me: 'I want you to come for a drive. I have something to say to you'.

We drove down to the Yarra Boulevard, not far from where I first formally proposed to Marie. He started explaining that I had all sorts of responsibilities, that I was to look after my mother and that when he died I was to make sure the house in Wallace Avenue was sold.

'She can't live in that vast old house by herself. She will want to. But you mustn't let her. Find her something else smaller and more comfortable.'

I remembered the heart attack before our wedding.

'But you're all right now. You are as fit as can be', I answered.

Dad started to cry. I couldn't believe this. Here was the Victoria Cross winner, the tough campaigner, the man who had always been in command of his emotions, weeping.

'Keith', he said, 'when you come down from Brisbane next Christmas, I won't be here. I'll be dead'.

'That can't be true', I replied. 'Surely something can be done. What about the doctors?'

'Nothing can be done. They have told me. You will find absolutely everything is in order. I have arranged it with Perpetual Trustees.'

He was true to his word. His affairs were impeccably arranged, and sadly his forecast for his life was accurate, also. On 2 March 1957, six days before his sixty-second birthday, he collapsed and died on his way home from the Moonee Valley races. He was a committee member of the Moonee Valley Racing Club. My mother was incredibly brave, but I made the mistake of later telling her of the talk in the car on the Yarra Boulevard.

'Why didn't he tell me?', she said. 'Why didn't he tell me?'

There was a funeral with full military honours at Christ Church, South Yarra, on 5 March. There were 800 people present and 300 wreaths. There were seven First World War Victoria Cross winners present: G. Ingram, L. McCarthy, W. Jackson, W. Peeler, W. Ruthven, W. D. Joynt and R. V. Moon. There was also James Rogers, 82 years old, the sole surviving VC winner from the Boer War.

Bishop J. D. McKie, the senior Church of England chaplain of Southern Command, gave the funeral oration. I remember the casket was draped with the Australian flag and on top was Dad's dress sword, something I had never seen before, and an officer's cap and a wreath. The pall bearers were eight regular Army officers, and as for his VC, that was carried on a cushion by another regular officer, Captain M. T. Frost. It was a sunny morning and that part of Melbourne came almost to a standstill. The traffic lights in Punt Road were turned off and police controlled the traffic, which banked up all the way along Toorak and Punt roads. A procession of cars nearly 2 kilometres long went all the way to the Springvale Crematorium.

My mother survived the ordeal of the funeral with great dignity, but it was not easy following Dad's last instructions. She did not want to leave that huge old house, Ste Anne's, and she announced emphatically that she would not live with her children. She would keep her independence.

So there she was in a house with twenty or more rooms, a building I used to think was haunted. We would send David to stay with her. She loved that. David made drinks for her and unquestionably became the world's most skilled 7-year-old at mixing gin and tonics.

Eventually she moved into a maisonette in Irving Road, Toorak. There she still carried on her magnificent cooking, making Madeira cakes and Christmas pudding. Every Sunday for lunch she would cook an enormous wing rib of beef for any of her family who could come to eat it. She believed grandmothers should be the kind of people their grandchildren would never forget, so she kept in constant touch with all of hers, making sure she knew everything they were doing and plying them with gifts. She died on 21 November 1974. Her grandchildren wept at her funeral.

Marie and I moved from Brisbane to Melbourne on 20 December 1957. There were a number of reasons: it was important to be near my mother, and John Waters, Editor-in-Chief of the Herald and Weekly Times, said he needed a columnist for the *Sun News-Pictorial*. Could I start immediately – like on 31 December? Dad was no longer in Flinders Street. I was not the boss's son any more. So I became the daily columnist for the *Sun News-Pictorial*, a job that kept me busy for twenty-seven years.

CHAPTER TEN

APITS

We returned to Melbourne with mixed feelings, although by now we were used to being uprooted and moved. It is the same whenever you leave any city, any house where you have been happy. In every move you die just a little. Melbourne in the 1950s and 1960s was a curious, inhibited city, suffering from an inferiority complex. It had never quite overcome the shock, the trauma of those terrible days in 1893 when the banks closed their doors and so-called Marvellous Melbourne went into depression. In the first half of the twentieth century its suburbs had sprawled outwards but, apart from the Manchester Unity building, the Hotel Australia and the illustrious picture palaces, there had been few new public buildings in the city itself. Furthermore, its politicians and its moral attitudes were still utterly Victorian.

The Melbourne Sunday was world famous. Where else on earth, with the possible exception of Adelaide, could one find a city in which absolutely nothing happened on a Sunday, in which the biggest excitement was to go either to the Botanic Gardens or to Essendon Airport – an alternative of gazing in composed decorum at the swans or at the aeroplanes. Brian Fitzpatrick, the historian, wrote sardonically that the Melbourne Sunday had a tranquillity, a pure beauty. Why, it was a work of art, like the *Winged Victory of Samothrace*, the Two Minutes' Silence or *La Giaconda*! Our Winged Victory meant no sport, no movies, no theatre, no hotels, no human activity that would interfere with church going.

It was a shock also to return to the agony of 6 o'clock closing. In Queensland the hotels closed at 10 p.m. and we couldn't help but notice the contrast. Melbourne was a city of drunks. Any night at 6.15 p.m. the scene was the same: ejected drunks vomiting in the gutter outside Young and Jackson's Hotel, opposite St Paul's Cathedral.

The favoured drinking pubs for reporters on the *Herald* and the *Sun* were the Astoria on the corner of Flinders Lane and Exhibition Street, where Collins Place now is, and the Phoenix in Flinders Street. They were both classics of their time: dung-coloured lino on the floor, dung-coloured lino on the bar and no furniture or creature comforts. They seemed to be affected by the government attitude that hotels were immoral: too many comforts would encourage drinking.

In the late afternoon there was a terrible urgency. A male would leave the office at, say, 5.20 p.m., gather four or five friends and reach the hotel bar at 5.30 p.m. It was a male world; in keeping with the Victorian morality of Melbourne females were not permitted in public bars. For women there was the apartheid of the ladies' lounge where drinks were much more expensive.

Picture the scene. There was a large clock on the wall, invariably set fast because the police came round at 6 p.m. to make sure the bar was cleared. Yes, time was desperate. It was part of the male code of honour for everyone in a school to buy a round of drinks, but there was the time problem. There was only one solution: all the rounds had to be bought in one hit. The bar was as crowded as a peak-hour train; nowhere to put your five or six beers. If there was no windowsill or ledge available they went on the floor between your feet. You had to down those beers before the barmaid or barman started to shriek for everybody out at 6 p.m. No easy task that. By 6.05 or 6.10 he or she would be shrieking, 'For Chrissake gentlemen, do you wan' us to lose our licence'.

Ah, but there was nevertheless a charm and Victorian elegance about the Melbourne of the 1950s, a comfortable, opulent, very English elegance. After all, the land had been settled by the English, all homesick for 'home', so they planted English trees and English shrubs and put up public buildings that looked as if they belonged in Manchester or Birmingham. The Fitzroy Gardens was all elms, planted on either side of public paths, that, would you believe, were to the design of the Union Jack.

Six o'clock closing came to an end in February 1966. Already a new building boom was under way and the old Melbourne steadily began to disappear. At first it was exciting getting new buildings. The ICI building was the first to go up, in about 1960, followed by the CRA building in 1962. For a brief period we gloried in the thought that these were the tallest in the country and even called them skyscrapers.

Too late we realised that many of the great old buildings that had come down should have been saved. I would like to think that I had a hand in rescuing the Windsor Hotel, the Princess Theatre, the Regent Theatre and at least the façades of the Rialto and the Olderfleet buildings, but for twenty-five years it seemed as if I was always standing by for the death of another building, the Requiem Mass for another piece of history. I had a curious ally, big, bluff old Jim Whelan. His father, also called Jim, had founded Whelan The Wrecker in 1892. Whenever another building received its death sentence and was due to be wrecked Jim gave me the tip. He knew as much about old Melbourne as anyone alive. He loved the place and went about his wrecking with an air of sadness; he enjoyed wrecking the horrid and the ugly, but lovely pieces of history, that was a different matter. It caused him genuine pain to pull them down and he carefully preserved sacred relics, windows, doors, cornices, sculptured heads, exquisitely carved pieces of marble.

It was in 1962, when the CRA building in Collins Street was brand new, that I said to Jim: 'How would you like to pull down one of these awful modern filing cabinets? Take the CRA building in Collins Street. Would it be difficult?'.

His eyes shone. 'It'd be easy', he answered. 'I'd put up a scaffolding all round, then just start from the top and work down, floor by floor.'

It was a prophetic discussion. In 1987 the next generation of Whelans, Tony, Owen and Myles, did exactly that. The CRA became the first of the post-war generation of office towers to feel the wrecker's hammer. Nobody missed the CRA, an extremely ugly building that looked like a long drawer that had been pulled out of the ground. The construction of that tower was really the death of the old Collins Street because it replaced the stately Melbourne Mansions, one of the last establishments in the city where people actually lived.

Melbourne used to be a city of little hotels on every corner, all with good counter lunches. For example, there was the Port

Phillip Club Hotel in Flinders Street opposite the railway station, which dated right back to the 1860s. It had a marvellous oyster bar, where one could buy a dozen oysters plus bread and butter for 2 shillings and 6 pence. It did have at least half a dozen beds made up, as the law decreed for hotels, but this was a venerable establishment, dedicated almost entirely to the drinking man, and it contained a labyrinth of bars. In the public bar there were great punkahs, mechanically operated. In the summer they creaked back and forth, making little ripples across the surface of the beer.

The Cathedral Hotel, the noble home of the Anglican drinkers, was another. Down it came, as, too, did Scotts in Collins Street, so beloved by all the graziers. Up the so-called Paris end of Collins Street we lost the Occidental, on the corner of Collins and Exhibition streets. Legend had it that Nellie Melba once slept at the Occidental. Its counter lunch of liver and onions was utterly famous. The bar from the Occidental was used in the movie *On the Beach*, and Ava Gardner actually placed her pretty elbow upon it. The Occidental was replaced with – to my mind – the quite useless Reserve Bank.

The Oriental opposite was more illustrious. In the old days the owner was Pearson Tewksbury, who made a fortune out of gold. The story goes that he was a guest at the Oriental in 1910. When the manager insulted his wife Tewksbury stormed out of the hotel, bought it and returned some time later, presumably with the statement, 'I have news for you'.

Dame Nellie Melba actually did sleep at the Oriental. There is a suspicion that Dame Nellie spent a night in every resting place, bar the Melbourne Club. Alas, poor Oriental, she came down in 1972 to make way for the Collins Place towers.

The most grievous loss of all was Menzies Hotel at the corner of Bourke and William streets. When it was rebuilt in 1867 the *Argus* described it as absolutely the finest in the colonies, 'unique but by no means *outré*'. It remained the finest in the colonies until Mr Whelan had to wreck it in 1969. Everybody stayed there – George Augustus Sala, Alexander Graham Bell, Toti Dal Monte, Fritz Kreisler, Ignaz Paderewski, Herbert Hoover, General MacArthur, Yehudi Menuhin and Danny Kaye. In 1904 Paderewski called over the head waiter and demanded: 'Tell me, who is your chef? Is he a chef, is he a tailor or is he a carpenter?'.

Down a side lane there was the Governor's Entrance. Very

private. You see, it was not done for the governor to be seen entering an establishment that sold spirituous liquors. Menzies became the black tower of the BHP headquarters. Why there? They could have built their headquarters just as easily down at Mordialloc.

I grieved also for the Federal Hotel at the corner of Collins and King streets. Mr Whelan pulled that down in March 1972. What a crime it was. No sane government should have allowed it. The Federal was our most extraordinary piece of Victoriana. It was originally the Federal Coffee Palace, built for the Centenary Exhibition of 1888. It was to be the greatest, most exotic hotel Australia had seen. It had seven floors, an iron-framed dome, 400 rooms, its own ice plant, gaslight on all floors and an electric bell in every room. The exterior was remarkable in that not a square millimetre went undecorated; there were marvellous twiddly bits and sculptured figures of all kinds, including massive ladies who represented every State except, curiously, Western Australia. High up was a mixed-up sculptured scene of plump, naked girls and bearded boys. Over the grand portico there were two female figures arm in arm like gigantic lesbians. One had a breast exposed, and written below was the message, '*Restez Ici - Soyez le Bienvenu*'.

And what did we get in place of the Federal Hotel? - twenty-four storeys of the very dull Enterprise House, which actually housed the Victorian Health Department. Like BHP the Health Department could have been just as happy in Mordialloc.

There were so many other buildings that I loved. There was the Eastern Market in Exhibition Street. Here there were important shops that sold second-hand books. Down below there was a sedate, spacious, superbly untidy hardware store. Behind its counters were assistants who could answer incredible queries such as: 'I would like some screws about that long and this wide, and I want some cement and steel plates and things to build a barbecue. What have you got?'. The Eastern Market, which at one time housed phrenologists, fortune-tellers and magicians, was replaced with the Southern Cross Hotel. Never again did we have phrenologists or a good hardware store in the city of Melbourne, only hardware supermarkets that had no interest in the helpless do-it-yourself amateur.

In 1967 we lost Cliveden Mansions in Wellington Parade. What a crime. It came down without a whimper. Sir Rupert Clarke had built it in 1887 for 91 117 pounds, an unbelievable sum when you consider that the working wage was 2 pounds a week. The immensely rich Sir Rupert had even kept a private regiment, the Rupertswood Battery. Cliveden Mansions had an enormous ballroom, a billiard-room, dining-rooms, twenty-eight bedrooms and, what was sensational in 1887, five bathrooms. There were seventeen rooms for servants. Its oak panelling had come from London and its expanses of stained glass from Italy. One huge stained-glass window depicted a gorgeous, plump Italian lady inviting all to enter, with the words, 'None Come Too Early – None Leave Too Late'. Alas, Cliveden came down to make way for a modern hotel, the Melbourne Hilton.

So that was Melbourne, a city going through a great metamorphosis when we arrived back in late 1957. There was much more for me to write about than in Brisbane and unquestionably it was a good time to return.

The job as columnist on Melbourne's *Sun News-Pictorial* began on New Year's Day 1958. Very naively I called on the *Sun* Editor, Frank Daly, and told him I was delighted to write this column, 'A Place in the Sun', but could we get rid of the corny title?

Frank Daly looked at me sourly. He gave me the names of distinguished people who had written the column, such as Howard Palmer, Stewart Legge and Peter Golding, and said: 'Mr Dunstan, "A Place in the Sun" is a column that started on the first day of the first issue of this newspaper back on 11 September 1922. We do not intend to change the title'.

I went upstairs to the archives and turned up the very first issue of the *Sun*. It was a tabloid in 1922, with plenty of pictures – a revolution in Australian journalism, when newspapers were broadsheets and front pages mostly carried classified ads. I turned up this column, 'A Place in the Sun', and a good column it was, too. It started with a paragraph about the Prime Minister, Mr W. M. Hughes. A shopkeeper in Carlton had put a peanut in his window and labelled it 'Billy Hughes'. One of the parliamentary Members pointed this out to the Prime Minister and said: 'It is a simply marvellous resemblance to you, Sir. None of the caricaturists have ever done you so well'.

'Are you sure it was a peanut?', growled Mr Hughes. 'I was in Carlton this afternoon.'

Noel Hawken of the *Herald*, a thoughtful journalist and perhaps the most graceful writer I encountered, filled my column for me many times in the next twenty-five years. Noel had graduated from the *Sydney Morning Herald* and the *Argus*. He was the leader writer for the *Herald* and an omnivorous reader, but unlike most of us he retained what he read. Had he been given his head what a different paper it would have been. He was far superior in intellect and wisdom to all his editors and managing directors. Hawken, with all his imagination and ideas, should have been editor of the *Herald* from the mid-1960s on. Critics have offered many reasons for the decline of the *Herald*, but I believe it was the consistent promotion of the wrong people.

It was Noel who coined the acronym APITS for the column. One could have confused it with a disease or perhaps an insecticide used to kill aphids on roses, but I always thought it sounded better than 'A Place in the Sun'.

Column writing was far more difficult then. It is not generally realised that huge social changes have taken place in the last thirty years. Mention drink in the column and there would be complaints to the editor. Sex is the funniest, most absurd of all human activities, but no one could mention it in a daily column. Human beings did not even copulate. The *Sun* ran a lively comic strip called 'Jane' that was syndicated from London. Jane liked to get her clothes off at least once a week, so we had artists forever busy putting bras back on Jane's naked breasts. Melburnians would be affronted at the sight of nipples, therefore they had to go. However, modesty went further than that. Every navel that appeared in a photograph had to be erased. There was a famous case in Brisbane where a farmer sued a newspaper after it painted out the genitals on a bull. It is surprising some proud young female did not sue the *Sun* over the loss of her navel.

One also had to be careful with references to the Almighty. Any appeals to God could be considered blasphemy. 'Damn' was a forbidden word. Put one 'damn' in the paper and there would be a thousand letters of protest. People were sensitive, too, about false teeth. I had a story about a farmer at Mansfield who left his teeth in a glass of water overnight. It was so cold that night, he awakened to find his teeth frozen in the glass. The editor killed the story. It was not right to suggest that people did not have their own teeth.

Every evening my column had to be inspected for social purity. Covering court stories was difficult. In court vile words were written down and handed up to the judge, who winced at the sight of them. 'Whore', 'harlot' and 'courtesan' were too awful for our newspaper. 'Lavatory' was never used; we could get away with 'toilet' but often the paper would resort to 'outhouse' or 'the smallest room in the house'.

The process of calling things what they are was slow. I can give you a timetable. 'Lavatories' and 'prostitutes' came in around 1963. We dropped 'houses of ill fame' in 1966 and started calling them 'brothels'. We were having 'sexual intercourse' by 1967 and we even wrote 'sodomy', which had been in the Bible for 2000 years. The show *Hair* changed much of our thinking.

By 1971 the word 'bloody' began to appear in print. What a shock that was. 'Bullshit' did not get there until 1974, and after that we descended to 'bugger'.

The ultimate breakthrough came in June 1979. The first paragraph of the *Age*'s coverage of a court case read: 'A magistrate found yesterday that a Skyhooks song with the refrain "Why don't you all get fucked" was not obscene'. Michael Davie, the *Age* Editor, received a visit from the vice squad, who said the police had received complaints from the public and the *Age* was liable for prosecution under Section 172 of the Police Offences Act. Davie was unabashed. He pointed out that almost every milk bar was selling paperbacks that contained this word, and he had the impression even children in the street were using it.

I announced all this in triumph in a column for the *Bulletin*, pointing out that 'fuck' was in John Ash's *Complete Dictionary of the English Language* in 1775, and pushed it home with A. P. Herbert's famous 'Ode to Four Letter Words':

> *Let us banish the use of four letter words*
> *Whose meanings are never obscure.*
> *The Angles and Saxons, those bawdy old birds,*
> *Were vulgar, obscene and impure.*
> *But cherish the use of the wheedling phrase*
> *Which never says quite what you mean.*

> *You'd better be known for your hypocrite ways*
> *Than be vulgar, obscure or obscene.*

However, the *Bulletin* did not have the courage of the *Age*, and my story on the history of 'fuck' appeared with the word given very carefully as 'f _ _ _'.

At the height of all this moral purity a letter arrived from a nun. She was a Presentation nun who taught children at a convent in Moe, Victoria. She said that she liked reading the column every day but, even more astonishing, she liked to read it to her class as an example of good English. This left me in a more parlous plight than ever. As I wrote the column I kept thinking of not only the nun – would she approve what I am saying now? – but of her English class. English grammar was never my strong point. Finally I wrote back to the nun and said: 'You have ruined me. You now sit on top of my typewriter and I find it difficult to write a word'.

'I wouldn't worry too much about that', she replied. 'I am not easily shocked. I used to teach Germaine Greer.'

This was the start of a correspondence that went for twenty years. Sister C. was a born correspondent. She wrote warm, marvellous, entertaining letters. Yet we never met. One time she wrote that she was coming to the city and would be at St Patrick's Cathedral at 11 a.m. on Sunday morning. I went looking for Sister C. but never found her. In 1979 Marie and I went to live in California for three years and still we corresponded with Sister C., now living in the city. Our daughter Kate thought it appropriate to send her a copy of *84 Charing Cross Road*, the tale of a writer in New York who spent a lifetime corresponding with her bookseller in London. There was just one terrible flaw in this analogy. The bookseller, the male in the tale, died before the two had a chance to meet.

Marie and I returned to Melbourne, and this time we tried in earnest to arrange a meeting with Sister C. We set a date for dinner in South Yarra. The night came, 7.30 p.m. arrived. Sister C. should have been at our house. She rang to apologise. She could only leave the convent if she came with her 'minder' and the minder was ill. Fate had stepped in again. However, Kate insisted; she said she would be the minder. She picked her up from the convent and at last Sister C. came to dinner. She was nearly 70 years old. She had come to Melbourne from Ireland. Marie and I loved her instantly. She had a wild, fey sense of humour and was clearly a born teacher.

There was one other close association with the clergy. In 1984 the Anglican Church in Melbourne was taking an unconscionable time to find a new archbishop. Archbishop Dann had announced his pending retirement on 29 June 1983, but a year had gone by and still the selection board had not found a successor. The board could not make up its mind about David Penman, the 47-year-old Bishop for the Western Region of the Melbourne diocese. Some thought he was too Low Church, too different. In the 'Batman' column of the *Bulletin* I said the board had to do something because Penman was 'the last wombat in the paddock'.

Two years later I went to Bishopscourt to interview Archbishop David Penman.

'I have a bone to pick with you', he said.

'Why?'

He took me to his study and, with a grand gesture, said, 'Look!'. There must have been at least sixty wombats: little ceramic wombats, big ceramic wombats, wombat pictures, wombat posters, wombat tea-towels, stuffed furry wombats, wombat games, a wombat jigsaw, wombat tie-pins, an Australian flag in the shape of a wombat and even a great metal sign, clearly purloined from somewhere, which read, 'Beware of Wombats Next 5 Kilometres'. The archbishop explained that the remark about the 'last wombat' had gone into history. After his election a television station had sent him a toy wombat, and ever since wombats had just flowed, wombats of every shape, style and description. People were still sending them, so he had become a collector. When he had his dreadful heart attack in August 1989 Mrs Penman placed a wombat at the end of his bed.

Every columnist discovers that dealing with the public is an unusual experience. One of the most extraordinary people was Clive Bush, a retired bank manager of Copelen Street, South Yarra. He was the telegram-sending champion of the world. He lodged his telegrams at midnight to get the night-letter rate, and off they went, 300 words at a time, to the prime minister, the leader of the Opposition and all appropriate members of Parliament, demanding justice. Of course, APITS would always get its telegram. Clive presumed that when all else failed APITS would straighten out the nation.

There were people who came in with the biggest tomato in the world and the biggest pumpkin. I was grateful to the gentleman who posted me a live redback spider nicely parcelled in a matchbox. He wanted to prove that live redbacks were now available in Moorabbin.

I also remember with affection the day a fellow came down from Darwin and wanted to have a chat about things up there. Suddenly he said, 'Did you ever see a crocodile?'. Thereupon he pulled out of his bag a live crocodile a metre long. Naturally this called for a photograph. The Editor wasn't in, so we thought we would use his office. The picture session was going well until the Editor's secretary returned. She saw the crocodile, shrieked, burst into tears and left. The Editor came in, the crocodile took an instant dislike to him and it chased him round the desk. APITS stocks were not very high for the next month.

Random use of publicity could be dangerous. On one occasion I innocently mentioned a brand of pies. Next morning there was a gross of the most awful meat pies on my desk. It was difficult disposing of 144 cold pies at ten in the morning. Another time I mentioned quietly what a pity it was that crumpets were not sold in February – a stupid remark. A mountain of crumpets arrived that afternoon.

At least 60 per cent of all correspondence to a columnist comes from public relations people and another 30 per cent from charity organisations, all seeking free publicity. They will go to remarkable lengths to get it. One year there was a wild, sexy show at the Lido Theatre in Russell Street. A PR person had a great idea. One morning I came through the front door of the Herald and Weekly Times building and sensed something was up. There were giggles and peering eyes all down the corridor. The commissionaire, trying to be offhand, said: 'Oh, by the way, Keith, there's a young girl waiting for you in your office. She's naked'. My God, she was, too, except for a G-string. Her crafty PR person thought this was a great way to handle the publicity for the new show. I could not get her out of the office quickly enough. The crocodile was easier to handle.

There were many ways to fill a column. One of the best was to join in, take part in, some activity and in effect write the column from the inside. I had read about a columnist in Hawaii who wrote an abusive column on women and the easy, languid life of the housewife. One woman had replied, 'If you think it's so damned easy, why don't you try it yourself?'. So that's what happened. She took over the columnist's seat and he looked after her four kids for four days. It made hilarious reading. From then on I decided the way to get a good story was to get in there and do an activity myself. Many of these stories appear in a book, *Supporting a Column*, published by Cassell in 1966. I was a tennis linesman at Kooyong, an extra in *Lohengrin* with the Elizabethan Theatre Trust, second to Primo Carnera in the pro wrestling at Festival Hall, Father Christmas at Myer's, a Saxon in the battle of the Vikings on the Yarra and part of the vertebrae of the Chinese dragon at the Moomba parade.

In June 1972 the supersonic Concorde, which could fly at nigh twice the speed of sound, arrived in Melbourne with great éclat. It dropped its peculiar, insect-like nose and landed at Tullamarine. A public relations friend, Andrew Wise, suggested: 'Why not upstage it? What will this sonic boom machine ever mean to Melbourne?'. He looked round for the oldest, most lovable aeroplane he could find and came up with a Tiger Moth biplane made of wires and canvas and almost 50 years old. We called in the veteran pilot Arthur Schutt. We landed the Tiger on the main runway at Tullamarine and taxied right up under the tail of the Concorde. It made a very nice picture and everybody started looking at the Tiger.

Perhaps my favourite stunt took place on 27 March 1983. John Hopkins, with the Victorian College of the Arts Orchestra, put on a performance of the *Grand, Grand, Festival Overture* at the Melbourne Concert Hall. It was by Malcolm Arnold, an English composer. He wrote it to mock the pompous clichés of all the grand overtures. It calls for four shotguns, a floor polisher and three vacuum cleaners. As the overture progresses, the orchestra creates its own vacuum cleaner noises then, as in any beautiful concerto, the orchestra pauses while solo instruments take over. The grand finale comes when there are four shots from a gun and each of the mechanical cleaners is murdered by turn.

Jim McPherson at the Arts Centre put out the invitation: would I like the role of principal vacuum cleaner, playing with a full symphony orchestra? The offer was irresistible, the chance of a

Two grand Victorian buildings now lost to Melbourne.
Top: Federal Hotel, which advertised gaslight on all floors and even
electric bells. (La Trobe Collection, State Library of Victoria)
Bottom: Oriental Hotel, c. 1919, where Nellie Melba once stayed.
(La Trobe Collection, State Library of Victoria)

J. Stewart Legge. (Herald and
Weekly Times Limited)

E. W. Tipping. (Herald and
Weekly Times Limited)

Noel Hawken. (Herald and
Weekly Times Limited)

Sir John Williams. (Herald and
Weekly Times Limited)

Liberace was in town in the 1960s so I tried on his gear.

Anything for a column: levitation in 1984, courtesy of magician Doug Tremlett.

Sun cartoonist Jeff and I covered many Melbourne Cup days. It was formal gear and a Rolls-Royce for us in 1970.

Going to the 1977 Melbourne Cup: my trishaw driver was Tony Rafferty, Jeff's was Joe Marguccio.

The push-me-pull-you Melbourne Cup, 1975.

The Anti Football League provided Jeff with a rich source of satire.

Barry Humphries and his greatest honour, a Wilkie Medal presented by
Anti Football League President Douglas Wilkie.

The Honorary Secretary of the Anti Football League, K. D., displaying
his devotion.

The Anti Football League
Honorary Secretary and the finest
of all fund raisers, Fred Goding.

Ian Johnson, Melbourne Cricket Club Secretary, wonders about the
wisdom of burning a football on the sacred turf of the Melbourne
Cricket Ground.

lifetime. Fred Parslow was floor polisher, and the other two vacuum cleaners were Don Dunstan, former premier of South Australia, and Colette Mann, star of the television series *Prisoner*.

The thrill began with the dressing-room. Principal vacuum cleaner had a dressing-room of his own next to the conductor's, complete with name on door. The dressing-room had a wall-to-wall mirror, with lights all around, a piano, potted plants and an intercom mike over which came soft, female announcements, such as, 'Mr Dunstan, you're on-stage in five minutes'.

Finally we were on. Don Dunstan looked superb in a dazzling white sharkskin jacket. Colette was wearing stiff black taffeta with pearls, and Number One Vacuum Cleaner was in black dinner-jacket. My instrument was a huge industrial vacuum cleaner about the size of the golfmobile once used by President Eisenhower. Don Dunstan had an upright Hoover and Colette had a shoulder-strap job like a scuba-diving outfit. At the tune-up I was disappointed with the tone of my instrument. Don Dunstan agreed.

'I don't feel it makes a significant statement', he said.

While the orchestra played we kept busy, looking as if we were really sweeping. Then John Hopkins pointed his baton straight at me. I turned on my vacuum cleaner and played it with all the artistry I could manage. It had three notes – low, medium and shaggy. Then came the shots. First to go was Fred Parslow, and I thought he died nobly, with a nice sense of understatement, as befitted an old actor. Then Don slumped over his Hoover. The old prisoner, Colette, expired in grand style and, at the fourth bang, No. 1 VC collapsed over his sweepings. I did not receive any flowers but two lovely ladies did send me up an exquisite nineteenth-century-style feather duster.

There were some interesting characters in Melbourne journalism. I had a long association with Jeff Hook, the *Sun* artist. He came from Tasmania. His name was spelt 'Geoff' but he felt that looked terrible in a signature so he signed his cartoons 'Jeff' and always somewhere in the sketch hid a tiny hook. Sometimes he would forget to put in his hook and the switchboard would run hot with people ringing to say they could not find the hook. Nearly all of them would ring 'A Place in the Moon'. That was the normal place to ring, after the police, when people had a complaint.

Hook writes with his right hand and draws with his left. It is not easy to explain this extraordinary behaviour but many artists

are the same. Not only is Jeff a very good cartoonist; he also
has great skills as a black and white artist. Once we visited the
Boeing factory just out of Seattle. Here Boeing had a production
line of 747s in what the company claimed was the world's biggest
building, a building so large you could get a change of climate
with clouds forming inside. The Boeing public relations chief took
us on a grand tour. Jeff paused for ten minutes to make a sketch.
The PR chief was startled by the result.

'We had an artist in last month', he said. 'He stood right here,
and it took him a fortnight to make his drawing. When he finished
it wasn't as good as that.'

Another time we were at Lochsa Lodge, Idaho, in the United
States, and Jeff was making a sketch of the scene. A young man
stood behind him all the time he was sketching, always unnerving
for an artist. Finally the young man said: 'You know that's not
bad. You draw a bit. Ever thought of getting anything published?'.

Yes, he had had quite a bit published. I am constantly amazed
at the ruthless speed with which he can delineate the line of a
nose, the sweep of a jaw, the flab of a jowl. There is no sympathy
for Dunstan; always I come out with one eye and no teeth.

Every year, with Marie and Jeff's wife, Pauline, we went to
the Melbourne Cup, always by a different method. You must
appreciate that Flemington is difficult to get to on Cup Day so
our quest for the perfect system was like the hunt for the Holy
Grail. The first time we went to the Cup by Rolls-Royce. It was
a hired machine and we looked so rich that the collectors on the
gate at the members' entrance did not even ask whether we had
a ticket. We just swept in. Another year we went by speedboat
along the Maribyrnong – a somewhat smelly adventure. We went
in a beautiful coach drawn by four horses. We went by brewery
wagon. That did not make us popular with the police, because
traffic in Flemington Road had to be practically suspended to
make way for our majestic progress.

Another year a team of young gentlemen carried us all the way
in an eighteenth-century sedan chair hired from a theatrical firm.
It was a pleasant way to go, though a little wobbly perhaps.
Regrettably the not-quite-eighteenth-century fibreboard seat on
which Jeff was sitting collapsed, and he had a most uncomfortable
journey.

One year the Chairman of the Victorian Railways, Bill Gibbs, offered one of those push-me-pull-you hand trolleys used by railway gangers. This was lovely, the answer to a dream, the fulfilling of a lifelong ambition. They are a little hard to get going, but once Jeff and I – an uncoxed pair no less – got up a rhythm, both pushing and pulling, we made amazing speed. Mr Gibbs gave us the time and assured us the line would be free, but there was always the lurking fear that any second we might be run down by the Sydney express.

The most disastrous year was 1976. This was the year of the downpour, the great flood, when the members' car park went under water and we had the lovely sight of the very best Toorak fashions clinging to the skin, striped trousers rolled up to the knees and ladies' hats limp like wet blotting paper. Yet the dauntless Melbourne Cup spirit never flagged. The champagne drinking never faltered. This time the four of us rode to the Cup on two tandem bicycles, in formal gear, top hats and all. We were soaked from head to foot. On the way down the hill along Epsom Road the rain-soaked brakes on Marie's and my tandem decided they would no longer work. The tandem gathered speed to almost 60 kilometres per hour. We zig-zagged between cars and taxis. Suddenly there was a sixty-passenger bus in front of us. It seemed inevitable there would be a collision. I swung the handlebars, jumped the gutter, hit the footpath, scattering pedestrians, missed a lamp-post by 2 millimetres and came to a dead stop against a brick wall. We were close to eternity that day.

Did I say the most disastrous? No, perhaps 1977 was worse. We went to the races in two trishaws, flown out at immense expense for the occasion by Kay-Hertz Rent-a-Car and Singapore Airlines. Tony Rafferty and Joe Marguccio did the pedalling. Both were physical fitness men. Tony Rafferty in 1973 ran 5898 kilometres from Fremantle to Surfers Paradise, but he thought the journey to Flemington was the greater marathon. We parked the trishaws right next to the Rolls-Royce of Sir John Kerr, the Governor-General.

When we returned after the running of the Cup, the trishaws were gone. Those of you who have had cars stolen will know the experience of returning and gazing at the vacant bitumen in disbelief, half believing any second the car will materialise again.

It was the same with the trishaws. Surely somebody was having a joke, they would turn up any second. But they did not and we had to go home by train. I wrote further columns about the mystery of the missing trishaws, but years later they have still not been found.

There were many strange adventures with Jeff. Together we were sent to England, Ireland, Denmark, Austria, Holland and France. In 1970 we looked into the English stately home business and found that for a certain sum it was possible to be guests of the aristocracy for a week. We went to a real beauty of a stately home, Somerly Park in Hampshire, built by Samuel Wyatt in 1792. Our hostess, who did not want us to publish her name, was the daughter of a marquess and the widow of an earl. It was nearly 2 kilometres from the gates to the house. The family had peacocks. They had deer. And the garden, of course, was designed by Capability Brown. A butler in white jacket greeted us at the door, and he later pointed out the Gainsboroughs, the Van Dycks, the Canalettos and the Turners on the walls.

The countess had invited a friend who had actually met people from colonial Australia, and at 6.30 p.m. we gathered for drinks in the marvellous, stately drawing-room. There was a signed portrait of King Edward VII on the mantel. Just to get the conversation going Jeff and I chatted on about what a lively fellow he was with the ladies.

'He was my late husband's godfather', said the countess severely.

Of course, we had to dress for dinner, which took place in the dining hall around a classic baronial table. At the end of the meal the ladies retired, while Jeff and I sat alone to drink our port. I couldn't believe this. There were only four of us. But presumably Jeff and I had to talk about male things until we met the ladies again for coffee.

My bedroom was huge and in the centre was a four-poster bed complete with curtains. I wondered whether perhaps James I or even Elizabeth I had slept in it. At 3 a.m. I awoke with an agonised desire to go to the lavatory. The curtains on the four-poster bed enclosed me like a tomb. I peered out of the curtains and still all was total blackness. I could not find my way to the bedroom door let alone the bathroom, which was 50 metres down the passage. So I lay there, legs crossed, and suffered until first light.

Breakfast was also served in the dining hall: sausages and eggs on silver salvers. The countess and friend were not to be seen. We quietly departed.

Maybe the most spectacular place we visited was Las Brisas in Acapulco. Las Brisas was a hotel built 366 metres above Acapulco Bay, and it had 250 private cabanas and 250 swimming pools. The cabanas were built down the mountainside so that each one had the same startling view. Merle Oberon's house was immediately below. One reached one's cabana in one's own jeep with its striped canopy. Each cabana had coconut palms, hibiscus and orchids, and early every morning a gorgeous, black-haired Mexican employee called to float flowers in the swimming pool. People, such as Hugh Hefner in his personal, black DC9, used to fly to Las Brisas to stay.

Jeff and I moved into our cabana. I had to write my Acapulco story; Jeff had to do the black and white sketches for it. One remark did not get into the story. The employee who showed us to the cabana looked at us sideways – two men in this beautiful setting?

'Sir, would you like me to move the beds closer together?', he asked.

The explosion was awful. Jeff, the father of five, almost threw the poor Mexican into the hibiscus-flowered swimming pool.

There was one problem with column writing. The disturbing thought kept returning: should I be serious? Very early in my work in journalism I discovered that, although I was little use at formal dinners and never the life of the party, on paper I was quite good at making people laugh. What's more it was a peculiar knack. In the 1940s the *Sun* had given a 5–pound bonus for the funniest story written by any reporter during the week. Almost invariably I had won the bonus. Writing stories that amused people or stories that made people think 'My God, that's happened to me!' gave me more pleasure than anything else. I sat in trams and trains, watching people reading the *Courier-Mail* or the *Sun*, waiting for their reactions when they read the column. If they laughed or smiled my happiness was complete.

One day in Toowoomba, Queensland, I met a city business person. Naively I asked him if he read my column, and he replied: 'No, never give it a thought. I tell you how I read the paper.

I go straight to the finance page and read that. All the rest is garbage'. I learned a great deal from that.

My guilt about the non-seriousness of the column continued, so perhaps every ten columns I would change its character and become angry. One time I took up the torch for the union leader Norm Gallagher. He had been charged and ultimately sentenced to gaol for contempt of court. It seemed to me whatever we thought of Norm Gallagher and his union activities this was society's last resort, to attack him personally, and an outrageous breach of civil liberties. I came out on his side a second time when the police made a raid on his offices and not only took funds but huge quantities of union records. This was the type of assault, I thought, that would have done credit to a fascist state.

My editors were tolerant, and still are, but this was not what they expected. The correspondence was clear: people much preferred to be amused.

Modern journalists are much purer than they used to be. The young ones, I notice, are sober, drink little and are better behaved and much better educated than we were. Every year the top metropolitan dailies receive over a thousand applications from school leavers and young graduates to become journalists. At the most they accept eight to twelve. If I had to start all over again my chances of acceptance would be nil. My academic qualifications would fail me. The newspapers, if they wish, can take on young students who have graduated in the first dozen of the State. The danger is they might reject the characters, those who have the knack of running words together. I don't envy those who have the job of making the choice.

There were always characters around the Herald and Weekly Times building. One of the greatest was Jack Eddy. Jack was the *Herald*'s economist. He had this amazing gift: he not only knew his subject, he could make it intelligible to anybody, even me. Jack needed fortification. He would get off the train at Flinders Street Station, walk across the road to Young and Jackson's and have his first drink. Maybe he would have another at the Phoenix at the corner of Flinders and Exhibition streets. This had no effect on his performance; he still wrote with extraordinary lucidity. When 6 o'clock closing came to an end in February 1966 it was a sadness for Jack. Instead of hotels being open from 9 a.m. to 6 p.m. they

were now open from 10 a.m. to 10 p.m. When he stepped off
the train at 9 a.m. Flinders Street was drier than the Gibson Desert.
However, a distinguished coterie of *Herald* writers would gather
in the back bar of the Oriental Hotel. The back bar was neatly
out of sight and one could approach it by walking out of the
back door of the *Herald* and through the back entrance of the
lovely old Oriental. When the Oriental was pulled down to make
way for two lesser buildings, the ANZ tower and the Regent Hotel,
nothing was the same any more, and the Morning Tea Club
disbanded.

Another great character was E. W. Tipping. Bill Tipping started
the 'In Black and White' column for the *Herald* back in 1952 and
wrote it for fifteen years. When he stopped, it withered. Nobody
could quite repeat his skills. His career began at Melbourne
University. He became the *Herald*'s university correspondent, and
his talents were so great the accountants started to complain that
he was making too much money. In his last year he interviewed
Percy Grainger the composer. The result was a lovely piece,
showing all the Tipping style even then. He brought out the
rebellious, controversial Grainger character, revealing Grainger's
wicked preference for everything English over the much-fêted
German composers. The story was so good the *Herald* invited
him to work fulltime. Anyway it was cheaper to have him on
the staff.

Tipping was never a pretty writer. He did not believe in that
sort of thing. It was the same with the news commentaries he
made on 3DB: he wanted to give the impression he was talking
directly, as if across a dinner table. Nor did he believe in using
an unnecessary word. He delighted in the perfect column
paragraph of three or four lines. He believed that a paragraph
should be like a right cross – the true beauty of its impact should
come in the last fiftieth of a second.

Tipping was the best all-round reporter I encountered, whether
he was covering a flood, a bushfire or a classic event like the
Melbourne Cup. He changed his column for each of the editions,
and it was no easy task following him the next day. He loved
racing and on Cup Eve he would ask his readers 'What's Tipping
tipping?'. To my chagrin the racing writers were invariably wrong
and Tipping was invariably right. My tip always came last. One

time, in order to defeat Tipping, I thought I would tip the horse to come last, instead of picking the winner. I did that but failed again. The horse I tipped was beaten out of last position by a tail.

Bill Tipping died on 29 April 1970 after a protracted bout with cancer. He had worked long and hard for the mentally retarded, and the Tipping Foundation was named in his honour.

Another remarkable character was J. Stewart Legge. He tended to haunt me like a difficult conscience. Legge, son of a doctor, went to school at Scotch College and was cox of the crew. From there he proceeded to Melbourne University and for two years he was supposed to study medicine, but actually he was more interested in music. He was a devotee of Bernard Heinze and studied the organ under Dr A. E. Floyd. In all conscience he felt he could not expect his father to pay his bills any longer, and in 1931, during the worst days of the depression, he started on the *Argus* at 2 pounds a week. George Johnston, author of *My Brother Jack*, started on the same day. During the Second World War Legge reported the activities of the Pacific Fleet for the *Sun*, and he became everything from columnist to night chief of staff. He was a little man, always perfectly turned out in a white shirt and three-piece, perfectly tailored suit with handkerchief in the fob pocket. He looked like the chairman of a distinguished trustee company or the senior partner in an old firm of solicitors.

Every day Legge appeared before my desk, usually around 10.15 a.m. There would be a look of pain on his face and a spark of triumph in his eyes.

'Keith, oh dear, oh dear, oh dear.'

He had discovered an error in my column: the wrong mode of address used for an archdeacon, the name of a pre-First-World-War premier spelt incorrectly or maybe I had mauled the ancestry of a distinguished Melburnian family. I'd fight back, but Legge was always right. He had the most remarkable memory for detail, facts and useful general knowledge.

Legge was editor of *Who's Who in Australia* for three editions. He was very particular about the type of people who made its select pages. For example, while he was editor, John Halfpenny, then vice-president of the Amalgamated Metalworkers and Shipwrights' Union, did not make it. Officially those eligible for entry were 'people of official position, or appointments that would warrant their inclusion . . . or otherwise people who have made an important contribution to their sphere of life'. So no Mr Halfpenny.

'I am not concerned', said Mr Legge, 'with people whose role is public disruption'.

Nor did he like Germaine Greer.

'You would describe her as an phenomenon: she came and went. One successful book is not enough. That's why many authors are not there.'

He did not like television and radio 'personalities' or almost anybody in show business. Reluctantly, he put in Barry Humphries, but he would not have Mike Willesee, Paul Hogan, Ernie Sigley, Garry McDonald, Don Lane or even Graham Kennedy.

Stewart Legge's heart gave out on 24 April 1978. He was just on his way into the *Herald* to do some research on former Australian prime ministers.

Robert J. Gilmore was another of the old school, very precise. Accuracy was everything. He loved to be controversial, loved to take the opposite line to everyone else's and he had a gift for original and unusual stories.

In early 1949 Sir Keith Murdoch received a hand-written letter from Cecil Herbert Sharpley, an English-born member of the central committee of the Australian Communist Party. Sharpley said he had just resigned as a party member and he was ready to tell all to the *Herald*. Archer Thomas, the *Herald* Editor, called in R. J. Gilmore and told him to see Sharpley and find out what he had to offer. This was the great era of the Red Menace. Only twelve months before, R. G. Menzies had begun his attempts to ban the Communist Party. The Sharpley affair took on the air of a spy thriller.

Gilmore called Sharpley and they arranged a meeting. It was to be three days later, at 8 p.m. under the third lamp-post north of the Shepparton Hotel. Gilmore drove to Shepparton, booked into the hotel, had dinner, then met Sharpley under the street light. Sharpley was small and slight, with somewhat protuberant eyes, and surprisingly calm. Gilmore took him back to his room in the hotel, opened a bottle of Corio whisky, and some Schweppes ginger ale. He saw no reason to go beserk with *Herald* expenses.

Sharpley began to talk. Clearly it was all true. Gilmore wondered what risks Sharpley was taking. Sharpley thought there were several possibilities. They could run him off the road by car into the Yarra or they could try to do everything to discredit him.

The *Herald* arranged a bodyguard, Chris Coe, a valour badge winner, who had just retired from the police force. Sharpley and Coe secretly took adjoining rooms in a St Kilda hotel. And so Gilmore and Sharpley went to work. Sharpley wrote his story down on large pads, using a bottle of Swan ink and a steel-nibbed pen.

Within nine days the Sharpley series, put into shape by Gilmore, was running in the *Herald*. Sharpley told a story of union ballot-rigging and precisely how it was done. He wrote that most big strikes in Australia were neither decided on nor directed by the unions. They were called and run by the Communist Party. There was also a Flinders Street group, who were not necessarily actual members of the Communist Party. They were fellow-travellers, members of the Press whose job it was to get stories that were sympathetic to the cause into the paper. Gilmore announced he wanted no part of this. If Sharpley was going to name fellow journalists, he had to talk directly to Archer Thomas or Keith Murdoch. This he did. Among those Sharpley named were Kim Keane and Ian Aird. Keane was a New Zealander, an arts graduate and one of the company's cleverest journalists. Ian Aird was large, very witty, suffered terribly from gout and was yet another member of the brilliant team the *Herald* had in 1949. Aird specialised in short, potent movie reviews, so pithy he was banned from almost every theatre in town. No free tickets for Aird. He had to buy his own. Both Keane and Aird resigned and were a sad loss to the *Herald*.

The *Herald* ran the Sharpley series then brought out a book of the articles. It was described as 'a stark record of a programme of deliberate disruption. For every thinking man and woman'. Sharpley received 5000 pounds from the *Herald*, which was a big payment in 1949, and Bob Gilmore received a bonus of 150 pounds. This, too, he thought was generous, but then Murdoch added his own special touch. He did not want Gilmore to be out of pocket through tax. Murdoch worked out himself what the tax would be and added 52 pounds 13 shillings.

The Communist Party did all it could to discredit Sharpley. It announced that he was an alcoholic, that he had stolen 175 pounds from party funds and that he had been 'convicted of an offence under particularly disgusting circumstances'. The first two charges were fantasy. The third he admitted. He was fined 3 pounds in 1946 for urinating in the dark outside the Exhibition Building. What happened to him? He returned to England. Gilmore came across him again, in 1953. Sharpley was 'a bit hard up' on working man's wages, and he had written an article for the *Daily Telegraph* on ballot-rigging techniques.

The character of characters on the *Sun News-Pictorial* was Douglas Wilkie, the foreign affairs writer. Wilkie was born in 1908 at Wormhill, Derbyshire, the son of Allan Wilkie, the Shakespearean actor. When Wilkie, senior, toured Australia young Wilkie was a general roustabout and spear carrier. He claimed the pinnacle of his acting career on the boards was as a French soldier in *Henry V*. One of his jobs, particularly in Queensland, was shooing away goats when they tried to swallow the Wilkie Troupe posters. Goats adored the paste behind the bills, and Wilkie became a most competent goat shooer.

Wilkie said he became a journalist because it seemed the softest job around; furthermore he needed another job when there was a shortage of goats. Of course, he became the wittiest and most erudite of columnists. He adored to write his own headlines. Kevin Voltz in the *Sun* features department made a collection of them:

PUFFING BILLY ON THE RAILS

(on William McMahon criticising Britain over curbs to Australian exports)

COD'S WALLOP FOR NATO

(on the Cod War between Britain and Iceland, both members of NATO)

THOSE OLD SCHOOL THAIS

(when Thailand's new military government proved just as bad as the old constitutional one)

JEHOVAH'S FITNESS

(when Israeli troops mounted a successful raid on Lebanon)

CURRIED RICE FOR CANBERRA

(when the United States Ambassador in Canberra, Mr Walter
Rice, was ousted in favour of Mr Marshall Green)

BY HAMMER AND TICKLE

(when a Soviet trade delegation visited Australia to boost
Soviet–Australian trade)

MEIN KAMPF BED

(on Sir Henry Bolte returning from viewing West Germany and
its higher standard of living)

WHITLAM'S PRIVY ROLE

(after Gough Whitlam ended appeals to the Privy Council)

WOOL IN A CHINA SHOP

(on Australia's wool exports to China)

Wilkie, who inspired the Anti Football League, of which more
later, was an ideas machine. He had a little daily circuit, a sort
of milk round. He would wander round the reporters' room, natter
to the *Herald* columnist, chat to the *Sun* columnist, talk to the
Herald leader writers, visit the *Sun* cartoonist, all the time telling
stories, dropping Wilkieisms, feeding ideas.

Geoffrey Tebbutt was another great figure on the *Herald*. He
retired from journalism in 1972 and died in 1973. My most vivid
memory of Tebbutt is of a lean, white-haired figure, with a beak
of a nose, rushing to the *Herald* sub-editors' room before noon
with half a dozen proofs flying behind him like streamers. He
had discovered at least six errors in the first edition. The subs
would dread his daily probe, but they missed him when he left.
Indeed, this is my greatest fear with modern journalism. All the
old hands, the erudite ones, such as Legge, Hawken and Tebbutt,
have gone. I had a superb sub-editor, Kevin Voltz, who kept me
out of trouble for more than ten years. But now it is not the same;
often we journalists feel rudderless. The terrible errors that we
make go straight into the paper. The great computer technology
has not saved us.

CHAPTER ELEVEN

The Antis

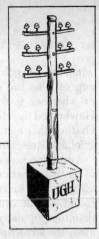

The great difficulty with the Anti Football League was getting people to believe that we were serious. The wife of a United States ambassador, Mrs Ed Clark, had the best line about Australia. She had the feeling she was living in a gymnasium, she said. Australians rarely seem to be beyond the sound of a bouncing ball. Almost since the first white settlement we have been obsessed with sport. As the nineteenth-century immigrants moved inland the first items they built in any town were the pub, the racetrack, the school and the church, often in that order.

In the 1860s, 1870s and 1880s when our scullers, boxers and cricketers began to win international fame, these were the people we adored. Sporting heroes were our national gods, infinitely preferable to nation-builders, pioneers, inventors, politicians and scientists. Thinkers, writers and poets rated not at all.

Henry Lawson in 'A Son of Southern Writers' wrote:

> In a Land where sport is sacred,
> Where the Labourer is God,
> You must pander to the people,
> Make a hero of a clod.

We were a nation of immigrants; most of us had left another place, another culture, and we were desperate for reassurance. In this land of sunshine we were capable of producing a super race. Sport helped overcome a national inferiority complex. Our idea of heaven was to beat the mother country, old England, beat her at anything. It was the satisfaction of the child showing itself superior to the parent.

We never changed in this. The national euphoria was unequalled when we won gold medals at the 1956 Olympic Games. The nation's cup of bliss ran over whenever an Australian won Wimbledon or when we took the Davis Cup. And the Prime Minister, Bob Hawke, led the cheering when we won the America's Cup in 1983. On the other hand we cannot bear to lose. It is matter of national grief and questions are asked in Parliament when we lose.

Australian newspapers give more space to sport than do those of any other nation on earth. In 1962 Professor Henry Mayer made an analytical survey of the contents of Australian newspapers. He found that the quality newspapers covered sport in more detail than the popular journals. These were the national averages: take away the advertisements and there was actually 41.4 per cent news space; of this, foreign news took 7.4 per cent, political-social-economic news 8.2 per cent, other news 10.8 per cent and sport 15 per cent.

Of all the sporting cities, the most dedicated, the most manic, is Melbourne. Melbourne attracts the biggest crowds for racing, the biggest crowds for tennis, the biggest crowds for cricket, and the crowds for football are more than double those of anywhere else in Australia. Living in Melbourne during the football season is like suffocating in a sauna bath; football seems to ooze out of one's pores. The sport dominates the newspapers, the radio and television. A good football story can gain preference over a landing on the moon, the death of a prime minister or the outbreak of the Third World War. Obituaries have gone out of fashion with Australian newspapers. Leaders of industry, famous professional people, politicians and actors die almost unnoticed except for the 'Deaths' column on page ninety-six. But say that leader of industry, that professional, that politician or that actor played in his youth for Richmond or Collingwood, then he makes page one.

The Anti Football League began on Sunday, 16 April 1967. The office of the *Sun News-Pictorial*, as always on a Sunday, was filled with football writers and famous ex-footballers teaming up with their ghost writers. There was no conversation but football. Douglas Wilkie, the foreign affairs writer, sighed and said: 'There must be a better life than this. Couldn't we start an anti-football organisation?' I suggested this in my column and the result was overwhelming. We seemed to touch a tortured heart in Melbourne.

I went to Lyle Turnbull, Editor of the *Sun*, and asked, 'What would you say if I used the column to start an anti-football league?'.

His shock was profound. He said nothing for several minutes. To his credit he finally replied: 'I suppose if we cater for people who love football we should also cater for those who detest it. Go ahead'.

Obviously we were going to need a badge. I thought it should be square – symbolic of something that would not bounce. It should be red, the colour of rebellion, and small, tasteful, like the badge of the Legion of Honour. AFL members could wear it. Other members would recognise it and know that here, at last, was a chance for an intelligent conversation. I wrote this in my column and the next morning there was a telephone call.

'My name is Alf Phillips. I'll design your badge for you.'

'Who are you, Mr Phillips?'

'We're in the business of making and designing badges', he replied. 'I work for K. G. Luke and Company.'

Sir Kenneth Luke, business person and breeder of Herefords, was also president of the Victorian Football League.

Very startled, I asked, 'Mr Phillips, you are having me on, aren't you?'.

'No', he answered, 'if there's a quid in it for you and a quid in it for Sir Kenneth, it'll be okay'.

K. G. Luke and Company subsequently made more than 100 000 badges, and every one of them had the company's name on the back. To be fair to Sir Kenneth, he did actually make a substantial donation to the AFL.

The next call came from Walter O'Donoghue, Advertising Manager at the Myer Emporium. Wally O'Donoghue had red, curly hair, a great imagination and a huge sense of humour.

'Look', he said, 'we'll back you in this thing. We'll put up 500 dollars for badges and sponsor it through Myer's. But you must realise you will never get it off the ground without a nice air of respectability. You must do it for charity and I suggest the Berry Street Babies Home'.

Berry Street was famous: it looked after the homeless, the foundling children.

All was now set. The idea was to launch the Anti Football League as the lead story in the *Sun*'s weekend magazine on Saturday, 17 June. On the Thursday Wally telephoned. He was very apologetic. His directors did not approve. An anti-football league would be very bad for Myer's image. The company also had a policy about fund raising. It just could not get involved in fund raising like this. It had not worked for charity before and it could not do it now.

This was disaster. The page was all made up ready to run in Saturday's *Sun* and it was too late to turn back. I now had to pay K. G. Luke's bill for the badges, 500 dollars'-worth. Five hundred dollars in 1967 on a journalist's salary seemed a great deal of money.

On Monday morning I went to the office and waited for the reaction. There was none. There was not a single letter and by lunch-time still nothing. I sat in misery. 'I should have known. Who would want to be anti-football in Melbourne? I have just lost 500 dollars.' At 1 p.m. there was a call from the post office: 'We didn't bring round your mail this morning because there's too much of it. How would you like it? We've got it all here in sacks'.

Every badge was gone by mid-afternoon and a desperate plea went to Mr Phillips for a new, quadrupled order. I hesitate to say the mail was entirely favourable. One writer said, 'If you don't like football why don't you do the decent thing, get out, go and live in Sydney, or even better Nome, Alaska'. Another wrote, 'Come to the Phoenix Hotel at 5 p.m. and I'll give you a knuckle sandwich'. A third said: 'This is typical of the cheap, nasty things you do. I never liked anything you wrote, never liked anything you said. What's more I can't stand your dull, flat, weak, smug, characterless face on television'. A surprising number said Wilkie and I were either communists or homosexuals. 'You got to be a commo or a poofter', one person wrote. 'It's the only way I can explain someone doing a thing like this in Melbourne.'

Yet other letters showed a huge sense of relief. For example:

Sir,

My mild pleasure out of football has been killed by the ever-present mass media playing each game in prospect, actuality and retrospect, and my Saturday night parties are ruined by the boredom of football conversation by the vocal minority.

Sincerely,

Ron Taft, Reader in Psychology,
University of Melbourne

And:

Sir,

I have many friends who, of economic necessity, must live in Melbourne, but find the intellectual climate absolutely stultifying as no intelligent conversation is possible whatsoever, following the orgy of weekend sport.

Yours, etc.,

L. Maginity, Caringbah

The Anti Football League very smartly produced cuff-links, earrings, T-shirts, sweat shirts and bumper stickers. We brought out a poster, which was most popular. It read in large letters 'THIS IS A FOOTBALL FREE ZONE'. All the football clubs had rousing songs, so we thought the AFL should have one also. Journalist David Rankine wrote the words. The chorus went like this:

> So all who are for us
> Come join in our chorus,
> What have you got to lose?
> I shun the game,
> Let's do the same.
> I've got the anti-football blues.

Doug Owen the folk-singer sang the words and Ron Tudor of W & G Records produced a record, which we sold for a dollar, again for the Berry Street Babies' Home. The flip side of the record was a problem, but we decided to do something for humanity. We felt what every home needed desperately was silence. We recorded two and half minutes of silence, which, according to Ron Tudor, was a most difficult thing to do technically. The silence was a huge success. Some people loved it so much they played it over and over again.

There were so many ways of raising money. By the 1960s the beauty contest had become a weary cliché. Why not for a change run a contest for females where beauty was no consideration whatever? We would run an anti-beauty competition where contestants could express their opinions on sport. The contest took place at the Hotel Australia on 19 July 1969. First prize was a 200-dollar wardrobe from Walton's and a fortnight's holiday at Surfers' Paradise, courtesy of Hotel Australia.

I had hoped that the winner would be plain to the point of ugly. She turned out to be not only extremely eloquent but also attractive. She was Pixie Rose, 18, of Middle Park. She said in her winning speech:

> The game is a national disease and children are brainwashed to it as soon as they can walk. If you don't like football in Melbourne they think you're some creature from Mars. My dentist is in Harrison House and the trees outside are an example of this hysteria. After tribunal nights there are streamers everywhere and limbs broken off the trees outside where fanatics have been climbing.

Pixie, or Peggy as we called her, was a loyal supporter of the AFL for the next decade.

Berry Street had a fund raiser, a master organiser, Fred Goding. Fred was a slim, slight little man, who appeared to be devotedly anti-football. I found out only years later that he had been first rover for Richmond in its years of greatness when it won all its premierships. Fred was keen to earn money on a large scale so we organised a series of raffles.

The AFL needed a focus, a rallying point. We instituted an Anti Football Day, which always took place on the eve of the Grand Final. The first time, we went to Ian Johnson, who was secretary of the Melbourne Cricket Club, and asked him for the ground-plan of the Melbourne Cricket Ground. Ian, who was less than devoted to football, said: "I will give you the plan, but you won't broadcast the fact, will you? If you do, I'll be ruined'.

We took the plan and printed anti-final tickets that were almost a replica of the tickets the VFL was selling for the Grand Final. We printed 120 000 tickets and our followers could buy a book of ten for 2 dollars. Purchase of a ticket gave a follower the privilege of staying away from the non-match. We considered the tickets great value because a purchaser could stay away not only from the non-match but also for the entire season. There was a further advantage: all tickets were numbered, all tickets were for various grandstands, so purchasers could nominate seats at the MCG that they found particularly undesirable and stay away from those. Before females were allowed (at last) into the Melbourne Cricket Club as members, many women bought tickets with great vehemence in the Members' Stand so that they could stay away from it. Indeed, women were always our best AFL members.

They made up two out of three of our entire membership and particularly included wives of footballers.

Lucky seats carried prizes. For the first non-match in 1972 the first prize was a Ford XL Cortina and the second prize a holiday for two to Singapore and Malaysia, courtesy of Qantas. It was a splendid money raiser for Berry Street.

We instituted our first Wilkie award in 1967, the very first year of the AFL, and from then on it became an annual event. The VFL awarded the Brownlow Medal, just before the finals, for the best and fairest player. The award was always conducted with huge radio, television and newspaper publicity. There needed to be an antidote for this. So we founded the Wilkie, in honour of Douglas Wilkie, the AFL President, and we awarded it to the male or female who had done least for football in the fairest manner.

We awarded the first Wilkie to the then prime minister, Harold Holt. We had noted that governors and, in particular, politicians liked to pick up popularity by associating themselves with a football club. Sir Robert Menzies was number one ticket holder at Carlton, Arthur Calwell was number one at North Melbourne, Sir John McEwen at Fitzroy and Billy Snedden at Melbourne. Gough Whitlam, whom one would have presumed had zero interest in Melbourne football, became the number one ticket holder at Geelong and also had himself photographed in a Collingwood guernsey.

But Harold Holt did none of this. We did careful research and discovered that never while he was a politician had he been seen at a football match. So in September 1967 we advised Mr Holt of his award. Two weeks went by and there was no answer. I telephoned his press secretary, Tony Eggleton, and said, 'Tony, the Prime Minister has received this extraordinary honour but we have received no reply'.

'Oh, I know he appreciates the honour', replied Eggleton. 'The trouble is he has an election coming up, and if word gets around it might be his downfall. I'll tell you what, he would be delighted to receive the award privately, with no photographs.'

So, on 11 September 1967, Bruce Matear, Chairman of the Berry Street Babies Home Appeal, presented Harold Holt with his medal. Holt explained that he had won his football colours at Wesley College in Melbourne and had even broken a collar-bone playing for Queen's College against Ormond College, at Melbourne University. But as for watching football, that was not for him.

'I like to play sport myself', he said. 'I like tennis and I like swimming. For example, I went spear fishing last weekend at Portsea'. We commented that anyone who went spear fishing at Portsea in frigid September deserved a medal.

Just three months later, on 17 December, at the very spot he had mentioned – Cheviot Beach near Portsea – Harold Holt went into the water and disappeared, presumed drowned.

Cyril Pearl, author of *The Girl with the Swansdown Seat*, *Wild Men of Sydney*, *Morrison of Peking* and *Dublin in Bloomtime*, was one of our most brilliant Wilkie winners. In angry letters to newspapers he described the various scourges that had plagued New South Wales. There was the dreadful louse phylloxera, which had swept across Victoria, virtually destroying a wine industry, then invaded New South Wales. Then there was the insidious pest prickly pear, which had come down from the north to devastate the farmlands. Now there was the equally horrid pest Australian Rules football, which was coming from Melbourne to contaminate Sydney.

We asked Cyril Pearl if he would fly from Sydney to accept his Wilkie award for 1972. He said yes he would, on condition that he could burn a football once kicked by the immortal Roy Cazaly.

We tried very hard to find a football that had been kicked by Cazaly, but it was impossible. Royce Hart of Richmond was an extraordinary hero in 1972. We did have a football that had been kicked by him. Would this do? Yes it would.

Anti Football Day was on 28 September. Fred Goding asked K. G. Luke to make the Wilkie Medal. It was a beautiful thing: large, gold and much more impressive than the Brownlow. Recipients wore it on a red ribbon hung around the neck. Mr Pearl in his acceptance speech said he felt like the Grand Ambassador Extraordinary from Uganda.

The ceremony took place in the middle of the Melbourne Cricket Ground. It felt quite eerie and awesome with the 60 000 AFL members who had paid to stay away. Nearby the Royal Australian Navy Band was practising for the imminent Grand Final. I asked the commander if he would play an appropriate tune while we burned the football.

'Certainly not', he replied, in clipped tones.

We placed the football on a little stove and lit it, but there was no result. We soaked it in kerosene: still no result.

'I told you so', Ian Johnson said. 'There are things you can do and can't do on the MCG. There is something special about the atmosphere of this place. The football will never burn. It won't be allowed.'

I must admit I started to feel guilty. It was a bit like taking one's pants off in St Paul's Cathedral. But suddenly the football began to burn. There was a marvellous column of black smoke and the sinister smell of burning leather. The Navy people relented. A sailor with a bugle came across and played 'The Last Post'. It was a most moving experience.

In 1974 first prize for our great non-football match was a Qantas trip for two to Bangkok. Colour television was the novelty of the moment so our second prize was a Sanyo colour television set. The Wilkie winner was Leon Hill, general manager of GTV9. Channel Nine was the first television station to have the courage to give up football match replays on Saturday nights.

We decided this time to bury a football at sea, and we felt it should be done properly with a tasteful old-time service. We hired all our gear from Formal Wear and our team, which included Fred Goding, looked fine, indeed, in top hats bound with black crêpe. We called almost every funeral director in Melbourne but not one would supply us with a hearse. Ultimately we were saved by a young gentleman, Ian Vinnicombe. He was a part-time taxi driver and, curiously, a member of the Collingwood Cheer Squad. Hearses, he said, had become most fashionable. He announced that he had a superb 1940 Dodge hearse that tipped the scale at just over 2 tonnes. He had bought it just ten months ago for 150 dollars from a funeral director in New South Wales.

We drove the hearse to Williamstown at a respectful 30 kilometres an hour. The idea was to hire a boat from Parson's Marina and have our burial at sea. Clearly the gods were against us. There was a true Melburnian storm, with 100–kilometre winds blowing straight from the Antarctic, and the wharf had all the atmosphere of a scene from *Hamlet*. All boating on the bay was banned.

There was only one thing to do: conduct our burial service at the end of the Williamstown Pier. We had a beautiful coffin for our football. I placed bricks in the bottom, bored holes in the lid and the four pallbearers gently, with appropriately mournful music, lowered the coffin into the sea.

'In loving memory of the ailing body of the once great Victorian Football League and its suffering attendances, we commit this expired body to the deep', we all intoned.

Then came disaster. Under pressure down below, the lid flew off, and the football popped to the surface like a cork. The wind caught it and soon it was scudding across the surface of the choppy sea. The last we saw of that football it was racing towards Port Phillip Heads, which stood out like the great goal posts in the sky. All four Melbourne television stations were there with their cameras. They made a great deal out of that story.

In 1977 our first prize was a holiday for two in Singapore, with two weeks at the Ming Court Hotel, courtesy of Qantas. Second prize was a Datsun car and third prize was the new, exciting gimmick of the year – a videotape recorder. Our charity now was the Multiple Sclerosis Society of Victoria. Fred Goding announced that the AFL in its first decade had raised 100 000 dollars.

Our Wilkie winner for 1977 was Kate Baillieu, television star of GTV9. Kate won her award by refusing to play in the Kerry's Angels all-female football team. The Angels were named in honour of the Nine network's proprietor, Kerry Packer. Kate Baillieu was a keen balloonist and she suggested that the best way to destroy her football was to explode it in mid-air. With two ballooning friends, Tony Norton and Bruce Blake, she created a beautiful thing, bright red and 4 metres long. We took the balloon to the centre of the MCG and attached a fuse. The theory was that the football would explode splendidly in mid-air.

The balloon went up, up, up, high into the sky, and was scooting towards Government House when, suddenly, it exploded. There was a sheet of flame and it went down like the ill-fated Hindenburg, right over Brunton Avenue, one of the big arterial roads into the city. Once again Ian Johnson was present. He grabbed me by the arm and said, 'I just hope you have got plenty of insurance'.

There was an hour of terror waiting for the report of some incinerated automobile, but the remains fell into the railway yards and not on the avenue.

In other years we cut up footballs with chain-saws, we hired magicians who made them disappear and in 1985 Wilkie winner

Barry Humphries, alias Sir Les Patterson, engaged a camel to eat a football. He had a little trouble. The camel was more interested after Barry had smothered the ball with cream cake.

The eating of footballs became popular. How wonderful it would be if we could recycle all footballs and turn them into food, we thought. We bought a fresh football, boiled it for several days, minced it and, with the aid of carrots, onions, tomatoes and lots of herbs, Peter Russell-Clarke, our cooking expert, turned it into a lovely curry. We served it nice and hot at our 1988 Wilkie award ceremony when Terry Lane, writer and ABC broadcaster, was our Wilkie winner.

Sometimes it seemed God was not quite on the side of anti-football. One year Robert Joyce, a sky-writing pilot, offered to draw the Anti Football League symbol across the Melburnian sky. We asked him if he could do it for us on the next Saturday, right above the Melbourne Cricket Ground where the Demons would be indulging in their regular clash with the Magpies.

Mr Joyce took off in his small aeroplane and he did indeed draw in smoke a wonderful anti-football cube plus the letters AFL. He had suggested the right height for our symbol would be 3000 metres. There was just one thing wrong with this, the wind at 3000 metres on that day was blowing at 160 kilometres an hour. By the time Robert Joyce had finished his sky writing the symbol was somewhere over Dandenong.

It all seemed a failure, a disaster. However, on the Tuesday morning this letter arrived from Mrs Lesley Dingle of Mitcham:

> During the season my husband carries his trannie round like a wart. And on Saturday afternoon he had it blaring – you know what – on the handle of his wheelbarrow.
>
> Well, just as we got to the forty-ninth barrowload of leaves, I reached breaking point. Thoughts of murder or suicide surged through my tortured mind and, in my hopelessness, I turned my eyes to heaven – and Oh miracle! Oh happy day! Hallelujah! There before my unbelieving gaze was THE CUBE!
>
> And, as I stood transfixed, an 'A' appeared and then the noble little aeroplane created an 'F' and an 'L'. I waved my rake in triumphant gestures and the transistor was struck dumb. After this great happening I now have the strength to go on living until the finals.

From time to time the AFL published *The Carefree Motorists'
Clean Air Guide to Victoria*. This was a series of exquisitely charted
courses that took members on routes comfortably free from all
football grounds. We discovered, however, that escaping from
football, keeping oneself football pure, on Grand Final Day was
extremely difficult.

In 1983 we had an idea. We hired the entire Princess Theatre
for a special matinée performance of *West Side Story*. We sealed
off the theatre and the plan was this: AFL members would be
able to enjoy a shrine of their own in which not a word about
the Grand Final would be uttered.

It was a failure. One character sat with an ear-plug in throughout
the entire performance. When poor Maria was pleading for a new
El Dorado 'Some Day' among the cut-throat gangs of New York,
this fellow was getting a blow-by-blow description about the thugs
on the Melbourne Cricket Ground. Then, at interval, I went out
to the men's lavatory and another four of them were tuning into
the football on their trannies. Heaven knows what went on in
the female lavatory, but I suspect it was worse.

The Anti Football League still survives; we still have Wilkie
Medals and many thousands of members. We now sell badges
from St John's Homes for Boys and Girls, at 18 Balwyn Road,
Canterbury, Melbourne.

The APITS column supported many societies of protest and
reform. One of them was the Pro Mini Club, which I proudly
believe helped set back Melbourne fashions at least ten years.

In 1965 the English model Jean Shrimpton arrived at the
Melbourne Derby in what we would call today a fairly modest
skirt. Barrie Watts wrote in the *Sun*:

> There she was, the world's highest paid model, snubbing the iron-
> clad conventions of fashionable Flemington in a dress five inches
> above the knee. NO hat, NO gloves, and NO stockings. The
> shockwaves were still rumbling around fashionable Melbourne last
> night when Jean Shrimpton – The Shrimp – swore she hadn't
> realised she was setting off such an outraged upheaval at Flemington
> on Saturday.

It did not take long for the young of Melbourne to awaken to the beauty of bare knees and bare thighs. Skirts became shorter and superbly shorter. By 1970 the fashion industry was alarmed. There is little material and little fashion in a miniskirt. Furthermore, as skirts became shorter and shorter, it was easy to economise by merely taking up the hems of existing clothes. It is not so easy when skirt lengths go the other way. The winter of 1970 saw the arrival of the maxiskirt, which went almost to the ankles. The Myer Emporium was so determined to establish this fashion it issued a decree that all female sales staff had to wear the new maxi.

The miniskirt was in peril and some of us thought the time had come to save it. Brian Goldsmith, President of the Multiple Sclerosis Society of Victoria, thought maybe we could set up a society as a fund raiser. Of course, we needed a badge. We called in Peter Russell-Clarke, a *Herald* cartoonist, to design one. His conception was brilliant: a pair of scissors to symbolise the cutting down of the maxiskirt, in the shape of the female form. We decided we would sell badges of imitation silver at 50 cents each for annual membership. Ah, but for life membership there would be a badge in imitation gold for a dollar. The silver badges cost us 15 cents each and the gold cost us 20 cents. The psychology was splendid. Few people wanted to be branded as miserable annual members, so nine out of ten went for gold. In the first three weeks alone we cleared 8000 dollars for the Multiple Sclerosis Society.

Letters poured in from males all over the globe. We had a Pro Mini Club branch among the RAAF in Malaysia and there was a Saigon branch for the Australian troops in Vietnam. There was such enthusiasm in Gippsland that the Traralgon Racing Club offered us a racing day. All women in miniskirts would be admitted free.

Brian Goldsmith believed this could be a marvellous means of raising cash for the Multiple Sclerosis Society. He organised a bus and we filled it with miniskirted fashion models. All afternoon they diligently went around the track selling Pro Mini Club badges and asking for donations to the Multiple Sclerosis Society. The models were so beautiful the money poured in. By 5 p.m. I thought the job they had done was so brilliant that I should take them into the club and buy them a drink. They accepted my offer with much enthusiasm. I was surprised by the extraordinarily exotic drinks that they ordered.

When we boarded the bus I told Brian I had thought the models were so wonderful that I had bought them all a drink.

'Oh, my God', he said, 'I had already done that'.

The effect of all those cocktails soon became evident. One of the models at the back of the bus announced, 'I'm too hot', and began to strip. Soon she was displaying a lovely pair of bare breasts. When we reached Drouin there were shrieks to the driver that they desperately needed a rest stop, so he obligingly pulled into a café. This was the signal for them all to go topless. There were squeals of laughter as they clambered out of the bus, showing much more than the Pro Mini Club had ever asked for. Brian shouted to them to make themselves respectable before showing themselves in the town but it made no difference. They were having a lovely time.

They went into the café, had soft drinks and went to the lavatory, while I tried to keep out of sight. The café proprietor took the naked invasion with surprising calm and we managed to get the models back on the bus. All the way back to Melbourne I sat, miserable, pondering my ruin. *Truth* newspaper, certainly, would get hold of this. I could see the headlines:

DUNSTAN'S NAKED HAREM
SENSATIONAL LURID BUS JOURNEY
CLERGY CONDEMN IMMORALITY

If Drouin had a local correspondent, that person mercifully missed the story. I wrote of the day's events in my column on Monday, but I was careful to censor my description of what had transpired on the way home.

On 28 October 1970 the Pro Mini Club held a rally in the plaza of the Southern Cross Hotel and invited all miniskirt wearers to attend. The day was frigid and wet. Attendance by young women in minis was almost zero. However, by extraordinary happenstance, the gallery on all levels was packed with enthusiastic males. There was some small opposition to the rally. Jonathan Crawford, the fashion designer, arrived with a team of models in maxiskirts. Mr Crawford, himself wearing a maxicoat, led the parade. He reminded me of Basil Rathbone in his nineteenth-century army greatcoat, when he played opposite Freddie Bartholomew in *Anna Karenina*.

Guests of honour were the former football stars Jack Dyer and Lou Richards. Richards told the crowd: 'I am in favour of the mini. I am a religious man. I have read the Bible right through and I have noticed that Adam's girlfriend wore the greatest mini ever'.

The stirring part of the meeting came when Mr Richards was asked to carry out a symbolic act: the cutting of a maxi down to mini size. Gina Blau, wife of Brian Goldsmith, modelled the maxi and Mr Richards, using a huge pair of gold scissors, hacked away until it turned into a jagged-edged but still delightful mini. Those present felt that the sight of Gina in this sensible, completely practical garment proved the justice of the cause, even if Mr Richards, as someone said, could hardly have gone any further above see level.

The campaign had a profound effect on Melbourne. Even when London, Paris, Rome, New York, Los Angeles and indeed the entire world had abandoned the miniskirt, mercifully it was still being worn in Collins Street.

In 1971 'A Place in the Sun' launched the National Distrust. There was a National Trust dedicated to preserving old buildings of great merit, but there was no similar organisation for getting rid of buildings of outstanding demerit, buildings that people could not stand. The newly formed National Distrust established various categories: C was noteworthy of destruction, B was 'should be pulled down at once' and A was 'outstandingly awful, worthy of destruction at all costs'.

Every year in January we gave our UGH awards. UGH stood for Ungodly Horror. We gave UGHs to car parks, UGHs to new buildings in the city and an UGH to the pure horror that was St Kilda Junction.

Jeff Hook designed our UGH award – a telegraph pole stuck in a block of concrete – and we published the illustration in the APITS column. The *Sun* Editor was very nervous about these UGHs.

'You take care', he said. 'Before long some builder or some architect is going to sue.'

One year a tyre firm in Elizabeth Street in the city won our top UGH. The owner had painted his building in a striking shade of puce. Having done this, he covered it with the entrails of automobiles, tyres, crank shafts, differentials and such. The day after the announcement there was a call on the telephone.

'Good morning. I notice that I am the winner of your UGH award.'

I groaned inwardly. Ah, yes, here it was, the writ at last.

'Yes Sir, that is correct. You did win our UGH award.'

'All right, where is it?', he asked.

'What do you mean, where is it?'

'Good God man, you say I have won an award. All right, I want it.'

That meant I had to spend half the weekend making the darned thing. When finished it stood nearly a metre high and was composed of concrete, a broom handle, cross-pieces of dowling and some of Marie Rose's beads for insulators. We sent it round to the tyre firm by taxi. The owner was thrilled. He displayed it in his front window for an entire year.

There were many other organisations championed in APITS. For example, there was the Scrooge Society for those who could not stand Christmas and were fed up with hunting for presents. There was one society of which I was particularly fond: the Society Against Progress. SAP believed that nothing was ever as good as it had been in the past, that things only deteriorated, never improved. SAP looked back with nostalgia to the days when the dollar was a splendid, unchangeable thing, not subject to absurd daily variations, and to the days when there were two postal deliveries on a week day and one on Saturday morning. Members mournfully remembered the time when wine was tax free, a glass of beer cost threepence, Myer's, David Jones, Walton's and Georges were happy to deliver an article free of charge, there were still parking spaces in the city and it was possible to breathe the air. In the old days we had not known about AIDS and there had been afternoon newspapers that carried news in the afternoons.

Everybody over 30 wanted to join the Society Against Progress, but, alas, it was not within our power to turn back the clock.

CHAPTER TWELVE

Jumping the generation gap

Writers are merciless. Everything that takes place, everything that impinges, is another raisin in the editorial pudding. During casual conversation or at dinner parties the haunted writer is hunting for material, checking over the conversation wondering what can be used. Columnists are the worst; their eyes and ears are on the alert, every waking hour. They are the worst because their need is the greatest. The column is a vast vacuum that sucks in all that is available and the vacuum is there daily. The columnist's family is caught in this ravenous drive, it becomes part of the notoriety. Unquestionably the trickiest time for me was in the 1960s and 1970s, when we lived in East Malvern.

The first house we ever actually owned was at 22 Central Park Road, East Malvern, just one block away from 13 Coppin Street where I was born. To say that we owned 22 Central Park is an exaggeration. We had a War Service Loan, a loan from the National Bank and a further loan from my mother. East Malvern was not Toorak, not as smart as Hawthorn or Camberwell and certainly not as affluent as Brighton. It was somewhere in between, comfortable middle class. The Reverend A. P. B. Bennie, then warden of St Paul's College in Sydney, commented: 'I know East Malvern very well. That's the suburb for spinsters and maiden aunts'.

Yes, our suburb was quiet and well-behaved; the Anglican Church team played cricket at Central Park on Saturday afternoons, splendid orchids grew in the park greenhouse. It was difficult to imagine anything untoward taking place in East Malvern. And it was utterly flat. The area from Central Park Road through to Dandenong Road was originally the site for the

Metropolitan Golf Course before land prices became too high and the club moved to Oakleigh. Our house was part of the glorious housing scheme, the grand subdivision of 1912, and we often wondered precisely where we were in the historic order of things. Was our house on the fourteenth green or was the fourth tee on our back lawn, close by our vegetable garden? The result of the great subdivision was pure Edwardiana. The houses in Central Park Road were variations on the one architectural theme: red-tile roof, red brick and stucco walls, with wooden additions at the back for kitchen and outhouses. They were built flat on the earth, with an eternal problem of rising damp.

At the end of Central Park Road, bounded by Wattletree Road, Burke Road and Kingston Street, was the lovely Central Park. John Landy, the world champion mile runner, used to train there. His parents lived opposite the park, in the area the real estate agents thought the better end of Central Park Road. Sometimes when I was jogging on foggy winter mornings he would pass me, perhaps two or three times in one circuit, and say 'Good morning'. One time the police picked him up in Central Park Road. There he was, running down the street in the dark, long after midnight. The wireless patrol thought anyone running along Central Park Road in the dark, wearing a track suit, had to be up to no good.

East Malvern was home to us for eighteen years. The three girls went to Korowa Anglican Girls' School, David went to Caulfield Grammar.

I always believed that good marriages begot good marriages. My mother and father had an extraordinary relationship. Although Dad was a forceful extrovert of a man, I cannot recall a cross word between them. Their example made a profound impression on Marie and me. If ever we had a tiff, if ever we had a cross word, the crisis was never so grave that I actually missed a meal. For one thing the cooking of Marie Rose was too good, and for another I needed her love.

Marie was, and is, an inspired and extremely inventive cook. My mother was a gifted cook, and she passed on to Marie all the remarkable family recipes, but, like a violinist, she had her repertoire and she never added to it. Marie has never been like that. She can cook, say, a great paella and never return to it again. She gets excitement and satisfaction from always trying out something new. In forty years of marriage almost every meal has been an adventure. There was the day, for example, at Calabasas in California when Marie discovered home pasta. There was no machine to make it: every piece had to be hand rolled, cut into strips and put out to dry. We had pasta on clothes-horses, chairs, towel rails, all around the apartment. Inevitably pieces dropped on the floor, so we had pasta underfoot, pasta sticking to the soles of our shoes, but the dish she made that night was one of the greatest of my life.

Marie thinks about food. There is ricotta gnocchi, that's good, but why not make a gnocchi with ricotta impregnated with fresh peas? So she will go to work, carefully crafting every individual piece. Yes, *gnocchi e piselli*, another culinary triumph. Like all great cooks she has a library of cookbooks, but her aim always is to use what is fresh, in season and available in the garden. Alas, sometimes it tends to destroy the pleasure of restaurants – the food always seems better at home.

It is absurd to think that you are in love when you get married. Love is something that is developed over the years through a hundred thousand shared experiences and mutual understandings. Love is like a forty-storey building, created piece by piece from all those thoughts you have had together, places you have been to, houses you have lived in, roads you have travelled. You learn to think each other's thoughts. Whenever I have been worried or groping for an idea for a newspaper article it has been amazing how often Marie has been first with the idea. That is why it is always a shock when the marriages of old friends break down. Are the partners really that different? It is hard to imagine the emotional earthquake that has taken place.

It is interesting how couples have special names for each other. 'Dear', 'Love', 'Precious', almost anything is better than the real name. It is a warning on the Richter earthquake scale when one comes out with the brutal, honest name. I don't enthuse over Keith. Marie prefers to be called Marie Rose, and particularly she likes to be called 'my Dove'. When the doves are around everything is fine.

Certainly there were tensions during the 1960s, and they were mostly male caused. Ours was a classic Australian household: it was the female who made all the sacrifices and it was the female who brought up the children. It is interesting to compare the last decades of this century with the 1950s or 1960s. Today it is normal

for both husband and wife to work. The joint earnings are vital
to pay for the children's education or to meet those interest rates.
So both husband and wife have to find ways to share the domestic
load, the cooking, the cleaning, the looking after of the children.
In the male-oriented world of the 1960s this did not seem possible.
The female did 95 per cent of the domestic work.

Marie would have loved to return to nursing. Every time she
went near a hospital she had a thrill of excitement. Just the smell
of antiseptic in the corridors evoked a desire to get back into
uniform and start working again. She had no chance to do that
until all the children had left home. They came first.

But there was the problem of one income. I worked out that,
even though I was on an A grade journalist's salary with a margin,
it was necessary to double my salary to keep four children at
public schools. This had its complications. Just as the Vatican in
Rome possessed its servants, so the Herald and Weekly Times
owned its journalists body and soul. The company considered that
the honour of working for it should be enough. It was a benevolent
organisation that looked after its employees in time of trouble,
but it was a mortal sin for any of its journalists to indulge in freelance
activities for Press, radio or television unless these were under
the company blanket. During the 1960s I did the 'Batman' column
for the *Bulletin* and wrote an advertising column for Georges
department store, news commentaries for 3DB radio and a
Saturday feature for the *Sun*, as well as a daily column.

The 'Batman' column began in 1961. Peter Hastings, Editor of
the *Bulletin*, chose the name in honour of John Batman, one of
Melbourne's founders. The column ran for four years before Frank
Daly, Editor of the *Sun*, began to detect curious similarities in
style between it and my *Sun* column. He called me into his office
and demanded to know whether I was Batman. I confessed that
I was. For quarter of an hour I was poised between resignation
and dismissal, but finally Daly agreed to keep my secret as long
as the *Sun* did not miss out on any stories.

The secret of Georges never leaked. Horrie Taafe, a master
merchandiser, opened the men's store at Georges in 1962. He
wanted a weekly advertising column on the front page of the
Age, something with a twist, that was both informative and
amusing. He asked me to do it for him, unsigned. So at one time

I had copy running in both the *Age* and the *Sun*. Just occasionally someone said: 'Did you see that ad for Georges in the *Age*? I think they're pinching your ideas'. Fortunately no one took it any further.

It was a tricky balancing act, always done at 5 o'clock in the morning before the house was awake. The Georges column had to be written on Tuesday morning, the *Bulletin* column on Wednesday morning and the feature article for Saturday's *Sun* on Thursday morning. News commentaries for 3DB three days a week were done at 5 p.m.

What drives a person to work like this? It is partly greed, partly hunger for recognition, partly fear – fear of that warning, 'You will end up as a hack sub-editor, working at 3 a.m.'. There was the even greater fear that if I stopped the ideas might stop, the curious knack God had given me might be taken away. Everything would come to an end. Even now, whenever there is a dry period and columns seem hard to find, that fear returns, and the thought comes to mind: 'There won't be any more. You're finished'.

There was one result from all this. Marie brought up the children. I worked every Sunday, so theoretically I had Friday and Saturday off, but often it was necessary to use Friday for research at the State Library. Saturday was the one family day.

To make matters worse often the column was on the move. Whenever a royal person, the Queen, the Queen Mother, Prince Philip, Prince Charles or Princess Alexandra, came to Australia, the *Sun* columnist had to trail behind. The *Sun* had to serve rural readers, therefore the *Sun* columnist had to keep touring around country areas. Week after week Marie was left alone with the children.

Marie and I had different views on religion. I said it was essential to go to church regularly. How otherwise could you have discipline with your religion, how else could you gain spiritual refreshment? You needed the stimulation that came from your fellow church members. Marie said no, sometimes she found church a dull rote. Real Christianity was looking after people, caring for others, being practical. She believed she could do far more good outside the walls of a church that often seemed merely self-indulgent.

Marie was true to her word. She looked after people's children in times of trouble. Rosemary, her niece, aged 15, came to us from Canberra because her mother was ill in hospital. Rosemary stayed for twelve months. She was not the only child that Marie took in. Perhaps the most intriguing of all was our exchange student.

All our own children were very different. David, the eldest, was very much a child of the 1960s. As a history student at Monash he was an agnostic, a radical and determined to change the world. Kate, our second daughter, seemed like the recreation of my grandmother Carnell, the one who had had all denominations in Ballarat praying for her when she was ill. Kate was talkative, clever at everything she touched and extremely ambitious. She was small, blonde and, like her father, abysmal at sport. Marie's heart constantly went out to her for Kate so desperately wanted to succeed in school sports. Time and again Marie watched Kate performing on the diving-board, trying to compete against girls larger and far more athletic. Kate never gave up. Our youngest child was Sarah – tall, blonde and, unlike Kate, athletic. Sarah was a natural mixer, always surrounded by friends and, like her mother, keen to care for others. Our eldest daughter was Jane, not a brilliant student but thoughtful and introspective. David was the radical, but Jane was the one who really wanted to mend the world, a natural for any cause that came her way. Jane wanted to find things out for herself, and in her eighteenth year, with single-minded purpose, she set about becoming an American Field Service student.

The AFS was then, and still is, a remarkable organisation for widening international understanding. American children aged 17 went out all over the world, to Japan, Europe, Africa, South America and Australia, and lived with families for a year. In turn people from these exchange countries sent their children to the United States to volunteer families, not necessarily ones that had sent their own children.

The selection process was very rigorous and the chances of acceptance maybe one in fifty. We thought Jane had little chance, but the interviews kept coming, until eventually the person who chaired the selection committee said she wanted to meet Jane. She wanted all the family to be present. It sounded like group therapy.

The interview was a disaster. We all sat round in our high-ceilinged Edwardian living-room, the space set aside for important visitors. It was after dinner and coffee was served. The interviewer was charming. She questioned us all about our interests. David, who was just the right age to be conscripted by ballot for battle in Vietnam, had just returned from an anti-war demonstration. He let loose with his anger and talked of the evil Americans who were creating havoc and slaughter with their indiscriminate B52 bombings of innocent Vietnamese. He told of the dropping of napalm and discussed the toadying of the Holt and Gorton governments to the United States. The interviewer listened with great attention.

She left soon after ten, and as soon as the door closed there was a cry of pain and floods of tears from Jane.

'Why did you tell her all that? Why did you have to go on about your wretched Vietnam, criticising the Americans? You've ruined it. They will never choose me now.'

'I haven't ruined anything', replied David. 'She came here, surely, expecting us to be honest.'

As it turned out he was right. Jane did receive the scholarship, and in July 1970 she flew to the United States to spend twelve months with a family in Toledo, Ohio, and have an academic year at an American high school. Jane was very nervous the day she flew off from the brand-new Tullamarine Airport. She hadn't realised the impact of the whole thing until the very last moment. Marie literally had to push her out onto the tarmac. But was she as worried as her parents? There was the terror as she flew off. What would her new American parents be like? Would they be kind to her?

Sam Downs and Mary Howard were kind to her, indeed. Sam was a senior executive with the Owens Illinois Glass Company in Toledo, Ohio. The Downs had three children of their own and were good church people. Sam at that stage did not smoke or drink, so that was the first adjustment. Jane had been used to an occasional glass of wine on the table. Not any more.

Jane went to the local school and it was almost as different from Korowa as it could be. Ottawa Hills High School was co-educational, with large numbers of high-spirited boys. The students had no uniform, it was wear what you like. Furthermore at Ottawa Hills students could study liberal arts, which utterly lived up to its name. If a child did not wish to turn up for class that was his or her prerogative. It was puzzling after all the tight discipline of Korowa to switch to the easy freedom at Ottawa Hills. One thing in particular struck her: how uninhibited the American children were. Jane remembered the American AFS students who had spoken at Korowa. She had been amazed by their easy eloquence in front of the microphone. It was the same here.

Education covered a broad spectrum at this American school, and the liberal arts teacher was particularly gifted. He helped make Jane's year fascinating. She could choose her own subjects within liberal arts; alas, none of them were much help for her future Matriculation exams, although they were splendid right then. She picked such areas as public speaking, poetry and American history. Her fine teacher inspired her to study the wonders of T. S. Eliot, and they made a special study of a famous American musical and how it was put together.

During the year the liberal arts teacher made the students do a thesis. Jane chose relations between blacks and whites in the United States. This was a matter of some wonder to Sam and Mary. Why would an Australian girl want to research such a difficult subject? Growing up in North Carolina, Sam and Mary had been very close to black repression, and here was Jane studying the activities of the Black Panthers and bringing home books by black radicals. Yet everyone was co-operative, and as a climax Jane spent several days at an all-black school in an industrial suburb of Toledo.

'At first I was pretty frightened', Jane recalls. 'But I think it made a difference being a foreign student and they asked questions about Australia. They didn't even know where Australia was. I remember they had this wonderful school assembly with music and they all clapped hands and sang. It was a real culture shock for me. Then I was billeted with a young black girl and her grandmother. We went out to a party where they played all the glorious black soul music I had never heard before.'

Jane wrote her thesis, and she finished it with the hope and dream that all the races might intermingle so there would be no blacks and whites, just a perfect world of beige. By coincidence it was an ideal that was also being suggested by the Australian Nobel Prize winner Sir Macfarlane Burnet.

It is not easy for a 17-year-old being away from home for a year. Winter in Ohio is dramatically cold and at times Jane wondered whether the warm sun would ever come again. One day a fellow student in class drew her a graph explaining what to look for as the first signs of spring. Yet there was the compensating excitement of travel. The Downs family took her home to North Carolina, to New York and to Niagara Falls. Then, at the end of the year, Jane had a bus tour across the United States with all the other AFS students, young people from Switzerland, Colombia, Cambodia, India – and, of course, Australia. It is a matter of debate how wise it is to send a child away right in the middle of year twelve; the academic years in Australia and the United States do not match, so in effect the visit actually disturbs two years not one. Year twelve is graduation year in the United States, a year of winding down. Year twelve in Australia is a climactic year of intense study. Whether it was good for Jane we are unsure, but it was very good for us. Sam Downs and Mary Howard became lifelong friends.

When Jane went off, we applied for a student in return. The result was fascinating. We had not realised at the time that the whole object of the group interview was to carefully match families. David had proved that radical socialists lived in peaceful Central Park Road. We received a radical in return.

Vivien Kane, 17, daughter of a medical family in Buffalo, New York State, arrived just in time for the January holidays of 1971. Vivien had lovely thick, brown hair, with just a glint of red. She wore very plain spectacles and not a hint of make-up, and she was carrying a guitar. The lack of make-up was part of the new mood: liberated females did not go in for such pathetic sexual lures.

There was that paralysing first moment of meeting, that twenty-fifth of a second before a word is spoken. We could see Vivien looking us over and thinking: 'My God! I've got to live with this lot for a whole year'. We no doubt were thinking precisely the same thing. But Kate and Sarah were carrying a big 'Welcome' notice with a caricature of Vivien done for us by Peter Russell-Clarke. There is nothing like good public relations. This helped overcome at least two hours of shyness. It was holiday time, so we immediately put Vivien in our old Humber and drove to a house we had hired at Lorne. The house had the inspired name Rufanredy.

Of course, Victorian holidays should never be in January. Schools should take their recess in late February or March when the weather is mild, soft, dry and sublime. In January it takes on all sorts of ingenious variations, both hot and cold, designed to torture campers. In January 1971 we had a week of rain, with southerly winds blowing straight from the Antarctic. Vivien looked at our little house, watched me trying to prepare a barbecue under an umbrella in the near blizzard and commented, 'Boy, what a dump!'.

Vivien grew on us slowly. The AFS theory was this: you were their parents, absolutely, for a year. The students called you Mum and Dad. Vivien did not find this easy; she tended to call us Marie and Keith. She was not only intelligent, she was very intelligent, indeed. She thought United States intervention in Vietnam was outrageous and that President Nixon was an evil, conniving man.

Vivien was Jewish, but she did not believe in God. Just over in Armadale there was a wonderful Jewish family who also had an AFS student, a Japanese-American from California. They would say: 'Isn't it amazing? You're Anglicans and you get a Jew. We're Jews and we get a Japanese Buddhist'.

When the great Jewish festivals came round Vivien always suggested that she go over to Armadale to see the Jewish family.

'Why?', Marie would ask. 'You're not religious.'

'No', replied Vivien, 'but they have such incredible food'.

Vivien, like our girls, went to Korowa School in Malvern. It was all part of the exchange plan. Local schools very generously accepted AFS students free of charge. She could not believe it when she saw the uniform: pleated tunic, blazer with badge on the pocket, straw hat, stockings, shoes, gloves. This was something out of the last century. Vivien's favourite expression was 'Oh my Gard!'. She said 'Oh my Gard' on this occasion and pleaded could she please take it home when the time came? Vivien was not sentimental about her Korowa uniform. She wanted to show this astonishing curio to all her friends.

Vivien never quite fitted in at Korowa. She made plenty of friends but the Australian school discipline was too much for her. All this business of wearing hat and gloves, virtually under the pain of death, seemed unbelievable. In the United States, unless a student was in a military academy, he or she went to school in jeans, a sloppy-joe sweat-shirt and sneakers. Vivien always walked home, through Central Park, with her long hair astray, hat off, trailing her maroon jumper behind her.

Then there were those radical views, which she never tried to keep quiet. The local United States consulate asked her to give talks at other schools. Vivien gave one and they never asked her a second time. She gave the audience her complete, unabridged views on American intervention in Vietnam.

Yet what strength of character she had. While fighting with the principal at Korowa she developed her own views on what should be done for suffering humanity. There was an appeal for donations to an organisation called the Brotherhood of Man Fund; she would work for that. Quite independently Vivien took part in walkathons, went from door to door, firm to firm, and raised over a thousand dollars.

She thought it was unfair, a terrible injustice, that students should be sent to Australia for year twelve. Just when they should be enjoying themselves what happened? They had to go through the torture of Australian Matriculation exams. Vivien did not study hard, and we did not think she took school work seriously. Whenever she felt lonely or found Korowa a little too much she would go to her room for hours and play the guitar. In her Matriculation she passed every subject with honours and very nearly topped the State in Australian History. She returned home at the end of 1971, went to college, then university, studied medicine and is now a radiologist.

In the 1960s and early 1970s there were times when it was a nightmare being a parent, and we wondered often where we had gone wrong and how things could have been done better. Sex, drugs, rock 'n' roll, it was all irresistible for the young. I remember going to rock festivals at Sunbury and again near Tocumwal up on the Murray, the reek of marijuana everywhere. One could even smell it in picture theatres in Melbourne.

Marie was smarter than I was; she was the first to detect it in our house at Central Park Road. One Saturday afternoon David was in the house with three or four of his friends. There was no doubt they had been smoking pot, grass – it had so many fancy names. It was time for a confrontation. Perhaps some people would have forbidden it outright. Marie, to her eternal credit, had a different approach.

'I don't know what you see in this stuff', she said. 'Why do you smoke it? If it's really so marvellous, I'd like to try some.'

We sat in what we called the family room, half a dozen of us around the coffee table. David rolled a cigarette from material that he had in a small bag. He did not roll his cigarette with one hand, but an old-time bushman would have approved his skill.

He lit the cigarette, puffed and passed it to his left. And so it went, round and round. This practice we found charming. Some would feel it was not sanitary, but there was a fellowship and togetherness about it. It was similar to passing the chalice at the altar.

As for the result, there was perhaps a feeling of elation but coupled with a sickness in the stomach. The sickness could have been caused by the worry and obvious drama of the occasion.

The argument continued: 'Is this all there is?' and 'Why do you do it?'. We smoked only the one cigarette. We never heard of them again at Central Park Road, and we like to think Marie's action helped circumvent a dangerous situation. Certainly David very quickly swore off drugs, and all those present became remarkably responsible, successful citizens.

Marie Rose was anything but a dove when real action was required. Apart from marijuana there was tobacco. David was an incessant smoker. She tried everything to rid him of the habit: cajoling, putting anti-tobacco literature by his bedside. As soon as she saw a cigarette she destroyed it, and she would cut up his cigarettes in front of him. She threw them on the floor and jumped on them. But her most inspired move was to appeal to his stomach. She took all his cigarette butts, made them into a cigarette sandwich and served it to him for lunch. That sandwich was so revolting poor David finally gave up the unequal battle.

The 1960s was the time to drop out, the time for an alternative society, the time to be anti-war. In the 1940s and the early 1950s it was exciting, different, to be left wing, to become a young communist. This was the way to straighten out and improve the world. But in 1969 there was disillusionment with both left and right: neither had anything to offer. Why should 19-year-olds be ordered by an Australian government to put on uniform to fight in Vietnam, in a war that was incredibly remote from Collins Street?

David while at Monash University took part with waterside workers in an anti-war demonstration at Williamstown. There was a clash with police. One huge policeman grabbed David by the hair, threw him into a police wagon and charged him with assault. Arrested at the same time was Laurie Carmichael, Communist Party member and Assistant Secretary of the Federated Ironworkers Association, plus his son, who was a draft resister.

David remembers Carmichael in the watch-house at Williamstown. The police had all the protesters locked in a cell together, and Carmichael was so angry that for three hours he would not talk to anyone.

When the case came before a magistrate, David's best defence seemed the law of probability. Here was this huge policeman who could, and probably did, play in the ruck for Collingwood. And here was David, 19 years old, a head and a half smaller. David was able to demonstrate how he had been thrown into the truck by his long hair. The magistrate saw the point and the case was dismissed.

The question was, what would his grandfather have thought? How would W. Dunstan, VC, have reacted to the news of his grandson being arrested for demonstrating against Australia's commitment to the Vietnam War? We could not answer that because he had been dead for more than a decade, but it seemed to me that had I been a Monash student in 1969–1970 I, too, would have been anti-war. Just as Harold Holt had followed in the wake of President Johnson, crying 'All the way with LBJ', so Australians, it seemed, were dying in Vietnam just to score good behaviour points with the United States.

There was a series of anti-Vietnam War marches, led by Dr Jim Cairns, MHR, who was to become federal treasurer in the Whitlam Labor Government. The biggest came on 8 March 1970, and it had the curious, even awkward, title of moratorium. A moratorium, according to the *Concise Oxford Dictionary*, is a legal authorisation to defer payment. The moratorium theoretically, then, was a stay, a pause, a time to think this thing out.

We are a peculiarly unemotional people, but rarely have I seen such crowds in the city. It was a Friday and shops in Bourke Street, fearing the worst, boarded up their windows. Myer, Buckley's and stores all along the route closed their doors.

It is interesting how you become educated by your children. The moral issues of the war, and indeed many other moral issues of the day, could easily have passed me by but for the daily debates across our breakfast table, debates that were difficult to win. I was told that if I did not believe in Australia being represented in Vietnam it would be an act of hypocrisy not to be at the march.

David and I marched together. First the crowd gathered at the Treasury Gardens, where we listened to folk songs and anti-war speeches. Then at 3 p.m., led by Jim Cairns, we started marching to the city, with the marchers chanting 'Stop the war' and 'We want peace'. At one stage Bourke Street was a solid mass of people from Spring Street all the way to Queen Street. We sat down on the tram tracks in front of Buckley's to listen to speeches, then we inched our way to the Town Hall, sat down again and listened to more speeches.

It seemed to me the crowd was exactly equal in size to the crowd that had come to the city for the Moomba parade the previous March. The official police estimate for the moratorium was 70 000. The official police estimate for the Moomba crowd was 500 000. The Victorian premier, Henry Bolte, said he was delighted with the figure: if 70 000 turned up for the moratorium, there were at least three-quarters of a million anti-moratorium people who had decided to stay away. The moratorium was a failure.

There was another moratorium on 18 September 1970. David and I marched again. There were many famous names in the march. Stephen Murray-Smith, the historian, was there. So, too, was Dr Bertram Wainer, the crusading abortionist. Wainer marched out front with Jim Cairns. This time the marchers chanted 'We shall overcome'.

It was not as dramatic or as deeply impressive as the first moratorium. Second-time-around events never are. The police estimate was now 20 000, the estimate by the *Sun News-Pictorial* was 40 000; Henry Bolte described the moratorium as 'a total flop'. Certainly there were at least 40 000, but this time it was a younger crowd, more student oriented. The earlier moratorium was particularly significant because it was a protest by people old and young and from all classes of the community.

Once again we sat down on the tram tracks in Bourke Street, and once again we heard stories of the futility of the war. The most telling moment of the march came when a voice over the loudspeakers gave us the list of the Australian dead. The voice came over in dull, flat tones. It was monotonous, but it was the monotony that drove the point home. It took fifteen minutes to read the names, more than enough time for us to absorb the horror that every one of them was a young Australian who had died in action and that there would be more to come.

In the 1960s and the 1970s the talk was all about the generation gap. There was a gap all right. We had seen a complete turn-around, from wowserdom, 6 o'clock closing and the sacred Sunday to the era of the Pill and sexual permissiveness. Once parents used to cover up, but not any more. Now mothers in the most respectable families were prepared to admit that their beloved daughters were living with 'a very nice boy' in Carlton. Even a vicar we knew told us sadly that his son was living in sin. Did he reject his son, forbid him the house? No, for what could he do? He had a choice between accepting the new moral behaviour or losing his son. The mental adjustment on the part of parents was enormous, and one wondered if ever again there would be such a rapid social change. Would the next generation, our children, have to cope with such a gap?

David was a typical captive of the times. In 1971 he was editor of the Monash University student newspaper, *Lot's Wife*. He ran a very dashing, lively, left-wing journal and Mrs Lot certainly lived up to her reputation. That year David was in trouble because the paper was running a campaign to exclude a series of advertisements from the Defence Department. The department was looking for university graduates, and, of course, anything to do with defence was anathema because of the Vietnam War. But David's real trouble came from an unexpected quarter.

Wendy Bacon, later an outstanding journalist, was a notorious radical. She had been the editor of *Tharunka*, the student newspaper at the University of New South Wales, and she loved to shock. She used obscenity as a weapon, not only against literary censorship but against every kind of repression. Wendy Bacon gave a lecture at Monash and unquestionably it was disturbing to tender sensibilities. She graphically described a sex festival in Copenhagen. The *pièce de résistance* was a live performance on stage. She told in picturesque terms of an act of bestiality involving a man, a goose and two women. *Lot's Wife* ran a complete, word-for-word report of her talk.

David was not present when Wendy Bacon gave the talk; the job was done entirely by one of his reporters. But he was the editor so he was the one arrested on charges of criminal obscenity and ordered to appear before a magistrate at the Port Melbourne Court. Why Port Melbourne? *Lot's Wife* was printed at Port

Melbourne. There were suggestions that this was a matter of some ingenuity on the part of the police. Port Melbourne was a working-class suburb where they could find an ideal magistrate and have the best chance of establishing a conviction. It wouldn't be so easy anywhere near Monash. Out there the new, sexually loose ideas would prevail.

A case like this could have been taken as simply a normal editorial hazard except that a frightening precedent had just taken place in London. Richard Neville, a young Australian and the Editor of *Oz*, had been sentenced to gaol for obscenity. Unquestionably the police were looking to this to establish an Australian benchmark. They, too, wanted a gaol sentence.

The Williamstown case had been a minor affair, but this one had us really worried. We called on our good friend Bill Thomson, senior partner in the legal firm of Read and Read. Thomson engaged a rising young barrister, Stephen Charles, who later was to become one of the Bar's most distinguished silks.

On the day, we gathered at the Port Melbourne Court and waited for the usual run of drunk and disorderlies, petty thefts and assaults to go through. Bill Thomson took David aside and told him to plead guilty.

'If you do that', he said, 'we can make a deal with the police and you will only get a suspended sentence. Look, you can't take any risks. If you get a conviction against your name you will never be able to become a lawyer.'

David was studying law-arts at Monash and the Thomson warning was dire, indeed.

'I can't plead guilty', David said.

'Why not?', roared Bill.

'Because I'm not guilty', replied David. 'I haven't done anything wrong. We were entitled to report a speech at Monash. It is simply a matter of freedom of speech. We weren't corrupting anyone. If I confess that I'm guilty I deny everything I stand for.'

'You will go to gaol.'

'I can't help that', said David.

'Well, there's nothing much that I can do, is there?', sighed Bill.

David had lined up a distinguished panel for his defence. First wicket down was Phillip Adams, film producer, columnist, advertising executive. Second wicket down was Ian Turner, professor of history at Monash. Third wicket down was Dr Bob

Birrell, sociologist. Phillip Adams, in his traditional black skivvy and black trousers, plus sports coat, turned up in his red Maserati sports car.

We waited and waited, becoming more and more worried. The petty thefts and other cases dragged on all morning and into the early afternoon. Finally, when our case did come up, things looked even worse than we feared. The magistrate was a little man, aged about 50, with horn-rimmed glasses. Marie nodded. Oh yes, we could see precisely why the police chose Port Melbourne. Here was the very magistrate they wanted. He looked the perfect pillar of Victorian respectability. David was practically in gaol already.

The charges were read, and Stephen Charles brought out the argument that *Lot's Wife* was restricted to a university audience and could hardly be described as a family newspaper. Students were open to every kind of literature and it was unlikely that this journal would corrupt them. He called Phillip Adams.

'Mr Adams, did you think those articles in *Lot's Wife* were obscene?', the magistrate asked.

No, he did not. Phillip was brilliant. He talked at length about how these articles were important for the enlightenment of a community that had been almost starved of sexual education. They were not obscene: they were merely statements of sexual fact and frank descriptions of sexual activities. If such writing was obscene, obscenity was in the eye of the beholder.

The 'nasty' little magistrate listened intently, then commented.

'Thank you, Mr Adams. I have been waiting a very long time for someone to define obscenity for me. The police have never done it. As far as I'm concerned the case is dismissed.'

There was a stunned silence. The police had been geared for a noble battle. Now suddenly it was all over, practically before they had started.

It was nearly 5 p.m. Phillip Adams's day was ruined. Just before he stepped into his Maserati he looked at Marie and looked at me.

'Have you got any more like that at home?'

It was a turning point for David. He was a rebel, but his anger became much better controlled. He never did become a lawyer. History was his first love and his particular passion was historical Melbourne. A history of the Melbourne City Council earned him a doctor of philosophy at Melbourne University.

How else do I remember the 1970s, that passionate period when Australia threw off the mores of a by-gone era and appeared to grow up? I remember it particularly for the end of Robert Paton Dalziel, dear friend since school days.

The outstanding trait of R. P. Dalziel was this: he never did anything that was predictable. When J. R. Darling asked him what he proposed to do after he left Geelong Grammar, Dalziel gave the opposite answer to the pious one expected.

'Make a lot of money', said he.

However, first he intended to study law.

'But you don't want to be a lawyer', we all said.

'No, but like learning to swim, there are occasions when it can be extraordinarily handy.'

His father, the old sea captain, had left him barely 5000 pounds. Dalziel's theory was that the 5000 would be just enough to pay his way through Trinity College at Melbourne University. It was more than enough. Even when he was sweating over torts and property and criminal law, Bob was studying the stock market and doing very well, indeed.

Come 1950–1951 there was a boom in uranium shares. Brokers were taking on staff, so Dalziel, the young lawyer, managed to get a job with Wallace Smith and Company. He had a natural gift for sharebroking, a real nose for finance, and he succeeded quickly. In 1954 he bought a seat on the Melbourne Stock Exchange, went into partnership with John Davies and started the firm of Davies and Dalziel.

Everything about Dalziel was neat. His features were small and neat, perhaps a trifle French, indicating his ancestry. His hair was very short – the sea captain would have approved of that – and invariably he wore a double-breasted, grey flannel suit and a black tie. He faced a thousand questions about that tie.

'In mourning, Bob? Have you lost a relative?'

'I am in mourning today for the economic policy of the Government.'

Or, when he became tired of that: 'I wear a black tie as a gesture to efficiency. When I get up in the morning what tie I wear is one less decision I have to make'.

The real reason was he hated any personal display, any kind of publicity. He wanted to be a back room operator, a manipulator. Flamboyance was not for him. Dalziel did not need a tie to put on a show, the show came from his personality and his sharp mind. He was a member of the Melbourne Club and his favourite game at lunch there was to taunt the other members. He would observe the tenor of the conversation – maybe the members were discussing the latest strike of the waterside workers, the need for banning the Communist Party or the awful R certificate movies depicting males and females copulating – then automatically take the opposite view, until the crusty members were very nearly beating the table with their fists.

Yes, he was unpredictable in everything. He made money, a lot of it. Just after his fortieth birthday, he telephoned me.

'I've retired.'

'You're joking.'

'No, I'm not. I finished at Davies and Dalziel this afternoon.'

'Tell me, Bob. Perhaps I can help. You've done something terrible, haven't you?'

'No, I haven't. I've just retired. There's no need any more to go on with sharebroking. It's a bore just doing the same thing over and over again. I've got enough money now, so I'm going to do nothing. That requires a very special skill, doing nothing.'

For a time Dalziel really did retire. He considered the mere making of money, once you had enough, a pointless exercise. In 1965 he bought a pearl-shell business in the Solomon Islands. This was very romantic, a throw back to his origins, we felt, a hankering after the seafaring life of his father. It proved to be a good way of losing money and he sold out in 1968.

Actually Dalziel did a great many things. He was a considerable force behind the scenes in the Liberal Party. Again this was his style, to be an influence without showing his nose. He tortured his fellow Liberals just as he tortured the members of the Melbourne Club.

In 1968 Roy Everard Ross, the quarry king, died and left nearly 9 million dollars to charity. Bob became the trustee of the R. E. Ross Foundation and chairman of Hillview Quarries. He set about his work diligently and many an orphanage for boys and girls, many an organisation such as the Multiple Sclerosis Society, received his cheque for thousands.

Now that he was in the quarry business he was the target for every environment group and good earth enthusiast. They won few arguments with R. P. Dalziel. He produced photographs that invariably proved his quarrying operations left the country better than he had found it.

In 1972 he went into the Freemasons Hospital to have a kidney removed. Yes, he could live on one kidney. But cancer was there, and he knew it was just a matter of time.

At the beginning of 1977 the doctors told him the time was quite definite: six months. As it turned out the time was a year.

'The reaper will not take me', he said, 'until the Government has abolished the inheritance tax'.

He liked the idea of a financial reason for staying alive and he managed his illness well until the Government bill went through. He was an extraordinary man. At all times he knew what the cancer was doing to his body, yet his good humour was unfailing, his brilliant, agile mind forever probing. Even when he was in the Austin Hospital, paralysed from the neck down, senior Liberals called him for advice.

I went to see him at the Austin Hospital almost every second day. Only once did I hear him complain. He cursed that dying was such an undignified business. He did not lose dignity in my eyes. Finally the pain became too much.

'I want to die', he told me. 'Find someone who will finish me off.'

I rang doctor after doctor.

'Can't we give him something? Surely there is a drug, an unnoticeable drug that will take him away easily, quietly?'

The doctors told me it was part of the Hippocratic oath that they heal people. It was not their job to murder.

'This is not murder, this is human relief.'

Only one said he would go to see Dalziel, but he would promise absolutely nothing. Dalziel died a few days later, on 13 February 1978. I don't know whether that doctor did anything. I did not ask him and the subject was never discussed.

Bob's wife, Elizabeth, endured all this. A flinty character, she was as brave as he. Soon after the funeral she said there was a history in her family of cardiac asthma and she would be dead within a year. Her prediction was precisely correct. They left two sons, Andrew and Matthew. The Dalziels I will always remember as my people of the 1970s.

Kate, David, Jane and Sarah, c. 1966.

Sarah and Kate welcome our exchange student, Vivien Kane, 1971.

Vivien Kane.

The Dunstan tandem team.

A triumph of the USA Bikecentennial, 1976: reaching the highest point on the transamerican trail, 3500 metres above sea level.

For Marie sometimes the Bikecentennial was sheer exhaustion.

Marie Rose wading through the floods in Kansas.

Friendly dogs in Kentucky.

End of the Bikecentennial.

Rodin plus Hook on twenty-five
years as a columnist, 1975.

'BAD NIGHT PLAYING THE TABLES, SIR?!'

How Jeff saw my journalistic
activities in Las Vegas, 1981.

The Carlton and United
commemorative beer can: more
trouble than it was worth.

A warning: the car park at Carlton and United headquarters is not for bikes.

The family, Easter 1990. Back row: Paula, Peter, Sarah, Steve, K. D. with Zoe, Andrew and David. Second back row: Jack, Charlie, Sam, Kate holding George, and Jane. Second front row: Tom, Marie Rose and Hannah. Front row: Tim, Isabel, Ned and Henry.

CHAPTER THIRTEEN

Pedalling passion

You have heard of born-again Christians. Born-again cyclists are similar. My conversion came on an autumn afternoon in 1964. Melbourne had a massive transport strike: no trains, no trams, no buses. Our house at Central Park Road, East Malvern, was 12 kilometres from Flinders Street. Just to write a funny newspaper column about alternative forms of transport I borrowed a bicycle from Malvern Star and rode to town.

It was not funny at all. I never got over it. Getting to town, battling with traffic or public transport had always been the most depressing part of the day. But this was enchanting, every day pedalling through parks, riding alongside the Yarra, dodging in and out of all the back streets of Prahran. Every day a different route. I spotted all sorts of fascinating buildings, interesting façades, wonderful chimneys and urns atop nineteenth-century parapets. I had never noticed them when in a car. What's more, there were the smells every night. I could enjoy the wonderful dishes the Greeks, the Lebanese and the Italians were having for dinner. Then it was quick. I discovered to my amazement that the bicycle, door to door, was faster than car, tram or train by a good ten minutes.

My bicycle in the office garage was the only one there, a lonely thing. In 1964 such behaviour was rare, indeed. This man, if not a ratbag, was an eccentric, a nut – a bicycle nut. There were even kindly queries and suggestions from good friends. Were my finances going badly? Could they lend me a little money to tide me over? Yet like any member of a minority I did not think I was a nut. It was the rest of the world that was strange. If the rest of the world was logical and sensible it would give up the pollution-breathing, human-killing internal combustion engine and ride the bicycle.

There was a curious hostility to the bicycle on the road. Motorists wound down their windows and shouted abuse. 'Get off the road, you fucking idiot', was a common, kindly cry of encouragement. One afternoon in Prahran four youths in a Holden opened the doors of their car as they went past and tried to wipe me off. I had a little rear-vision mirror attached to my glasses, which had been made for a dentist, so I saw what was happening and fled to the footpath.

A pioneer of the bicycle was Victoria's Minister for Transport, Brian Dixon. He asked me to be foundation president of the Victorian Bicycle Institute. At this time there were no facilities for bicycles, no bicycle paths. We had the theory that no Melburnian was more than 5 kilometres from a railway station. If only we could encourage public transport to carry bicycles or to provide good lock-up facilities at railway stations we could improve physical fitness and at the same time solve Melbourne's traffic problems. Hostility remained. There was little interest from the railways, nil from the Country Roads Board or the Road Traffic Authority and I remember the Chairman of the Board of Works, Mr Croxford, telling me that there was no place for the bicycle on Victoria's roads and that if he had his way the bicycle would be banned.

The immediate effect of taking up regular bicycle riding was a 6-kilogram loss in weight. Never since have I had to worry about weight problems. I used to suffer arthritic pains in the hip and knees. These disappeared.

The most frequent line of objection I received was: 'Frankly, I think you're crazy. I'd ride a bike myself, but not in all this traffic'.

Here is my survival record for twenty-four years of bicycling over more than 200 000 kilometres: no serious accidents; a few minor spills. One day my tyre got caught in the tram lines in Toorak Road and I went straight over the handlebars. Everybody in Melbourne does that – once! It is not an experience you wish to repeat. Another time I hit a car door and almost landed in the arms of a lady Jaguar driver. You are also inclined to do that once, and again you learn quickly. The biggest danger is the non-looking car-door-opener.

I belong to a little dining group called the Stringer's Club. Every year we give an award to the restaurant that has provided us with the greatest enjoyment during the year. In 1977 we gave our award, a silver pie, to Clichy restaurant in Collingwood. We thought it would be a nice idea to celebrate the occasion properly so I took along a bottle of Veuve Cliquot. The proprietor of Clichy, the ebullient Sigmund Jorgensen, was so pleased he opened another bottle of the widow Cliquot, and another, and another. When I returned to my bicycle, which was waiting patiently in Peel Street, I found it would not stay still. I put a leg over it and fell on the other side. I tried from that side and again fell on the other side. At the third go I managed to get on and wobbled home to South Yarra. Next morning I found I could not get out of bed. I did not ride again for six weeks. Lesson three: alcohol and bikes do not mix.

In Los Angeles in 1980 I bought one of the new, fancy bicycle computers. It did everything. It gave the speed, maximum speed, daily distance, total distance, time, pedal rate and more. I took this wondrous thing to the highest hill I could find. Down I went, my eyes on the bicycle computer, fascinated as my speed mounted to 30, 40, 45, 60, 65 kilometres an hour. Suddenly in front of me there was a semi-trailer, parked right across the road. I threw the bicycle sideways and hit the bitumen. The result: two broken ribs and a lacerated face. I was not wearing a helmet. I was only going out for five minutes so why worry? Lesson four: always watch what you are doing and never venture out the gate without a helmet.

But I believe people can survive almost anywhere on a bicycle, and I believe that with slow, careful travel I am safer than in a car. It takes several months to get used to the proximity of fast-moving cars and maybe a year to become truly traffic canny. There is the fun of studying maps and devising fascinating routes, through parks, over foot bridges, down lanes to avoid traffic. Oddly enough, the thicker the traffic, the safer the cyclist is. It is the high-speed highways with no side safety lanes that inspire the greatest terror.

The true joy of cycling is getting out in the country and touring.

It is here that you discover what a remarkably efficient instrument the modern geared bicycle has become. You might start by riding 5, 10 or 15 kilometres. This will grow to 20, then forty. Once you have gone that far the rest is easy. One hundred to 200 kilometres a day is within your reach.

In 1976 Marie and I went on our ultimate bike ride, across the United States. Freda Morgan, wife of John Morgan, Editor-in-Chief of the Herald and Weekly Times, read about the projected ride in a magazine. At first she had a hankering to go herself. This was not possible, but John Morgan saw the potential for a good story, so why not dispatch Dunstan, with cartoonist Jeff to do the illustrations?

All sorts of ideas had been worked out to celebrate the bicentennial of the United States. One of them was a great hand-holding ceremony, a human chain from coast to coast. This did not eventuate but the bike ride did. The ride was the idea of two young American couples, Dan and Lys Burden and Greg and June Siple. The plot for the ride really began in 1972 when the Siples and the Burdens decided on perhaps the most astonishing bike route ever, from the top of Alaska right down to the bottom of Argentina. The Siples made it all the way. The trip took them three and a half years. Dan Burden covered 15 200 kilometres then succumbed to hepatitis in Argentina. Dan was a lovely, laid-back character, 191 centimetres tall, with a big moustache. Greg Siple was famous for his 'Eskimo roll'. With his feet strapped into his pedals he could do a complete Catherine wheel on his bike. Hands on ground, over, Eureka.

We received the complete plan and route for the bicentennial bike ride, called, believe it or not, Bikecentennial 76. It was formidable. Start at Reedsport, Oregon, work our way north to Missoula, Montana, near the Canadian border, follow the line of the Rocky Mountains south to Pueblo, Colorado, then continue down into the plains of Kansas, and finally head in a straight line across to Virginia and the Atlantic Ocean – some 6800 kilometres, at an average of about 90 kilometres a day.

We trained for months in preparation. We did much of our riding on the road from Moe to Walhalla in Victoria. The spectacular part was Mt Erica and a 260-metre rise known to all bicyclists as Shit Hill. This was because the bikers always made the inevitable remark when first they gazed upon it, 'Aw, shit!'. We were to discover later that Shit Hill was a nothing, barely worth a raised eyebrow.

Enthusiasts came from all over the world to take part in the big Bikecentennial ride. There were contingents from England, Japan and Germany and an astonishing 160 people from Holland. There were twenty-six from Australia and we all flew together in the one Qantas aircraft, our bicycles stowed below in cardboard cartons. Our actual luggage for the three months' ride was very little because all of it had to be carried on our bikes. I remember saying to Marie: 'Darling, guess how many pairs of shoes you will be able to take? One!'.

There was a last-minute message from the most famous cyclist of all, Sir Hubert Opperman. He was in the habit of sending what he called Oppygrams. This one read: 'Eat little and often, look out for maniacs going downhill and keep your chamois well greased'.

Already we had been educated in the mysteries of the chamois. Bicycling shorts, like old footy boots, have their shortcomings. One never wears underpants. The shorts must be worn next to the skin. Sewn into the crotch is a leather insert. For a happy crotch this must be kept well greased with Vaseline. Marie and other ladies in the party looked at the unlovely shorts and said, 'Nothing in God's earth will ever get me into a pair of those'. They were all wearing them within three days.

We had a stopover at Honolulu and the full team took time off to sit on the beach at Waikiki. It was then that Marie gained a faint idea of what makes up a true cyclist. The scene out in front was one of the most beautiful on earth. Over yonder was Diamond Head, the sun was shining out of a stainless sky, the sea was even bluer than Elizabeth Taylor's eyes and young women of every shade and hue were stretched out on the sand, wearing very little. The conversation went like this.

'I don't reckon myself there's anything better than a Campagnolo derailleur.'

'What do you use with it?'

'Aw, a 14-32 sprocket. Works pretty well.'

'I got a Shimano, myself – 14-34.'

'A ten-speed?'

'No, a fifteen-speed. I put on a little twenty-eight chain wheel.
We'll need 'em.'

Nothing really diverts true bicycle nuts. They didn't even notice
Waikiki.

We started from Reedsport in Oregon on 18 May. We went
in groups of twelve or thirteen. In our group there were nine
Americans, a 20-year-old Englishman, on leave from Cambridge,
and four Australians, including Marie, myself and Jeff Hook. The
fourth was Fred Smith, a 50-year-old plasterer from Alexandra
in Victoria and an ex-professional cyclist.

It was a fascinating group. There was Don Hartley, 66, an ex-
employee of the Santa Fe Railroad and his wife Norma, fifty-
four. Don was from Tennessee and had a lovely Southern accent.
He had a passion for pie, which he pronounced 'pah'. 'Ah'll just
have a li'l piece of blueberry pah', he would murmur. He loved
strawberry pah, apple pah, pecan pah, blueberry pah . . . But 'The
pah ah'm lookin' for is a hoolaberry pah', he always said.

We wondered and wondered about hoolaberry pie. We even
asked for it in shops, but nobody had heard of it. Eventually we
discovered it was a myth, like Norman Lindsay's Magic Pudding.
Hoolaberry pie was the ultimate pie, the pie of Don's dreams.
And Don was a dreamer. He took his riding slowly. He was the
tortoise that always got there faster than the young ones – except
that he took no notice of directions and often went the wrong
way. His wife had a whistle, so whenever Don was out of sight
there would be this blast from it. We thought it was like the mating
call between two birds.

As a 51-year-old it was interesting to discover that age did not
matter. There were teenagers and there were riders over seventy.
There was even one old fellow, named Clarence Pickard, who
was 86 and turned up in a silver pith helmet and neck-to-knee
underwear. Clarence lasted for 1600 kilometres before he went
down with bronchitis.

Then there was Cyril Henry from Dublin. Cyril was 66, red
in the face and had a shock of white hair that stood up like
Insulwool. Cyril thought the ride actually started from Portland,
so he arrived there ready to go, only to discover his group was
leaving the following morning from Reedsport, 250 kilometres to
the south. Instead of taking a bus he hopped on his bike, gear
and all, and rode the 250 kilometres in ten hours.

'It's a wee bit tiring when you are not sure of the way', he said later.

The ride would have been easier had there been a gentle start. By the third day we were right into the mountains and we had to climb 1525 metres to get through the Santiam Pass. Originally we were supposed to go through the McKenzie Pass but this was under 8 metres of snow. It was then we discovered how unprepared we were.

Our panniers were fully loaded with 18 to 20 kilograms of gear, plus sleeping-bags. Pain came first to the knees, then to the back and ultimately to the cheeks of our behinds, intense pain so that we wanted to stand all the time. I developed blisters on my posterior. If any cyclist was going to give it up it was going to be here. Marie showed extraordinary courage. She was ill and the changes in diet took a terrible toll. Age 50 is an unpredictable time in the female life cycle. Marie found the menopause hard enough without the Rockies as well, but she struggled up that mountain. Fred Smith was the strongest; he went up, he went down. He even pedalled beside some of the weaker riders and gave them a push.

There could be no delays because a new group passed through every twenty-four hours, and every night the bike inn was booked. A bike inn was a church hall, a church, a gymnasium, a tent, a municipal building and, on our third night, actually a Benedictine monastery. Several times we slept in Indian tepees or wigwams. That was a rare experience. Tepees are made with skins stretched across long poles that come to an apex. Because Indians always light fires in their tepees there has to be a gap at the top to release the smoke. The 'chimney' is also a convenient inlet for any available rain.

Sleeping in bike inns was extremely good for straightening the back. We had tiny blow-up back-packing mattresses, designed to provide comfort only from the top of the shoulder down to the suffering behind. On a hard, slippery floor it required a miracle of judgement to remain poised and asleep on this little concoction. As for a pillow – one filled one's sleeping-bag cover with one's track suit.

Then, of course, we all slept, males and females, in the one room. The young, we noticed, paired off very early and rides of even up to 160 kilometres did not diminish their ardour. Ardour could come at any hour; say, at two or three in the morning. Marie, Jeff and I would be fascinated by noises of sleeping-bags unzipping and zipping, followed by even more eloquent noises, which reverberated through the bike inn.

One of our team was Chip Haines, a cartoonist from Florida. He had a marvellous bicycle that had cost him 850 dollars, with every conceivable gadget including compass and thermometer. Every night Chip sat cross-legged like a Sioux brave in front of his sleeping-bag and, regardless of all noise around him, slipped into meditation, a total trance. No doubt it helped solve his problems. Chip was busy reading *Zen and the Art of Motor Cycle Maintenance*. This was the story of a father and son and friend who were touring through the mountains of the United States, precisely where we were. The message was this: when toiling, straining up the mountain, the object is not just to reach the top but also to enjoy and observe on the way.

After Oregon, we pedalled north through Montana to Missoula, then south through Yellowstone National Park in Wyoming. The sign outside Yellowstone Park read: 'Beware of Grizzly Bears – They are Dangerous. Keep Your Windows Closed at All Times'. This was disconcerting news. It brought to mind the old lion park joke, 'Englishmen on bicycles admitted free'.

We pedalled for 35 kilometres through Yellowstone and spotted bison, elk and antelope but mercifully not a single bear. A ranger told us he had not seen one for two years. But several days later one of the cross-country riders lost his bicycle for twenty hours. He thought it had been stolen so informed the police. They found it in the bush, covered with scratch marks. A bear, looking for food in his pannier bags, had carried it there. Unquestionably it was the strangest bear story since Davy Crockett.

The ride was carefully charted along back roads: no main highways and never did we enter towns with populations larger than 35 000. For the first 2400 kilometres we seemed rarely out of national parks, State forests and wilderness reserves. I thought it the most continuously beautiful country I had ever seen. I still dream of the calm and the eternal quiet of those Rockies, the scent of Ponderosa pines and the urgent, rushing rivers of Oregon.

Sometimes we were in sunshine, often we rode in rain and for two days we pedalled through falling snow. However, not rain, snow or even hail is the enemy of the cyclist. The greatest menace is wind. In Wyoming the wind came up daily at 10 a.m. precisely, almost as if God had suddenly thrown a switch. We rose before dawn in an attempt to defeat it, but as soon as that wind came up cycling speed dropped to little over walking pace. The only solution was draughting: cyclists pedalling in a human chain, nose wheel no more than 3 centimetres behind the wheel in front, and everyone taking turns of being leader and accepting the full force of the wind. The weather was anything but kind to the skin. We started to look like a bunch of Navajos. Marie's greatest problem was her lips, which became so sore she finally had to cycle in a surgical mask.

We crossed the great divide of the Rockies four times, but the hardest day was crossing the Hoosier Pass at 3500 metres. We started at 7.30 a.m., rode 80 kilometres before we tackled the pass and then climbed 1300 metres. All day we pushed, averaging, it seemed, about 6 kilometres an hour. Our bicycles had three chain wheels on the front and a cluster of five gears at the back, giving a combination of fifteen gears. We pedalled up the Hoosier Pass in bottom gear, feet going round like food mixers. It was nearly 6 p.m. by the time we reached the top. Many times on the way up, tempers had become strained. At the top Marie put down her bike and started kicking it.

'What are you doing that for?'

'I hate the bloody thing', she said.

But then exhilaration, a feeling of achievement took over. We had a formal leader who had been trained for the job by the Bikecentennial organisation. He was a remarkable young man called David Canha, 25 years old and a student marine biologist. He had carried 200 crackers in his panniers all the way from Reedsport. He lit them and their noise reverberated loudly as we all cheered. You would have thought we had climbed Mt Everest. We looked down at the most majestic of sights, rocky, snow-covered peaks going for ever into the distance.

From then on it was all downhill to Pueblo, riding marvellous descents that went for 40 to 45 kilometres, free-wheeling, with the wind in our faces. Before, I had always ridden behind Marie to make sure nothing went wrong – respectfully behind, the way Prince Philip always walks behind Queen Elizabeth, with his hands behind his back. But now Marie was becoming very fit, indeed, and it was no longer a case of staying respectfully behind; it was the very devil keeping up with her. She showed particular skills on gravel. Her method of coping with dangerous gravel roads was not to hesitate, not to go slowly, but instead to pedal full-speed ahead. Invariably she arrived ten minutes before everybody else. The group called her the Gravel Queen.

Jeff was a very strong and highly entertaining bike rider. Occasionally at the height of his sufferings he gave vent to anger. For example, at Wisdom, Montana, named in honour of the supposed sagacity of President Jefferson, our bike inn was the show grounds, and Jeff's bedroom was a cattle stall. He was so enraged he proposed to write to President Nixon to give him a piece of wisdom. He never did. Jeff's rage always subsided quickly. Sadly we had to say goodbye to him in Pueblo. He had an important appointment back home in Melbourne: the birth of his daughter Sarah Jane.

The food was interesting. We developed voracious, teenage appetites. Oppy had given the advice eat little and often. The terror of long-distance cyclists is 'hunger flatness', and it is true that the body is similar to a paddle steamer: once the fuel stops burning the steam dies. We ate more in a day than in a week at home. Our handlebar bags were filled with nuts, raisins, Hershey bars, M & Ms, jelly beans, Granola bars, sesame seed bars. We learned how to steer and handle gears with one hand and eat with the other.

We paid for our meals in advance, 5 dollars a day to cover the lot. This money we pooled and it was amazing how far it went. Usually we cooked our own food. Fred Smith carried the large aluminium pot, Dave Canha carried the little fuel stove, the rest of us carried the other necessary items. We had a one-pot cookbook that detailed all the health-giving recipes that could be contrived in one saucepan.

My most vivid memory is of peanut butter. Americans were obsessed by peanut butter: it was a special elixir, treated with all the national reverence that Australians accord Vegemite. They purchased it in 4.5-litre jars and ate it with everything, even putting it in porridge. Sandwiches at lunch could only be described as breathtaking in every sense of the word. The idea was to take a layer of brown bread, spread it with a centimetre or two of peanut butter, cover that with honey, add dried fruit and maybe sliced apple, celery or tomato, a slab of cheese or salami, and complete the internal bliss with some slices of banana, then apply the lid, another slice of brown bread. The calories involved could not be reckoned even on a computer.

Of course, the group always looked out for good pie stops. After we passed the half-way mark we met groups travelling from east to west, so word of the absolutely best pie towns and cafés was passed up and down the line.

There was a rest day every ten days. This gave us an opportunity to meet riders from other groups. For example, we met Albert Schultze, a welder from Alice Springs. Albert was a marvellous character; he utterly fascinated the Americans. Albert had a great beard like that of John O'Hara Burke of Burke and Wills fame. He wore a blue beret and a faded pair of buttoned up the front overalls. He smoked an old pipe – some achievement when riding a bike – and attached to his bike was a fair dinkum, blackened bushie's billy. Every so often he stopped and boiled up a cup of tea. He carried his water in a milk bottle and most of his gear balanced precariously on his handlebars.

Albert's sister, Wilma, was there, too. Wilma had a road-house at Buchan in East Gippsland. Wilma and Albert had not seen each other for twenty-four years so she talked her brother into making the trip. Albert thought they would be doing it by motorbike and he was startled when he found out there were no motors involved, only muscles. Wilma was an indomitable rider. Her fame spread way ahead of her. Always she was the perfect lady. I remember Dan Burden, the tour director, telling us some time before we met her, 'There's a lady, honest, who is riding the trail on a lady's bicycle in skirt, nylon stockings and high-heeled shoes'.

Joe Martin was another unusual character. Joe was an air traffic controller who worked for the Department of Transport in Melbourne. Bikecentennial offered two different trips: the slow trip of 65 to 145 kilometres a day or the fast trip of 160 to 225 kilometres a day. Joe, 58 years old, chose the fast trip. He sailed past us in Colorado. He was carrying almost no gear, beyond a change of clothing. He didn't even have a sleeping-bag. We asked him how he endured sleeping on some of the hard floors of bike inns. Joe had the answer. He pumped up the three spare tyres he was carrying.

After leaving the mountains of Colorado we were into the plains of Kansas. There were not only fields of wheat, but oceans of wheat, oceans with curved horizons going on for ever, and we realised this was the true wealth of the United States. Now we had to start riding at 5.30 a.m. to avoid the heat. We pedalled off in the blackness, then saw the dawn come up a blaze of red, spreading over the gold of the wheat. After days of near 40-degree temperatures the rains came, and it rained steadily for three days - 280 millimetres of it - causing a dam to burst at a town charmingly called El Dorado. We packed all our spare clothing in plastic carry bags and our sleeping-bags in plastic rubbish bags. Rain seeped everywhere and our handlebar bags filled like little lakes. Water first seeped down our necks, then penetrated our 'waterproof' trousers, trickled down to our knees and finally filled our boots. Once we were thoroughly wet it did not matter any more. After the dam burst the roads were under water and all one day we had to walk, water up to our knees. Fred Smith was so terrified of water damaging the bottom bracket of his bike, he carried his machine, plus pannier bags, on his back. I took a photograph of Marie, very wet, indeed, standing in front of a sign that said, 'Be Thankful to God'.

On, on into southern Missouri and the Ozarks. This was the country that inspired Al Capp's comic strip 'Li'l Abner', and it revealed once again a very important truth: there is no such place as the United States. It is really fifty different countries with fifty different accents. In the Ozarks it was definitely a different language.

One day we met an elderly gentleman in front of a grocery store.

'Whar yur headin'?'

'Yorktown, Virginia', we told him.

'Whar yur frum?'

'Melbourne, Australia.'

'Orrrrstralia, huh? Thar sure is a furr peace.'

It took us an hour to work out what he'd said. He meant that Australia was a far-off place.

The locals were sensitive about their comic-strip image. They refused to concede that they had a distinctive way of speaking, which was really a type of eighteenth-century English. Their answer was always this: 'We ain't got no accent. It is them furriners that's got the accent'.

One needed a glossary to understand the language. A Springfield, Missouri, editor, Dale Freeman, provided us with a few essential definitions:

tar   A motor car rides on tars.

rang   When they got married he put a rang on her finger.

crame   Everyone loves vanilla ice crame.

are   He shot an are into the air, it fell to earth Ah know not whir.

dork   It gets real dork when the sun goes dahn.

grub   He grub her from behind.

hep   He can't hep it, he was borned attaway.

flare   A rose is the purtiest flare there is.

walled   That girl of hern was too walled (wild) for mah boy.

yurp   France is in Yurp.

There were nice phrases, too: 'Duller than a widder woman's axe', 'Scarce as preachers in paradise' and 'He looked like he'd been chawin' terbac an spittin' agin the wind'. This was interesting. I particularly liked the fellow I met in a bar at Pittsburg, Missouri.

'Say someh'n. Keep on talkin' thar. Ah lake to har yuh cos you talk so funny', he said.

The Ozarks had not entirely escaped the rich stream of modern culture – Big Boy Hamburgers, Burger King, Colonel Sanders and McDonald's – but much of the region was primitive. Several times out on the road we came across Mennonites, members of a Christian sect that spurned the twentieth century and everything associated with it. Some were in horse-drawn covered wagons. We saw a father, mother and children in a horse-drawn buggy. Father had a beard, big hat and rough trousers supported by braces. Mother looked like an eighteenth-century Quaker, in long, grey dress, with sleeves down to the wrists and a close-fitting bonnet.

We crossed the Mississippi and pushed on into Kentucky, which we had thought was the land of blue grass and racehorses. We saw few racehorses but an astonishing number of dogs. I have put up with cringing dogs in Indonesia, Aboriginal dogs north of Tennant Creek, stray dogs in Port Moresby and a whole cacophony of dogs at Cruft's Dog Show in London, but nothing to compare with the vast kennel of Missouri and Kentucky. The average farm in those States had about five dogs, and four out of the five detested bicyclists. I have consulted many authorities on why barkers do not like bikers. The most popular theory is this: dogs are fascinated by the sparkle of light on the moving spokes. Rubbish! They jump to the attack before they even see the light of the spokes. A more plausible theory is that they are irritated by supersonic sounds given off by the bicycles or by the clicking of the free wheel. Maybe. I believe the dog reasons like this: people who ride bikes when there are other more comfortable modes of transport are fair game; they are almost helpless and it is fun to watch their terror.

Repeatedly I was attacked by dogs. One member of our party was attacked by two dogs at the same time. He went off the road, hit a log, crashed on his back and was out of action for several days. Beagles were shocking, Dobermanns were terrifying and almost all terriers were anti-bicycle. Worst were German shepherds. The jumbo-sized dogs like Great Danes and St Bernards, oddly enough, loved us.

Some riders used their bicycle pumps to try to beat off the dogs, like cavalrymen wielding swords in the Charge of the Light Brigade. Albert Schultze carried a large mallet and biffed the dogs over the head. The popular weapon, however, was a pressure can of anti-dog spray. It was called Halt, sold for 2 dollars 50 cents and was standard issue for posties in the United States. The label on the can read: 'Contains capsaicin. Strongly irritating to eyes, nose and skin. Will instantly repel and subdue dogs when sprayed into face and eyes'. There was one strapping group leader who carried her can of Halt on her belt, like Jesse James toted his six-gun. She could knock down a German shepherd at ten paces.

Marie would not have a bar of this. She said it was cruel to the dogs. Bravely she would stop, get off her bike and talk to them in a Southern accent. It seemed to work every time, and soon tails were wagging. The only trouble was the dogs fell in love with her. On one occasion a German shepherd followed her for over 40 kilometres.

Everything about Kentucky was unexpected. We had not expected to see such poverty. We saw houses with earthen floors, no appliances and outside pit lavatories. Unemployment in some areas was up around 20 per cent. I have never seen so much rubbish;

the citizens just left it in bags by the side of the road. I later asked Dan Burden, 'Why did you chart the route through Kentucky?'.

'We took you through some of the best parts of the States, so we thought you should see some of the other side too', he replied.

There was another thing we had discovered. Drinking saloons were common in the West, but once you crossed the Mississippi they all but disappeared. We cycled 1600 kilometres without seeing a pub and that is hard for anyone on a bike. But I thought all would be well in Kentucky. This, surely, was one of the whisky capitals of the world. Everybody had heard of Kentucky bourbon. Our route kept clear of all that. We found there were 120 counties in Kentucky and ninety-two of them were dry, as the result of local option.

We were in a very dry town, Hodgenville, Kentucky, when it occurred to me that there must be a story in this. Who would tell it to me? Ah yes, go to see the local newspaper editor; he would have to be a good drinker. So I called in at the local paper and asked to see the editor. Soon a young lady came out and said, 'Miss Phillips will see you now'.

Miss Phillips was tall and grey haired. As I asked questions about the licensing laws of Kentucky she began to look more and more severe, until finally she said: 'Before we proceed with this interview I think there is something I should make perfectly clear. I have been a total abstainer for thirty years. I will show you something'.

She stood up and revealed that one leg was in a brace.

'I was knocked down by a drunken driver when I was 21 years old.'

That put an end to my inquiries, but I did discover that Elijah Craig was credited with the invention of bourbon back in 1785. He sold it for 25 cents a gallon. It is one of the ironies of life that Elijah Craig was a hell-fire Baptist preacher. As for the famous moonshine, it had gone into a decline. We were told that in the 1950s moonshine (illegal liquor) produced in the hills made up 20 per cent of all the Kentucky whisky produced. Now it was hard to get, even a novelty.

We read in the Louisville *Courier Journal* that the security system around the mountains was splendid. When a 'Fed' or anyone who looked even faintly like a cop or a 'revenooer' was in the district, the thing to do was to ring a dinner bell. The alarm would be picked up by others, until the entire area echoed to the slow, metallic clank of dinner bells.

We rode through West Virginia and Virginia. The countryside was a lush green, elms and beeches throwing leafy shade right across the road. It all looked historic, expensive and luxurious. The farmhouses tended to be white-columned, four-storied *Gone with the Wind* mansions, with stables twice the size of mere houses back in Missouri.

Suddenly it was all over. We finished at a place called Camp Chickahominy on a lake surrounded by a million mosquitoes. It was named after a long-forgotten tribe of Indians. For us it meant the end of the transamerican trail, a time of sadness. I felt I had lost my freedom. I could have gone right on pedalling up the East Coast to Canada.

Inside the camp, waiting to greet us, was Dan Burden, the astonishing man who dreamed up the crazy idea of sending thousands of people on push-bikes across the nation. He had prepared a beautiful victory cake in the shape of the United States. It depicted all the States and the Bikecentennial route and gave the total distance, 4246.8 miles. This he served with ice-cream and punch. Marie and I were left with a deep respect for our Malvern Stars. They had carried us, plus our luggage, all that way, through snow, heat and flood. I worked out our times and average speeds and estimated that our suffering pedals had turned over 1 448 000 times.

It was a United States far different from what we had expected. How shall I put it? Before, I had spent my time in big cities such as New York, Los Angeles and San Francisco. Rural America was another place again. The people were much simpler, even naive. Small-town America was not rich, the houses never Hollywood grand. We were told we would be mugged, our bicycles stolen. That never happened. We became so trusting we left them unlocked outside cafés and stores.

Religion was very strong. In each town there were always churches, expensive churches in the main street, and often these were Baptist. There would be a bookshop, but inevitably it was a religious bookshop. I found it hard to buy a newspaper in many towns and almost impossible to get a news magazine like *Time* or *Newsweek*. The towns were introspective, calm and often beautiful. As I cycled I thought: 'These are the sort of towns that sent kids off to Vietnam. The people couldn't have had the faintest idea what it was about and when a boy came back in a coffin the shock must have been profound'.

The social centre of each town was the Dairy Queen ice-cream shop, rather than any pub, and the boredom of the young was similar to that endured in Australian country towns. 'Cruisin', that phenomenon so beautifully described by Tom Wolfe, was all the go. Every night we saw teenage boys and girls out in their fat-tyred Mustangs and Camaros, just going round and round and round in the modern sexual parade.

We found the people extraordinarily warm and generous. Sometimes they stood by the side of the road offering soft drinks. I particularly remember Mr and Mrs Parker of Hebron, Colorado, and their three sons. Their object was to greet every cyclist who went through. Mrs Parker was cooking thirty-two dozen cookies a day. At harvest-time the whole family had to work full pressure in the fields, so they put up an apologetic sign saying sorry, they couldn't get out for personal greetings, but coffee, fruit juice and cookies were available in the garage.

The Bikecentennial Trans-America Trail is still there. There is a Bikecentennial organisation, which operates in Missoula, Montana, and bikers have followed the tracks of the pioneers of 1976, ever since.

After we returned to Australia we became fascinated by tandem bicycles. The tandem has a number of advantages. For one thing if you are travelling with your partner there are no arguments about pace. Your partner cannot burn you off on the hills; you are compelled to travel at the same pace. For this reason it is a gloriously sociable machine. You can chat all the time and the person who rides behind, technically known as the stoker, can give helpful advice. Backside drivers are not unknown on tandems.

There is one disadvantage. There is much audience reaction from the side of the road. Ninety-nine people out of a hundred make the same comment, 'Ahhhhh, you know the one at the back's not pushing'.

Marie, an utterly devoted stoker, has never taken kindly to this comment. Indeed anyone who has ever ridden a tandem knows instantly when the partner has eased off the power. Yet tandem riding is a lovely experience, a thing apart, as exhilarating as skiing or high-speed skating. Feed your stoker adequately, give him or her plenty of muesli bars and you can get speeds around 40 kilometres per hour.

Most tandems have a deep and abiding problem – they require much to stop them. They build up extraordinary momentum and stopping them needs three and a half times the power required to stop a normal bicycle. Their spokes break and they go through cotter pins as if they were peanuts.

In late 1976 I decided it would be lovely to have a tandem that suffered none of these problems, a touring machine that would take us with our luggage over 1000 kilometres or more. I noticed there was a tandem shop in London, so I wrote the owners a letter, asking them to make me one. There was no reply. The English tend to be like that.

I tried all over Australia to find a suitable tandem, with no success. Then I saw an advertisement in a United States magazine: 'Mail Order Tandems with a Difference. All you have to do is install the pedals, adjust the seats and ride them home from the airport. Yes, we ship to the nearest jetport wherever you are'.

The ad did say in the small print that the average price for these tandems was about 1200 dollars. Good tandems are made to measure. You must have the right frame size for the pilot up forward and the right size for the stoker down aft.

The man making the tandems was Bill McCready of Bud's Bike Shop, Claremont, California. I was so desperate for this machine I got out of bed at 4 a.m. and telephoned him direct. He took my requirements, recommended the ideal bike for Marie and me and told me how it would be assembled. The frame was to be made by the tandem specialists the Taylor Brothers of Stockton-on-Tees, Cleveland County, England. The gears, cranks and chain wheels were to come from France. The brakes, ah, they would be something – massive cantilever caliper brakes from France, plus newly invented Phil Wood disc brakes from California, enough to stop a truck. Each wheel was to have a remarkable forty spokes and there would be special sealed hubs and bottom bracket. The saddles were also to be American, and the seat pillars were to be made by Campagnolo of Italy.

I hung up the receiver, sent my 500-dollar deposit and dreamed of the beauty of this thing. Nine months went by and nothing happened. I telephoned again.

'What's happened to my bike?', I asked Mr McCready.

'We still haven't received your frame from the Taylor Brothers in England.'

He explained that Messrs Taylor made all their frames by hand and then indulged in the most beautiful paintwork, lovingly applied coat after coat. I got the picture. It was like producing Lancias for Malcolm Fraser. I asked why, if Taylor Brothers were slow, did Bud's Bike Shop not get its frames elsewhere? Mr McCready was shocked.

'When you are dealing with the best in the world there isn't anyone else.'

What with the passage of time, the bike that was originally to cost 1200 dollars rose to 1600 dollars. It was in July, just over a year since I had first contacted Mr McCready, that a call came from a Customs agent.

'Your bike has arrived.'

Oh joy.

'There are a few problems', the agent continued. 'Qantas want 225 dollars for air freight.'

'Ye-es.'

'And you won't get the bike until you have paid a bill of 1063 dollars 13 cents for sales and customs duty.'

'WHATTTT? You've got it wrong.'

'No, that's right, 1063 dollars and 13 cents.'

'But, but . . . Nobody in history ever paid duty like that. This is a bicycle. Do they think it's a Mercedes?'

'I'm sure you will get a refund. What you must do is write to two bicycle manufacturers and get letters from them explaining that they do not propose to make such a bike in Australia.'

I didn't write to two, I wrote to three, who between them made 90 per cent of the bicycles manufactured in Australia. I wrote to everyone in sight: to the ministers for business and consumer affairs, even to the Federal Treasurer. However, after the arguing had been going on for five months a bike manufacturer who made kiddie tandems for joy rides announced sure, he could make a bike like mine. My case was ruined and the 1063 dollars 13 cents was not returned.

Marie did some arithmetic. She was very understanding.

'Do you realise', she said sweetly, 'your bicycle has cost just on 3000 dollars?'.

But she had to admit the Taylor Brothers frame turned out to be everything we had hoped it would be. The bike gave us far more than 3000 dollars'-worth of pleasure, and, unlike automobiles, which tend to give up after 100 000 kilometres or so, this vehicle was for ever.

By curious irony, within twelve months we were back in California, living almost within bike-riding distance of Bud's Bike Shop. What's more the Bikecentennial organisation ran other rides. In 1980, with Jeff and Pauline Hook, we rode the Mississippi Trail. There were many of the old team with us, such as Don and Norma Hartley. We picked up the Mississippi River at Lake Itasca, Minnesota, near the Canadian border. There the river was just a trickle. It was important to take a running leap across the rivulet to be able to say later, 'I leaped across the Mississippi'. There was a sign at Lake Itasca that said, 'Here 1475 feet above the ocean the mighty Mississippi begins to flow its winding way 2582 miles to the Gulf of Mexico'.

At least we did not have to tackle the Rockies this time, and theoretically it was all downhill. Marie and I rode our Taylor Brothers tandem.

Ever since the days of our wind-up gramophone, when we played Paul Robeson singing 'Old Man River', we had dreamed of one day seeing the romantic Mississippi. Every night we camped by its banks and discovered the real truth. It was one of the most important commercial waterways in the world. Mark Twain once reported that the railroads were complaining of the unfair competition from the river. One hundred years later things had not changed. All night long we heard the barges chugging up and down. One time I spotted a tugboat pushing twenty-two vast container barges. We were told the tugs, misleadingly titled 'two-boats', could push anything up to forty barges at a time. And what barges. They were worth 2 million dollars each and could carry as many as sixty 25-tonne semi-trailers.

Restless, huge, extraordinarily powerful: by the time we had ridden a thousand kilometres the Mississippi was nearly 2 kilometres across. We visited Hannibal where Mark Twain spent his childhood. The river was the inspiration for all those wonderful stories about Tom Sawyer and Huckleberry Finn. It's a wonder Huck survived: I wouldn't let a kid of mine ride a log raft in a fit. The river was chocolate-grey. Vicious currents raised little waves; trees, boxes and hunks of debris moved past at high speed and from side to side. The river was immense. If you had a hankering for walking on water it would take you at least forty minutes to stroll across.

There were many other rides. Marie and I went on the annual Great Victorian Bike Ride and the Australian Bicentennial Bike Ride from Melbourne to Sydney in 1988. Jeff and I went on a tour of Denmark; again no Rocky Mountains. One time we were pedalling up a gentle rise and a German alongside us announced in guttural tones, 'You are now crossing the Danish Alps'.

'The Danish Alps?'

'Yes, this is the highest point in Denmark. You are 150 metres up.'

Then in 1983 I went on a tour of China. It was a comfort at last to go to a place where the automobile was in the minority. In China there were 700 million bicycles. We entered China via Macau and pedalled through southern China, all around Guangzhou and through Guangdong Province. The Chinese ride heavy, single-speed bicycles that weight about 20 kilograms. Our ten-speed Taiwanese lightweights, provided by Himalaya Bicycle Tours, were a constant source of wonder. Whenever we stopped in a village or town a crowd of 500 or more crowded around, curious not so much about us as about our bicycles. They would get down on their hands and knees to look at the gears, then ask for a demonstration.

However, one day early in the tour we received our come-uppance. We were cycling near Shiqi, on our way to see one of the great dams built by Mao Zedong just before the Cultural Revolution, when we were caught in a typhoon blowing out of the South China Sea. Alas our Taiwanese bikes had no mudguards. I don't think I have ever been so wet. To make matters worse, we were riding on gravel roads, so we were soon covered in mud from helmet to bicycle shoe. When we arrived at the dam an elderly Chinese came over on his bicycle. I thought he was just another who wanted to admire the technical wonders of my bike. But no, he pointed to his bike, which had huge metal mudguards, then pointed to mine, which had none. He placed a forefinger to his head and made a circular motion to indicate that I was out of my mind. It was not the first time I had been called a nut.

CHAPTER FOURTEEN

The virus

Most journalists have a dream of writing something else, a film script, a play, a book, an item beyond daily news. Everything they write is ephemeral: news today, gone the next. So often as a columnist I received the message, 'Yes, I read your column, usually in the smallest room in the house'. The symbolism of that message did not go unnoticed.

Then there was the other message, the dire warning made by Dad, 'There is no money in journalism'. My father's words about journalists being miserably underpaid were all too true. So in 1959 I started writing radio scripts for Crawford Productions.

I began with worthy sagas about Australian achievement, then for nigh on five years I wrote scripts for the police series 'D24', which could almost be called the forerunner of television's 'Homicide'. Every week Dorothy Crawford sent me a synopsis of some murder or vile crime, taken from the police files. Crawfords believed it was important to improve the public image of the police, so the message of 'D24' was always that the police were decent, honest and ultimately triumphant. I turned each synopsis into a half-hour radio play, for which I received what even then did not seem a princely sum, 10 pounds a script.

Dorothy Crawford, Hector Crawford's sister, could have been putting on plays for Laurence Olivier. Her standards were high. She sent back scripts two or three times until she got what she wanted. I found it exhausting murdering some creature every week. We went through all the famous hangings. One episode concerned Frances Knorr, the baby farmer who specialised in taking in unwanted babies for cash, on the pretence that she would be a loving foster mother, then murdered them. Frances Knorr was hanged at the Melbourne Gaol on 15 January 1894. Female fiends made good subjects for scripts. Another splendid 'D24' episode was about Martha Needle, who poisoned her whole family because she wanted to marry a young carpenter named Otto Juncken. Martha swore her innocence right up to the moment on 22 October 1894 when the hangman pulled the lever. We had knivings, garrottings, armed raids, famous exploits of bushrangers, the death of Squizzy Taylor: 'D24' was a splendid blood-stained history of local crime.

The plays were put together at radio studios in the city. Dorothy decreed that there were never to be more than five main characters in any script; one more actor to be paid and the expense would be too high. The stars nearly always were Keith Eden and Patricia Kennedy, two astonishing actors for whom I had the greatest admiration. They could do any accent, feign any instant emotion, including dying splendidly on the gallows. They stood round the microphone, no time even for rehearsal, and plunged straight into the script live, while a technician in the studio handled sound effects ranging from sea gull cries to car doors slamming, steps on stairs, shots and the occasional axe on the back of a neck.

Colin Bednall, the person who launched me into column writing, was now managing director of GTV9, and he asked for a full-length, two-hour radio drama. I gave him an outline of a tale about a gambling-addicted, saucy, middle-aged female who lived in Fitzroy. She ran an illegal tote in a disused church hall. The tote had defences in depth and an early-warning system that would have done credit to the United States Air Force, but still she was constantly raided by the police. I thought it a racy story, but it did not please Colin Bednall. My gifts for character creation were never quite good enough. The play, as they say, did not go to air.

One merciless deadline with a daily column was bad enough, but script writing for compassionless editors who called up even at midnight was too hard. Besides, there was always the dream of producing a book, something in hard covers. The first book was *The Paddock That Grew*, the history of the Melbourne Cricket Club. I have talked of the magical events in life: marriage, the arrival of each child – nothing equals that – going solo, the discovery of music, the first byline. And, oh yes, the arrival of the first book.

The scene comes back very clearly. The year was 1962. The first copy of *The Paddock* was delivered to the Herald office in a cardboard box. I took it home, then at 5 p.m. I hauled out the volume, solid, hard covered, eternal. I put it on the kitchen table, walked around it three times and purred. My God, it had happened.

The Paddock was published by Cassell and Company. The manager of Cassell Australia was an elderly gentleman, Cyril Denny. He was one of the old school, nothing extravagant about him. He served barley water to his staff in the morning and in the evening.

Very excited I went in to see Cassell and said, 'What do you think of my book, Mr Denny?'.

He gave me a long look and without a smile answered: 'Keith, I have been here a long time. I have published a lot of books and I have never read any of them'.

The next book was *Supporting a Column* in 1964, followed by *Wowsers* in 1966. Two men, Cyril Pearl and Phillip Garrett, had a remarkable influence on my early book-writing career. Cyril, author of *Wild Men of Sydney*, *Morrison of Peking* and many other books, relished poking fun at the absurdities of society. He loved to steal notepaper from the Naval and Military Club and then, under its letterhead, write outrageous, pompous letters to the *Herald* and the *Age*, signing them Major-General Fitzhenry (ret). Nobody ever checked to find out whether this general really existed.

Cyril told me that he knew the head of the research department at the La Trobe Library, Phil Garrett.

'Phil', he said, 'is amazing. He knows where every body is buried and every extraordinary, unknown story in Melbourne. The truth is he has written most of the books for the so-called historians here, but they have never acknowledged him'.

I discovered all this was true, and I formed an alliance with Phillip Garrett that was to last for fifteen years. He would point to stories, like a water diviner with a wand, and I would go hunting. Almost invariably I found the elusive substance for a book. Phillip Garrett taught me that research in a library is not a dull, dusty affair, but something that can be immensely exciting. He was a quiet, shy person whose greatest love was to get into one of the pubs around Carlton, late in the day, and just talk.

Our first project together was *Wowsers*, a history of Australian prudery. Phillip told me I would have to go through every issue of the *Bulletin* from its inception, a formidable task. Yet it was not dull; it was like fishing. I would go for days without making a catch, then suddenly I would find a fact, an extraordinary happening that proved an entire historical theory. I would find it perhaps in an old journal, such as *Bell's Life* or *Melbourne Punch*. When that happened I became so excited I wanted to stand up and shout: 'Look, I've found it. It's there. I've got it, I've struck gold'.

Oh no, behave yourself. You are in the solemn sanctum of the reading room. No noise is permitted here whatever. So I would have to wait an hour or two and explain my excitement to Marie when I got home.

Phil was a genius for finding the off-beat story. He told me about the first cremation in Melbourne, which took place on the beach at Black Rock in April 1895. Cremation in the nineteenth century was considered outrageous, appalling. However, there was a small group who believed in it and fought for it. In 1895 J. R. Le Pine the undertaker agreed to cremate the late Mrs Henniker of 8 William Street, Richmond, who had died at the age of eighty-three. He picked a remote spot on the seashore between Half Moon Bay and Black Rock. His assistants used 3 tonnes of firewood and a keg of kerosene. They took the hearse, with the body in an elaborate coffin, almost to the beach, then placed poor Mrs Henniker among the logs. No clergyman was there and Mr Frederick Henniker, Mrs Henniker's only son, lit the match. It was described in Parliament as 'a scandalous and horrible occurrence', but there was no law against it and so we won cremation.

Phil Garrett also introduced me to William Henry Judkins. Judkins was a little wisp of a man who was for ever collapsing from ill-health. In 1906 he was superintendent of the Social Reform Bureau, which he had founded, and editor of the church journal *Review of Reviews*. Judkins, although apparently of poor physique, was a battery of energy. He was in the newspapers daily, thundering against sin in all its forms. His blast-off point was the Pleasant Sunday Afternoon at the Wesley Church in Lonsdale Street, Melbourne. With Mr Judkins as the speaker it should have been more aptly named the Blood-curdling Afternoon or a Sensational Afternoon at the Wesley Church. He could shake the very dust off the church rafters. There was a new exposé every week: gambling at bridge parties, Sunday drinking and a hundred other sins. He stood outside hotels on Sundays counting the number of people who went in and out. He was strong in his condemnation of the wickedness of barmaids, those voluptuous sirens who enticed men into hotels to partake of the demon drink, thereby leading them to ruin. Particularly he railed against John Wren, who ran that 'sink of evil', the illegal Collingwood Tote. He was against the brothels of Lonsdale Street, two-up and the pony tracks, and he used to say there were forty-four places of evil in Melbourne where the law was broken. Judkins was the name of the day. Little boys ran up to him, called him names and threw things at him. He was the ultimate wowser.

I followed his career in the newspaper room at the State Library. It is a curious thing about research: you move into an era to such a degree that eventually you feel you are there, living in that day as if you had taken a trip in H. G. Wells's time machine. I had started writing a book to mock the wowsers, but later I was not in a mocking mood and I gained a respect for the extraordinary courage of little Mr Judkins.

After 1908 Judkins's appearances were fewer and fewer. He went to Sydney in 1910 to fight a great prohibition battle, although it was clear he was very ill. Yet when everyone thought Judkins was finished, he came back to preach his old hell-fire, standing on crutches. Then one night, working alone, I read that on Tuesday, 3 September 1912, William Henry Judkins died of cancer. He was only forty-three. I felt I had lost a friend. I left my books and went off to have a cup of coffee, close to tears.

Wowsers poured out with passion. I had a distaste for this society that imposed controls over what books we read and what art shows we went to and told us how we should behave on Sunday. I believed utterly that the absurd Methodists, Baptists and Presbyterians had held back our society for a century or more. It was their censorship that stopped the exchange of ideas on book and film, it was their restrictions that stopped sex education and produced a race of inhibited, even dangerous, people. Once people were better educated there would no longer be a need for pornography, and sex abuse, child molestation, rape and abortion would disappear. I am not sure about any of this any more. Who knows? Perhaps old Judkins had something. Perhaps it all requires more time, another fifty or a hundred years, but in the 1990s pornography has not disappeared, it has proliferated. Rape, abortion and child abuse are more prevalent, and as for alcohol, perhaps we are a little wiser, but it still causes more havoc than all other drugs.

Another man whom I admire deeply, and who has had a great influence on me, is Barry Humphries. I met him first when he was a university student doing his Piescape and Forkscape sculptures. At the opening of his Piescape exhibition he put his elbow in a bowl of tomato sauce to test the sauce for the correct temperature and then drank it. What was left he poured over his head. This, he said, was a tribute to our great national drink. One picture was called *I Was Eating a Pie and I Coughed*. The beauty of such modern art, he said, was this: it could not possibly last more than two days.

Barry went through a period of alcoholism, which caused him great suffering. It was ironic perhaps that he launched *Wowsers* at almost the height of his troubles. His drinking became so bad that his father, Mr J. A. E. Humphries, used to sit in my office at the *Sun*, wondering where Barry was and hoping that he just might turn up.

Indeed, I was very disturbed that he might not turn up for the launching of *Wowsers*, which was to take place at Dan Murphy's Cellars in Chapel Street, Prahran. But that was not the Humphries style. No matter what his state, no matter how ill he was, he never missed a curtain call. He went further than that. Instead of my giving him a present, he presented me with a magnificent Hutton's Hams advertising mirror, 150 centimetres by 60 centimetres. It depicted the little Hutton's man, in his high hat, so famous at the turn of the century. There he was, thrusting another character out of the way with a 'Don't argue, Hutton's Hams are best'.

My mother was offended by this. Her father had been manager of Farmer's Hams and Bacon, a far superior ham she felt, and it was Hutton's that took over Farmer's in Ballarat and ended Farmer's Hams for ever. She decided she would not sleep until she found a Farmer's mirror, and she did, in a grocer's shop in Toorak. I don't know how she got it, for she was a very shy lady, but I think she almost tore it off the wall. We still have both mirrors splendidly displayed, side by side.

Although Barry did turn up for the launching of *Wowsers*, he had been drinking a great deal of brandy. He gave another marvellous Humphries performance, which was reported on radio and television, but the strain was there. Marie put him in the car at Murphy's car park and for half an hour he sobbed.

In 1970 Barry was charged with being drunk and disorderly, and three days later he was beaten up at a hotel in Richmond. That was the turning point. He had a number of very good friends who helped him through his troubles and he has not drunk since.

Barry was extraordinarily generous with his ideas. It was at his suggestion that I wrote *Knockers*, a book that has run through many editions. He kicked it off very well: 'Don't bother to rebuke Keith Dunstan for having documented our most endearing vice between the covers of this book. It won't sell'.

He had another idea for a bestseller for me, *Ratbags*. He even suggested a range of ratbags who should go into the book – Bea Miles, Frank Thring, Percy Grainger, Germaine Greer and, of course, John Barry Humphries. In the foreword he wrote:

> What is a Ratbag? A Ratbag is a man who saves all his dead matches for that tea tray he knows he will never make. A Ratbag writes letters to Raquel Welch enclosing his photograph and a stamped, addressed envelope.
>
> If you're a vegetarian, a Jehovah's Witness birdwatcher with five-colored Biros in your breast pocket and you belong to a sky-diving club, you are a potential Ratbag.
>
> If you are a hippy over nineteen who thinks Shakespeare was a woman, Hitler was Jewish and if Beethoven were alive today he would be writing TV jingles, you are a transitional Ratbag.
>
> But if you read *The Great Gatsby* once a year, if you can whistle the Brahms Hungarian Dances, don't have a television set, grow your own marijuana and have just ghost-written the autobiography of a surfrider, you are a terminal or raving Ratbag.

There were other books – *Sports*, a history of Australia's obsession with sport, *The Store on the Hill*, a history of Georges, the illustrious old store in Collins Street, Melbourne, and then in 1987, after four years' labour, *The Amber Nectar*, a history of Carlton and United Breweries. Given that CUB in its time had swallowed more than sixty other breweries, *The Amber Nectar* was virtually the story of brewing in Australia.

The Amber Nectar was the idea of Paul Ormonde, Public Affairs Director of CUB. It all seemed so simple at the start, but when I began digging at the brewery I was horrified. Where were the old records? They virtually did not exist.

You see, brewers are suspicious, careful people. They have had to be. Except for the Bible Belt in the United States and the choicer parts of the Middle East, Australia endured the most virulent temperance people in the world. In sumptuous wowser pockets such as Melbourne and Adelaide this continued until the 1960s. The brewers were always under attack so they retired to their fortresses. Not only did they not reveal any information, they never spoke to the Press. When R. F. G. Fogarty was chairman and general manager of CUB he employed an old Army mate, Ginger Burke. Ginger theoretically was the public relations officer, but actually he was the anti-PR officer. It was Ginger's job to keep all reference to CUB out of the papers.

R. F. G. Fogarty had a rule. He never gave interviews. Eventually, by using every wile as a newspaper columnist, I did manage to make friends with him. He gave me careful 'leaks' for my column in the *Sun News-Pictorial*. One day he called up.

'Keith, we have a new can. Come and look at it.'

I entered the bluestone fortress in Bouverie Street and went into the sacred chamber. 'Old Foge', a term one dared use only behind his back, pulled out the new 26-ounce Foster's Lager can. He gave it to me. It was empty.

'Do something with that', he said.

It was not an earth-shaking story, but anything to do with beer is news. I took the can back to the office and showed it to the Picture Editor.

'Hard to photograph that', he said. 'Why don't you take it over to the Phoenix Hotel and photograph it with Lou Richards?'

This I did.

Three months later CUB was renovating the ancient Duke of Wellington Hotel in Flinders Street. Legend had it that once cock fighting used to take place at the Duke. 'I'll ring my old mate Foge', I thought. 'He'll tell me about it.'

His secretary replied coolly to my call. There were no little lies such as 'Mr Fogarty is in conference'. No, she said, 'Mr Fogarty doesn't want to speak to you'.

So I thought, 'All right, Brian Breheny, the Assistant General Manager, he'll talk to me'. Mr Breheny wasn't available. Well, how about Dr Carl Resch, the head brewer? Couldn't get him. So I went right round the building. Not one official would come to the phone. As a last resort I rang Ginger Burke.

'Hey, Ginger, what's going on? Am I on the black list?'

Ginger explained: 'You see Keith, you had the old man's big can photographed with Lou Richards. He doesn't like Lou Richards. So he has put out the word that nobody in the entire company is to talk to you'.

The ban went on. Fogarty died on 27 February 1967. Brian Breheny took over and actually threw a party for the Press. Every media person, as he or she left the brewery, received a present of a carton of beer. Brian Breheny looked at me, smiled clearly the smile of forgiveness, and said, 'You deserve two cartons'.

But all the suspicions were still there when the suggestion came in 1983 that a book was necessary for CUB's centenary. We argued over a contract for a year. Word came back from the management that they wanted to see every chapter and approve it before I proceeded further. As far as I was concerned the book was mine; any interference and not a word would be written. Finally, when I decided to reject the project altogether, my historian son, David, suggested that the History Institute act as an independent arbitrator. Any suggested amendments were to be put to the institute. So we proceeded. As it happened an arbitrator was never necessary. CUB did suggest some changes but only to save me from inevitable libel writs.

There were other problems. When I started research, wherever I turned doors seemed to close. Brewers were very sensitive souls. Not only did they not reveal information to newspapers, but newspapers also did not write about breweries. They dared not offend delicate Presbyterian, Methodist and Baptist sensibilities.

I needed official records. I went to the CUB management and asked for old records and all board minutes, please. There were none, they said.

'We don't keep board minutes.'

Mercifully and wonderfully everything changed after the big Elders IXL takeover. I asked again.

'Certainly.'

There was a splendid, patient keeper of the books, named Joyce Grimshaw. She said: 'Not only do we have the minutes of CUB, I think I can find you the original minutes of the Foster Brewing Company'.

Indeed, they were all there in a locked vault, carefully handwritten in ancient, leather volumes. It was an enchanting moment when I opened the first volume. I felt I had just discovered Lasseter's long-lost gold reef.

The launching of *The Amber Nectar* was on 18 November 1987. The Managing Director of CUB, Peter Bartels, produced a big surprise, a special beer for the launching, an unbelievable thrill for the author. CUB had done it only twice before, the first time for the television star Bert Newton and the second time for one of their top executives. The can carried my photograph, signature and the message 'Commemorating the launch of "The Amber Nectar" November 18, 1987'.

Actually I began to regret I ever saw that beer can. The book launch took place at the Hotel Windsor, and the roll-up of Press, radio and television reporters was splendid. Alas, their interest in the book was only slight. What fascinated them was this: Dunstan had received a huge quantity of free beer. You see, I was a victim of modern engineering. CUB either had to give me a large quantity of cans or have them destroyed. Beer canning is a very high-speed operation and the absolute minimum run on the canning line is 1000 cans. The launching was at 11 a.m., not a strong drinking time even for journalists, and the guests disposed of maybe only sixty cans. CUB could not sell the rest, so after the launching Paul Ormonde asked would I mind if they delivered about 940 cans to my house? I said modestly, 'Thank you very much'.

From then on we were under siege. I received more than 300 letters from beer can collectors, asking for cans. I had a notice printed and sent out, announcing that a large cache of cans for collection would be available at the *Age* office during Easter 1988. All the cans went in two hours. In the following days we were telephoned morning and night. The number of beer can collectors in Australia was beyond belief. They had an association and they swopped cans. Rare cans fetched high prices. The beer can enthusiasts seemed worse even than butterfly collectors or hunters after old snuff-boxes. Some sent photographs of their collections, of living-rooms lined with beer cans from floor to ceiling. One wondered how they endured such constant alcoholic decoration, but no doubt it gave them a feeling of comfort. The problem grew and grew. The international can mafia took over – there were requests from collectors as far off as Wisconsin and Surrey. Some sent rare local cans, believing an exchange would be irresistible.

I tried to answer their requests. Still the letters came. Some offered cash, 50 dollars a can, but I thought if I accepted money it would become worse. Bob Millington, the *Age* 'News of the Day' columnist, published my appeal, 'Please stop, there are no more cans', but they did not believe me and it was eighteen months before the letters stopped arriving.

After *Ratbags* there was a three-year break in book production. In May 1979 John Morgan, Editor-in-Chief of the Herald and Weekly Times, said the company needed a representative on the West Coast of the United States. Would the Dunstans be prepared to set up residence in San Francisco? This was an offer almost as beautiful as the one made by Sir Keith Murdoch precisely thirty years earlier, when he had asked us to go to New York. We would, indeed.

Just two weeks before we were due to leave Morgan had another announcement. There was little point in having a representative in San Francisco. Los Angeles was the place. Three-quarters of the population was in southern California, the movie industry was there, the aerospace industry was there. Everything really happened down south. Would we please make our headquarters in LA.

This was awful news. I was almost too terrified to break it to Marie. We remembered Los Angeles as being hot, smog laden, automobile ridden, an awful conglomerate of widely tossed suburbs, with perhaps a city centre but not a place where anyone lived or wanted to be. We moaned, but there was no turning back now. Our tickets had been bought, our house in South Yarra had been let, even our bicycles had been boxed and made ready for departure.

Our only contact in Los Angeles was an Englishman, Ronald Clarke, the West Coast representative of the Reuters News Agency.

Upon arriving, I went into the Reuters office in downtown LA and asked for Mr Clarke.

'Oh, he never comes in here', said a receptionist.

'Never?'

'Well, maybe once a month to pick up his pay.'

'Where is he, then?'

'He works from his home out at Woodland Hills.'

'Where's that?'

'It's about 30 miles north from here. You get there by taking your car out along the Ventura Freeway.'

'But I haven't got a car.'

The receptionist shrugged. She knew anyone without a car in Los Angeles should go away and cut his throat.

'But he can't work out there. It's impossible.'

'Oh no. He's right. He's got his teleprinter, his computer. Everybody does that.'

This was our first discovery of the new era in journalism. Most of the London newspapers had representatives on the West Coast but none of them worked right in LA. They all had their computers and I had to do the same.

I rented a word processor from Reuters, a machine called a Teleram. Laughably it was classed as portable. Actually it weighed nigh on 30 kilograms, and it almost dragged my arm out of its socket when I took it aboard an aeroplane. The portable I acquired seven years later had more than 100 times the memory, worked at twice the speed and weighed only 2 kilograms.

The Teleram had a built-in modem and sent messages over the telephone wires to the Reuters computer in New York, which then relayed the copy to Sydney. I always admired its chirpy style. When it made connection with New York a message came on the screen: 'Hi! This is your Reuters computer'. Then when the message had gone through it would say: 'So long! That's all folks!'. One time in four it did not work at all; and on these occasions I came close to kicking its computer teeth in.

The Teleram had one dreadful failing, electrostatic energy. Southern California is about as dry as the Simpson Desert. In summer the temperatures were regularly around 38 degrees Celsius and, with carpets made of nylon, conditions were perfect for this alarming behaviour. It was possible actually to see a spark go from the fingers to the metal case of the Teleram. When this happened there was a complete wipe-out; everything on the screen disappeared. Sometimes I had been labouring for several hours, written 2000 or more words on the shortcomings of President Jimmy Carter, when zap, everything was gone and I had to start all over again. Eventually I discovered there was one solution: the Teleram had to be earthed at all times. So I had to type in bare feet. But then I would forget to take off my shoes and disaster would strike again. Where did all those stories go? They were so irretrievable. There had to be some great black hole that held the long-lost tales that were zapped away into non-existence.

Yet the Teleram was the answer, the forerunner of all the word processors that made it possible for so many of us to work away from newspaper offices. It had to be carted everywhere. For example, there was that moment in history when *Columbia*, the first space shuttle, landed at Edwards Air Force Base in October 1981. California was specially moved by this space event because the astronauts were coming home to virtually their own backyard, the great Mojave Desert. The world's Press congregated at Edwards. Months before we had had to book our own special telephone connection.

I remember sitting out in the makeshift Press room on a frigid desert morning, working very carefully in bare feet to make sure I did not lose my historic message. Some people had camped all night around the base, others had driven out at two, three or four in the morning. By dawn the crowd had built to an astonishing 150 000 people. Of course, everybody had to be there. There were the astronauts Buzz Aldrin, Scott Carpenter and Wally Scherer. From the entertainment world we had Roy Rogers, Dale Evans, John Denver and Frank Sinatra. Then there were some distinguished movie spacemen: Leonard Nimoy, Spock no less, and William Shatner from *Star Trek*.

The desert, a pale ochre in colour, like so much of California, reminded me of home. The country was flat and it could have been the very land, say, north of Broken Hill or around Coober Pedy in South Australia. It was devoid of all trees except the curious Joshua trees, 3 to 4 metres high, with strange, gesticulating fingers. Undoubtedly the trees were named after the prophet Joshua and these were his outstretched fingers, yearning after God.

For the crowd at Edwards Air Force Base the moment of greatest tension came when *Columbia* fired its retro-active rockets over the Indian Ocean. This was the time of the re-entry, with temperatures boosted to 806 degrees Celsius. A television commentator, with an air of gloom, was announcing: 'For sixteen minutes we will not know whether the flight has been a success. We will not know whether the astronauts have come through it alive'.

So we waited and waited, nobody saying much, while those minutes ticked by. Then the silence was broken. There were cheers across the great Air Force base as if it were a football final. *Columbia* was 47 000 metres over Big Sur and we could hear a Southern drawl, 'We're comin' right down the chute – right on the money'.

At 10.17 a.m. there were two loud bangs like anti-aircraft fire. *Columbia* had passed through the sound barrier. It was all over with such astonishing speed. First we saw a sparkle, a glint of metal 4000 metres up. There were screams of 'There it is' as *Columbia* came into full view. Then it just dropped like a gliding brick, flattened out, appeared to rise a trifle and finally landed, as predicted, 'as sweetly as a feather'.

I was astonished at the size of the space shuttle. It was as big as a DC9. It had a curious nose-down, tail-up appearance. *Columbia* almost gave the impression it was exhausted.

Helicopters swooped overhead. There was a sniffer team to check for dangerous gases, vehicles with umbilical cords to cool *Columbia* down and to clean out its entrails, fire carts, transport wagons and, not the least, a tow vehicle that was to bring the craft in at 4.5 kilometres per hour, a process that took four hours. Some come-down after travelling at 26 715 kilometres per hour.

It was several hours before we were able to interview the astronauts, John Young and Robert Crippen, whereas the entire landing had been over in twenty seconds. It was a remarkably moving event. I interviewed one lady, Louise Wolfe of Fullarton, California, who said: 'This is the first time we have had a chance of seeing real spacemen come to earth. For me this is history. I wasn't there for Christopher Columbus, but, look, I saw the arrival of the space shuttle'.

To Marie's and my surprise, and despite all our dire misgivings, we learned to love Los Angeles. Oh yes, there were lots of druggies, a high rate of crime, astonishing, weird religious sects, psychopaths and sexual crazies, but I think the rate per head of population was little different from that back home in South Yarra. Nobody actually knew how big the Los Angeles population was; the estimate was about 11 million. Nobody was sure where Los Angeles began or ended; the guess was it was about 120 by 80 kilometres. It was a string of eighty communities loosely tied together. Deer wandered through the Hollywood hills, and farmers still produced vegetables, strawberries and oranges in the most remarkable places.

We settled at Calabasas, beyond the smog and just beyond Woodland Hills where we had first met the Reuters man, Ron Clarke. We bought a condominium overlooking an exquisite lake. There was a swimming pool where Marie could swim, and we played tennis almost every afternoon.

Los Angeles, of course, was the ultimate victim of the automobile. It had no public transport system worthy of the name and 600 kilometres of freeways. You could drive on freeways all day, twenty-four hours a day, without ever retracing your steps and without ever leaving Los Angeles. The creature who did not own a car in Los Angeles was indeed lost beyond redemption. I can never forget the breaking-in agonies. We bought a Chevrolet but the insurance company declared that, unless we acquired Californian licences immediately, the car would be impounded. They laughed at our international licences so carefully purchased in Melbourne. In California they did not even recognise interstate licences let alone the international variety. So I went into the Department of Motor Vehicles in Hollywood. There were at least 500 people battling to get a licence all at the one time. I queued for over four hours. But not everyone queued. During the morning I saw the pop singer Rod Stewart sweep in. Rod's hairdo was tinted a beautiful shade of canary and he had a nice blonde creature on his arm. Rod swept through and won his licence in ten minutes. It pays to be a celebrity in LA.

First I had to pass a two-page written test in Californian road law, then do a thorough eye test. Finally along came the examiner, a bearded black gentleman who had to fold up like a deck-chair to get into the car. He made me drive interminably around Hollywood, but fortunately he was not over-interested in my driving. He just kept complaining about the summer heat.

'Man, can't you get any more air-condishnin' outa this car?'

Miraculously I received a pass. My driving licence called for both a colour photograph and a thumbprint. There's no coyness about fingerprinting with the LA police.

There was still the terror of those freeways. Just getting on and off called for immense skill. I looked at the four lanes of pounding traffic and was terrified. I went up the ramp at 30 kilometres per hour, prepared to inch my way into the stream. Immediately there was a deafening outbreak of beeping from behind. Malibus, Eldorados, Comaros, Thunderbirds and Bonnevilles were going out of their eight-cylinder minds.

I consulted Ron Clarke.

'There is just one way to get on the freeway. Close your eyes, put your foot down on the accelerator and go like hell.'

I had no trouble after that.

There was never a shortage of stories in Los Angeles. For example, there were wonderful places like Forest Lawn. In a curious, inverse way we came to love it, making it almost top of the list for our sight-seeing visitors, after the J. Paul Getty Museum. Forest Lawn was the inspiration for Evelyn Waugh's extraordinary novel *The Loved One*. You will remember he called the book *The Loved One* because death in California was such a horrid idea it was never mentioned, and anyone who had gone to the great beyond was always called a 'loved one'. The place where they made their departure was Forest Lawn, built to be so spellbinding that it was almost a Disneyland for loved ones.

In 1963 Jessica Mitford, one of the brilliant Mitford sisters from England, satirised Forest Lawn all over again in *The American Way of Death*. She described the entrance gates as the largest in the world, 'twice as wide and six feet higher than those at Buckingham Palace'. This was absolutely true, but that wasn't all. Forest Lawn really saved tourists wasting their time looking at the art treasures of Europe. Forest Lawn had them all. It had reproduced almost the entire works of Michelangelo. There was the huge statue of *Moses*, the lovely *Pietà* from the Vatican, the Medici *Madonna of Bruges*, *Day* and *Night* from the Medici Chapel in Florence, plus Michelangelo's *David*, carved out of a single block of Carrara marble, just like the original. Actually Forest Lawn has had two copies of *David*. The first came crashing down in the earthquake of 1971. The new one was built with a stainless steel rod up one leg and was mounted on Teflon so the next time the earth moves, God willing, *David* will stay aloft.

What else? There was da Vinci's *Last Supper*, reproduced in stained glass, and *The Crucifixion* by Polish artist Jan Stryka, the largest painting in the United States, if not the world, 60 metres long and 14 metres high. To see it visitors had to go into a vast theatre and listen to the story of the last days of Jesus, in quadrophonic sound, before lights went on, curtains rolled back and the Los Angeles Philharmonic played Tchaikovsky's Pathétique Symphony as the picture came into view. After that the curtains closed and the picture was replaced by another equally large one, *The Resurrection*. This time the music was Handel's 'Hallelujah Chorus'.

Regrettably, above all, editors in Australia yearned for stories about movie stars. Messages would arrive night and day, saying please interview Frank Sinatra, Bob Hope, Jack Nicholson, Meryl Streep, Michael Caine – notwithstanding that in most cases it would be easier to get a private hour alone with President Carter and no trouble at all, in comparison, to have a chat with the rising Ronald Reagan. After conniving, pleading and describing the huge, enthusiastic audience in Australia, where people were actually English speaking, it was possible to get interviews with a great many of the stars: people such as Liza Minelli, Cher, Johnny Cash, Johnny Mathis, Nastassja Kinski, Julio Iglesias, Phyllis Diller, Willie Nelson, Dorothy Lamour, Debbie Reynolds, Vincent Price, Cleo Lane and Sammy Davis, junior.

Often it meant finding them in regrettable places like Las Vegas or Lake Tahoe. One time Marie and I went to Hurrah's at Lake Tahoe to see Sammy Davis. Our hotel room had two bathrooms and three television sets. There was a television set in each bathroom, and the windows were sealed to keep out the light on the presumption that guests only went to bed in the day-time. Night-time was for gambling and looking at Sammy.

Almost once a month we went across the desert to Las Vegas. There we stayed at Caesar's Palace, which had almost as much statuary as Forest Lawn, including another gigantic reproduction of Michelangelo's *David*, again made out of a solid block of Carrara marble. One almost hoped Michelangelo, wherever he was, received royalties. Celebrities performed in the Circus Maximus where the ushers were dressed as Roman legionnaires and people such as Sammy received 150 000 dollars a week.

It was here, too, that I interviewed the astonishing Willie Nelson. He had his hair in plaits and his face looked as if it had been trampled upon by too much drinking and far too many one-night stands. He admitted he had been a good whisky man. He had wonderful stories about his first wife, Martha, a full-blooded Cherokee. They had a stormy marriage and, according to Willie, one time she threw a fork at him and it stuck in his rib-cage, humming like a tuning-fork. Then there was the time he came home drunk and passed out in bed. Martha sewed the sheet tightly over his head until he was like a body ready for burial. Then, when he awoke, she beat him with a broomstick. Their marriage after such an event was not destined to be a long one.

Our stay in Los Angeles was never as lonely as we expected. All three daughters came to the States while we were there. The most remarkable visit was by Kate, the journalist, who was married on 1 February 1980 in an adventure almost as great as ours back in 1949.

Our close friendship with Milton and Sylvia Johnson went back nigh on forty years, and it seemed a bonus when Kate and their son Andrew also became close friends. Andrew was an engineer like his father, and he melted my heart immediately because he was a good bicycle rider. Soon after we left for California the beautiful Kate–Andrew romance seemed to come apart. Andrew left with a friend to sail on a small yacht to England. Kate went in the opposite direction. She bought an air ticket and decided to stay a month or two with us in Calabasas. It seemed that the Kate–Andrew episode was over.

Actually it was just starting. There is nothing like a long cruise on a small boat for thinking, and Andrew missed Kate desperately. He terminated his boat trip at Singapore and sent a cable to Kate at Calabasas: 'I love you. Will you marry me?'.

Kate replied, 'Come and see'.

It was not easy finding a plane from Singapore to Los Angeles. Andrew had to travel via Canada and the airline lost his luggage on the way. He arrived in Los Angeles with only the clothes that he was wearing and feeling decidedly nervous. Kate had held him in suspense, but the answer was 'Yes'.

The marriage took place at the Prince of Peace Episcopalian Church in Woodland Hills, just near Calabasas. We thought marriage in the US would be a happy, easy come, easy go affair, but that was not the case. The vicar at the Prince of Peace was even more stern than our vicar back home. Two days before the marriage he insisted on giving the betrothed couple his standard lecture.

'Don't come back to me again', he said. 'I only marry people once. This is for life.'

They were married in the presence of a small group of our American friends, including Vivien Kane, the student who lived with us for a year. She came from Philadelphia to be with her Australian 'sister'. Kate and Andrew made a beautiful couple. I particularly thought so, because Andrew, having no wardrobe, had to borrow one of my best suits for the occasion. What a honeymoon. They went to a firm called Rent-a-Wreck and hired a huge convertible tourer. It was so grand they looked like Hollywood stars of the early 1970s as off they drove on a grand tour to San Diego, Las Vegas and round to San Francisco.

Jane came over to visit us, with her American husband, Steve Beckley. Sarah also joined us for a marvellous six-week holiday and became infected by the biking mania of her parents. She bicycled along the edge of the Grand Canyon in Colorado and for several thousand kilometres along the banks of the Mississippi River. She too discovered the joys of sleeping in a mini-tent on the hard ground and being bitten by what is often described as the national bird of Minnesota, the mosquito.

So what happened to our children? David, once known as Steamboat, made a career as a historian and a writer. He married Paula, who became a senior teacher at Lauriston, then Korowa. Jane was a nurse at the Royal Melbourne Hospital. She and Steve, a potter and teacher, settled at Maldon. Kate and Andrew returned to Australia. Kate, after working for the *Age*, went into television, reporting, news casting and production. Andrew diversified into computer engineering. Sarah, our youngest, became an advertising account executive and married Peter Cudlipp, an advertising director. This was our ultimate blessing, four very happy marriages, which provided us with eleven grandchildren.

In 1982 Marie and I arrived back in Australia and just before Christmas I returned to the old harness of writing 'A Place in the Sun'. Rod Donelly, Editor of the *Sun*, brought out an unnerving poster to celebrate the return: 'Dunstan is back'. Very likely it confused a number of people and made them think Don Dunstan had returned as premier of South Australia.

At first it was fun to be writing the old column again, but it was amazing how much Melbourne worked to a tight calendar: summer heat, Moomba, football, Melbourne Cup, cricket, Christmas. The same stories kept coming back and back and back. I retired from the *Sun* and worked as a freelance journalist, although still writing regular Saturday pieces for the Herald and Weekly Times. In August 1985 Max Suich, chief editorial executive of James Fairfax and Son, asked if I would write a weekly column for the *Age* and the *Sydney Morning Herald* and regular articles for the *Good Weekend* magazine. I had been hanging around Flinders Street ever since I first visited there as a small boy with my father, and there were some terrible feelings of misgiving and guilt as I walked out for the last time. But there had to be a change, there had to be a new direction. Marie Rose, who is always the brave one in making decisions, said: 'Do it. You will regret it for ever if you don't'. The Max Suich invitation was irresistible and temporary retirement was over.

As Thea Astley once said, writing is a virus. People who get the bug don't know how to get rid of it. One really needs a pill to make one stop.

INDEX